PENGUIN BOOKS

Talking about O'Dwyer

C. K. Stead made his name as one of the new New Zealand poets of the 1950s and 60s and his book *The New Poetic* gave him, quite early in his career, an international identity as a literary critic. He also published short stories, and his first novel, *Smith's Dream* (1971) became the movie *Sleeping Dogs*, launching the careers of director Roger Donaldson and actor Sam Neill. In 1986 Stead took early retirement from his Professorship of English at the University of Auckland to write full-time. He has won a number of literary awards and prizes, was made a CBE in 1985, and is one of only two New Zealanders to be elected a Fellow of the Royal Society of Literature. He is currently working with Roger Donaldson on a movie script of his novel *Villa Vittoria*. *Talking About O'Dwyer* is his tenth work of fiction. Stead is married with three children (one of whom is the novelist Charlotte Grimshaw) and several grandchildren.

Talking about
O'Dwyer

C. K. Stead

PENGUIN BOOKS

PENGUIN BOOKS

Penguin Books (NZ) Ltd, cnr Airborne and Rosedale Roads, Albany,
Auckland 1310, New Zealand
Penguin Books Ltd, 27 Wrights Lane, London W8 5TZ, England
Penguin USA, 375 Hudson Street, New York, NY 10014, United States
Penguin Books Australia Ltd, 487 Maroondah Highway, Ringwood,
Australia 3134
Penguin Books Canada Ltd, 10 Alcorn Avenue, Toronto, Ontario,
Canada M4V 3B2
Penguin Books (South Africa) Pty Ltd, 4 Pallinghurst Road, Parktown,
Johannesburg 2193, South Africa
Penguin Books India (P) Ltd, 11, Community Centre, Panchsheel Park,
New Delhi 110 017, India

Penguin Books Ltd, Registered Offices: Harmondsworth, Middlesex, England

First published by Penguin Books (NZ) Ltd, 1999

3 5 7 9 10 8 6 4 2

Editorial Services by Michael Gifkins & Associates
Designed and typeset by Egan-Reid Ltd, Auckland, NZ
Printed in Australia by Australian Print Group, Maryborough

Top cover photograph: 'A soldier during manoeuvres on the Cassino Battlefront,
Italy.' Alexander Turnbull Library, National Library of New Zealand, Te Puna
Mātauranga o Aotearoa. DA-05505

The assistance of Creative New Zealand towards the publication
of this book is gratefully acknowledged by the publisher.

Acknowledgements

Special thanks to Kay Stead who grew up in Henderson
to Rob Dyer whose father Major (later Lt Col) Humphrey Dyer
fought in Crete as a Pakeha officer in the Maori Battalion
to Ljiljana Scuric and Jadranka Pintaric my good friends in Croatia
to Alan Ross from whose life I have borrowed a brief naval episode
to New Zealand National Archives and New Zealand Defence Force
Archives for access to official war records
and to Creative New Zealand for financial assistance.

i.m. Parata Heta Thompson
killed in Crete 24.5.41

Across lands and seas I've come,
brother, to take of you this last leave
giving what we give to the dead
a voice for their silence.
No righting the wrong done
by Fate that took you
from those you loved—
only this gift of sad speech:
Brother for ever, for ever
     haere ra!

(Catullus 101, trans. CKS)

ONE

The Makutu

'I GIVE YOU CHURCH AND QUEEN, MR BURSAR.'

'Church and Queen.'

That over, they can settle to it. O'Dwyer is dead. Two days ago. Obits in this morning's *Times, Guardian, Independent.* Funeral service and cremation tomorrow.

The hard fact of it is the talk tonight around the table in the panelled room under the candle chandelier where the dons of Bardolph's College retire from high table for dessert, leaving the undergraduates at their long benches in the dining hall watched over by past Masters in gilded frames.

Clockwise around the table goes the port wearing about its neck a silver medallion that says PORT, and followed, always at a respectful distance, by the claret and the sauterne, the fruit and the chocolate, and the little silver snuff box. And around goes the talk of Donovan O'Dwyer.

A big man. (Too big for his boots.)

A grand drinking companion. (A boozer.)

Irish. (Not Irish-born.)

A New Zealander. (Spent all his working life in Oxford.)

A Blue, a first in Greats. (Too good a start for such a long decline.)

Fought with NZ Div in Greece and Crete, North Africa and

Italy. (And the old soldier nostalgia was correspondingly long-winded.)

Commanded a company. (But that didn't last.)

A good father. (Fatherer rather—both in and out of wedlock.)

Claimed by New Zealand as a favourite son. (But they didn't have to live with the sod.)

And wasn't it a company of the Maori Battalion?

It was (Mike Newall explains), but to begin with its senior officers were Pakeha.

White men. Well, there you are then.

Will they talk about me like this when the time comes? Mike asks himself, and knows they won't. No he doesn't know (he corrects himself), but thinks it unlikely.

Michael Francis Newall, also New Zealand-born, also Irish by descent, but orange not green. Enemies by heredity, he and Donovan O'Dwyer (and something of that there was, from the mother's milk on either side); but bound, here in Oxford, by the nearer bond, the more recent nationalism—a shared nostalgia for the land of their childhood and youth.

More than acquaintances, and less than friends—Mike, twenty years younger, lacking the war, the wounds, the campaign medals, the Mentioned in Dispatches.

Never to have marched with Death—seen it, risked it, brought it about—Mike has felt this sometimes, almost as a failing in himself. Has wished life had taken him, too, to the edge and let him look over. Has thought he might—just might—have proved himself equal to the moment, worthy of the trust; and in any case would like to know. It gave Don a claim to dominance, the senior not just in years but in experience—something that couldn't ever be taken away.

On the other hand it's Mike who has prospered academically. Professor M. F. Newall, internationally (if modestly) recognised for his work on the philosophy of Wittgenstein, while Donovan O'Dwyer's name has come to be associated with certain Oxford pubs—the Gardener's Arms, the Victoria Arms, the Lamb and Flag, the Eagle and Child—whichever one (and each served a lengthy term) he was making his liquid HQ, his centre of operations.

O'Dwyer, the ancient history man whose fame is (as today's obits don't quite conceal) that he talked it all away; whose early promise turned to past promise, and then to forgotten promise. So many pints, glasses, bottles, nips, doubles. 'History flows through me, Mike,' he said once, taken short in a lane just off the High, and stopping to piss against a wall, 'but it doesn't hang around to have its picture taken.'

It was what always restored the balance between them—that, and Mike's knowledge of the secret of the makutu.

It's a summer evening, Trinity term just approaching its end, and the light out there in the garden quad seems reluctant to leave; but as they sit on, eating three kinds of berries with one kind of cream, revolving the bottles, pulling once and then, later, a second time, on the rope that brings the disapproving butler to replenish, it fades, as old soldiers are supposed to fade, and they're left at last under the wavering illumination of the candle chandelier.

'And what's this I'm hearing about you, young Newall?'

It's Bertie Winterstoke, sitting beside him, who asks this, when the bones of Donovan O'Dwyer seem for the moment picked clean. Winterstoke is eighty, tall and thin, with boyish-blue old-boy eyes, a lot of untidy white hair, and a large ugly hearing aid that looks just one technological step beyond the ear trumpet. O'Dwyer's contemporary and friend, Bertie likes to keep up the joke that Mike, twenty years his junior, is 'young'. Or perhaps he sometimes forgets it's no longer true.

He has been away from Oxford for some months, and is catching up on the gossip. The question is murmured, a discreet note posted directly into his neighbour's ear. It's the hour when the port, or the claret, or the sauterne (which were preceded by excellent wines over four courses at the high table) opens a few last gates. But Mike is wary. 'About me? That I've been on a jaunt to Croatia?'

'No, no. That was long ago wasn't it?'

'I've been again. Just back.'

'Ah.'

But of course this is not what Winterstoke means. No escape. Mike says it cheerfully. 'You mean our divorce.'

'That's it,' says Winterstoke, relieved that he hasn't, after all, blundered in where he's not wanted. 'That is what I've been hearing. So it's final. Sad news, dear boy.'

'Well . . .' Mike shrugs, fiddles with his spoon, and decides, since Winterstoke has been away he won't have heard the quip he's used, and perhaps overused, to cover the pain and embarrassment of it. 'We'd had a very long disengagement. It was time to untie the knot.'

Winterstoke chortles obligingly. And then: 'No. But look here, I'm sorry to hear it, Michael. I hoped you might . . . You know?'

'Afraid not, Bertie. No chance of that.'

'A pity. I admired Gillian. I do admire her.'

'I'm sure she deserves it.'

'A beautiful woman.'

'Certainly,' Mike agrees.

'Courageous. Articulate. Not afraid to speak her mind.'

Mike feels he could do without these reminders. Perhaps the noble lord would like to try his luck with her. But he acknowledges their justness: 'Yes indeed. All of that.' After a moment he adds, 'Too much, I sometimes thought.'

'Ah well, we bring it on ourselves, Michael. We like them intelligent and then we complain when they develop balls. Beat us at our own game.'

'You mean talking, do you?' Gillian was always formidably articulate.

'Handing it out, dear boy. Margaret Thatcher's handbag. If we'd had feminism without the atomic bomb, we could have had the women's infantry.' He shrugs, looking across the table at the Master's female guest, who is listening. 'I should shut up. Careless talk costs lives, they used to tell us during the war. But there's a point, I think.'

He shovels a load of berries on board, and closes his mouth on them, where it seems whatever needs to happen next happens almost without the aid of mastication. After a few sideways movements of the lower jaw, and a pause which has also given him time to reflect, he swallows and tries again.

'And we, of course . . . I mean chaps. We get softer, don't we? Is it just age, or something in the water? Have you become a weeper, Michael?'

Professor M. F. Newall, recognised for work on some of the drier corners of Wittgenstein's *Tractatus*, who has recently been shedding rather more tears than a man is supposed to, doesn't reply.

'Play me the Last Post,' Winterstoke says, 'and I'm a goner.'

Mike has had his share, more than his share, of those good wines, and for just a moment he seems to hear the Last Post, and imagines the grave of Joe Panapa on the island of Crete. He stares out across the garden quad. The gothic gingerbread opposite deliquesces, then pulls itself together.

'And you can afford it, can you?' Winterstoke asks.

'The divorce?' Mike is glad to get the subject into its practical frame. 'Now you mention it, Bertie, no I can't. I might have to pitch a tent down by the canal and tidy myself every evening to claim my dining rights.'

Winterstoke opens his mouth and puts his head back, miming laughter. His long greenish teeth are tinged berry-red. 'My dear chap, that's pretty much my life you describe.'

The butler is reaching up to the candles with a snuffer on a pole as the fellows rise in ones and twos to make their way into the common room where they began, almost three hours ago, with a glass of champagne. There's coffee waiting now, a box of cigarettes, even brandy and cigars if anyone should want them. Mike excuses himself.

'Must take a leak.' He means it as an exit, an escape, but Winterstoke comes too.

'A life peer must pee,' he says as they make their way down the stairs. And then, as they stand side by side at the porcelain: 'A painful time for you, Michael. I know. Feel for you. Been through it myself.'

Mike mumbles his thanks, shaking off and zipping up. 'The trip to Croatia was good. Change of scene and so on.'

'What about the home front,' Winterstoke persists. 'How are you coping there?'

'Getting used to it,' Mike says. 'Living alone, I mean.'

'One does, of course. Mrs Cratchet helps in my case.' Mrs Cratchet is Bertie Winterstoke's home help.

'I don't have a Mrs Cratchet,' Mike says. From the wash-basin he asks, 'I'll see you at the wake?'

11

'The big man's send-off? You will, you will. Most assuredly. Why not a lunch afterwards?'

'Why not indeed?' Mike hesitates at the door.

'Don't wait for me, Argentina,' Winterstoke says, standing like a patient horse waiting for the starting gates to open. 'When you're young the penis has a mind of its own. At my age, it's the bladder.'

Out in the darkness of the quad Mike breathes deep and heads for the porter's lodge. But it's late, the door in the gate is locked for the night. He makes his way back through the garden quad, through a door in a wall, through another door, through a carpark and a set of tall iron gates. The doors and the iron gates require different keys which, with slow persistence, he manages.

Now—is it the fresh air?—as he makes his way along St Giles and up Woodstock Road, he begins to be conscious he's drunk. Quite considerably drunk. Appreciably.

Going past the grease-smelling van that sells hamburgers and chips outside the Radcliffe Infirmary, he decides he may have had a moment of sleeping on his feet. May still be having it. The legs are in motion and the body rides on them, dozing.

At a familiar corner he turns down a lane, pushes a little wooden gate open that doesn't (and never did) hang square on its hinges, follows the path under an enormous copper beech. At the front door he pulls out his keys again and finds what ought to be the right one. It takes concentration, a narrowing of the eyes, a steadying of the hand, to get it into the lock. It goes in, but won't turn.

Bloody hell! He doesn't live here any more. And Gillian has changed the locks.

There's a moment of the old outrage before he retreats, back along the path under the beech tree, as old perhaps as the house, which means two full centuries.

An upstairs window opens and a voice—the voice—comes down.

'Who's down there? What do you want?' And then, 'Oh it's you. What are you doing, Michael?'

He squints up at her and manages to say, 'Forgot . . .'

'What do you mean, forgot?' Her tone, he decides, is not

angry exactly; but snotty. Exasperated. The Wronged One standing on her Rights.

'Forgot,' he repeats. 'Past tense of the verb to forget.'

'I hope you're not drinking too much, Mike.'

A note of concern? But he's on a roll with the verb to forget. 'Has to do with loss of the power to recollect. Failure of memory. In extreme cases associated with certain forms of dementia. Al's heimer especially. You remember Al?'

By now she has slammed the window shut. He can still see her in there, behind glass, framed, a portrait of herself. The Provoked Wife. The Dark Madonna. The Angry Anglican. He hears her say something. He thinks (though it seems unlikely) it may have been, 'Piss off, for heaven's sake.'

He turns to go. Over his shoulder he makes a stab at a rude dismissive gesture and pushes through the little gate into the lane, his throat tightening again, the tears welling and spilling.

Just an average quiet night in North Oxford, he thinks, silently laughing as he silently weeps. But as he goes down Plantation Road he calms himself; reminds himself of his new Zen discipline, which forbids this kind of bad behaviour, this counting of old scores.

Drink less, think more, he tells himself; and repeats it.

Back at the little terrace house (also belonging to Bardolph's) which is his current address, and which secretly he likes very much, he has another pee, makes himself a mug of tea, goes upstairs to the study beside his bedroom, switches on his word processor and calls up the file in which he has been writing letters to his wife—his former wife. None of these has been sent. Not yet. Letters to Gillian. A book perhaps?

'Dear Former Wife and Sometime Sharer of the Newall Name,' he begins.

But he stops himself. This won't do. There have been times when he has written to her through half the night and been unable next day to think clearly and work efficiently. And in spite of everything, including unhappiness, he does want, is determined, to take control of his new life. This recent trip to Croatia has been good, as he told Winterstoke; but it has also unsettled him. And now there is the death of O'Dwyer. He goes to another file and begins a different letter.

'Dear Dalmatian,

'Donovan O'Dwyer is dead . . .'

He stops, feeling that so many ds in such a short space must be less than serious. He picks up one of his Zen books, opens it at random, and reads about Joshu who took up Zen at the age of sixty, began teaching at eighty, and continued for forty years. When a student came to him and said he had nothing in his mind, what should he do? Joshu replied, 'Throw it out.'

The student protested. 'If I have nothing, how can I throw it out?'

'Well, then,' Joshu said, 'carry it out.'

Mike turns over several dozen pages and reads, 'Roam about until exhausted and then, dropping to the ground, in this dropping *be whole.*'

❧

Gillian is there next morning at the funeral service, by which time Mike is sober and not a little ashamed. It's quite a crowd, though only a handful from Bardolph's. St Antony's, Donovan O'Dwyer's college, is strongly represented. There's an assortment of women of various ages, some of them alone and seeming to know no one. Everyone, Mike assumes, and not least Camille, O'Dwyer's famously long-suffering wife-now-widow, must be wondering, as he is wondering, is this one of Don's women? And what about her? And that one over there?

But then, following that logic, why not Gillian? Could she be one of the secret sorority? It's a thought that has never occurred to him before. It brings an unpleasant shudder. Why, after all, is she here?

He looks around for her again, sees her talking to Camille, embracing her, and remembers that they are friends from way back; that they belong to a group of Anglican women who meet every Saturday morning at the Café Rouge. Church women, but with balls, he thinks, the previous evening's small talk coming back to him.

And Winterstoke, tall, thin and bending in the breeze, has materialised beside him. 'When I used to drink with O'Dwyer,' the peer bugles, as if that talk hasn't been interrupted by some hours of sleep, 'he was bowling them over like there was no tomorrow. That was in his Lamb and Flag phase. Height of his powers. No stopping him. Booze, fags, and girls. Headlong. Must say I admired the brute. Such stamina.'

On Mike's other side Dr Sebastian Straw, Master of Bardolph's, listens, head down, leaning on his precautionary umbrella. 'Waste of a life, d'you think?'

'Oh no,' Winterstoke protests. 'Not at all. Never wasted a minute.'

As they take their places in the sombre crematorium chapel he murmurs, half to himself, half for Mike's ear, 'For we have done those things we ought not to have done, and our health is none the worse for it.'

It's a secular service—handsome reminiscences, good jokes, eloquent talk of soldiering, of scholarship, of family life, of pub life; even (with suitable circumlocutions and obliquities) of excesses and turpitudes. There are some references back to early years, to New Zealand, but not a lot. The returned serviceman aspect includes the lines about age not wearying nor the years condemning, intended surely, Mike points out (this is afterwards, to Winterstoke, in the courtyard again) for the ones who died in battle, not for the ones who survived and whom, like O'Dwyer, age has wearied and the years have condemned well and truly.

'It's embarrassing,' he protests. 'And such bad pastiche.'

'Antony and Cleo,' Winterstoke agrees. 'Age shall not wither her nor custom stale her infinite what's-his-name. But you know, dear boy, we old soldiers and old sailors are moved.'

'Of course. So am I, Bertie. That's probably why I complain. We shall not be moved, but we bloody are.'

They go over to offer Camille their condolences. She's standing with her daughter and two sons, composed, rather beautiful, in black but with a dash of red.

'Mike,' she says, taking him by both hands and drawing him aside. 'Will you give me a call sometime in the next few days? There's something I have to talk to you about. Something Don wanted you to do for him.'

'Wanted me to do?' He's surprised. He and O'Dwyer were never close.

'As a fellow-New Zealander.'

'Oh I see. Yes, of course.'

While Winterstoke says his piece Mike turns to Gillian standing nearby. 'I'm sorry about the disturbance last night, Gilly. Pissed, I'm afraid.'

'I don't mind the disturbance. But I hope you're all right, are you?'

'Yes, yes,' he assures her. 'Everything's under control.'

'Are you sure?'

'Quite sure.'

'I hope so, Mike. I worry about you.'

'Don't,' he says. And he squeezes her hand.

※

'Full marks to Oxford,' Mike says as he and Winterstoke settle afterwards at an out-of-doors table at the Trout at Wolvercote, looking out on the stone bridge, the weir and the fast-flowing river. 'Sometimes I wonder why I'm here. But where else could they do you such a send-off?'

'There's a lot to be said for a concentration of good minds in one place,' Winterstoke agrees. 'But you're right, you know. It would have been better without that going down of the sun stuff.'

'They'll do it for you, Bertie.'

'They would if I let them.'

'Well, how could you prevent it?'

'I don't intend to die, dear boy. Haven't the least intention.'

He's putting two pints down on the table between them, along with a numbered paddle that will signal where the lunches he has ordered should be delivered. There are peacocks in the garden, walking under trees and perching on outhouse roofs, their drooping tails now and then flaring into extravagant displays of greens and blues. Below the parapet the trout which give the pub its name appear and disappear, forever swimming to stay in one place. An old wooden footbridge, broken now, but which Mike thinks he remembers walking over when he was first in Oxford, goes halfway across and stops. Beyond trees on the opposite bank the Port Meadow takes itself off into a hazy distance out of which would come the humming and crooning of the A34 if it were not drowned here by the nearer turbulence of the weir.

'With me,' Winterstoke declares, 'O'Dwyer was something of an obsession. Not sure why. Sometimes thought of him as the bit of me that got lost along the way. Didn't like him altogether. But I envied him.'

'Gillian used to say I envied him. I denied it . . .'

'But it was true.'

'Yes.'

'You didn't know one another in New Zealand?'

'I saw him just once. I was a boy. He was a returned soldier. Captain O'Dwyer. He was in a spot of trouble.'

'When was he not?'

'Yes, of course. But this was rather different. He was—how can I explain? He was having a curse put on him.'

Winterstoke stares, refusing to be astonished. 'A curse. I see.'

'A makutu.'

'Something Maori.'

'Yes.'

'Was it serious?'

'The people who were there thought so. It's a bit like a fairy story. There was a bad fairy called Auntie Pixie . . .'

'You're pulling my leg of course.'

'Not at all.'

Winterstoke shakes his shaggy mane and stares. 'So why did I never hear this?'

'It's something he wouldn't have talked about.'

'But you knew.'

'I knew, because I was there when it happened. If it'd got about, it could only have come from me.'

'So discretion was more or less . . .'

'Enforced by circumstance. Yes. But now he's dead . . .'

'You're free to talk.' Winterstoke shakes his head again. 'I see. And no one knew.'

'Camille knew. And the daughter . . .'

'Helen.'

'Yes. She wrote a short story about it once, but I suppose people thought it was just fiction. She'd heard a version of what happened. It wasn't the whole truth, but it was close.'

Winterstoke frowns. 'O'Dwyer believed in this thing—this Mac-whatever?'

'Makutu. I think sometimes it suited him to believe it. He liked to pretend . . .'

Mike stops, then starts again. 'He had an idea that the gods had meant him to live his life in the land of his birth.'

'The gods?'

'So to speak. That it was his destiny . . .'

'New Zealand was?'

'Yes. So the first in Greats, and the fellowship at St Antony's, and all that, he came to see as the working out of the curse.'

'His successes?'

'Because they kept him here. And then the booze and the women . . . They were part of it too.'

'Oxford, booze and women. Not a bad curse.' Winterstoke sips his beer. 'But why did the bad fairy put a curse on him?'

'Why? Ah well . . .' Mike can't resist a dramatic pause. How many years has he waited for the chance to deliver this line? 'It was because he'd killed a man.'

Winterstoke frowns and makes a quick adjustment to his hearing aid. 'Could you say that again?'

'It was said he'd killed a man. One of his own Maori soldiers.'

Winterstoke's pleasure is immense. 'You mean we've just sent a murderer off into eternity, and no one knew?'

'I knew.'

Their lunches arrive, two plates of cod and chips with a large limp salad in a wooden bowl. They make space for the platters on their table. Winterstoke says, 'You're going to have to tell me about this, Michael. From the beginning.'

'From the beginning is a long story.'

The life peer smiles and opens his hands above the table. 'Take your time, brother. We're old men, and we have the summer before us.'

TWO

Wine and War

MIKE NEWALL GREW UP IN HENDERSON, THEN A NEARBY SETTLEMENT, now an outer suburb, of the city of Auckland which straddles a ten-kilometre-wide isthmus called by the Maori Tamaki-makau-rau—the place of a thousand lovers. The Henderson valley runs from the foothills of the Waitakere range, which shelters it from prevailing westerlies (but not from the rains they bring off the Tasman Sea) down to the upper reaches of the Waitemata, Auckland's eastern, and principal, harbour.

They were mostly Dalmatian settlers, poor gum-diggers and fishermen, who first saw the potential of cheap land that could be bought in the valley, and established orchards and vineyards there. In Mike's childhood New Zealand was still a beer-and-whisky culture, and the local wine was popularly known as Dally plonk. The appellation was affectionate but also disparaging. The wine might have deserved it, or it might have deserved better; but most of those who drank it would not have known good from bad. For them it was simply the cheapest and quickest bus route to the suburb of Inebriation.

Established by plebiscite at election time in New Zealand there were 'wet' areas where pubs could be built and liquor sold, and 'dry' areas where they could not. In the case of Henderson the divider between wet and dry was the local railway line, and

Mr Assid Corban, a Lebanese who had planted vines and was making wine, found his house and sheds on the dry side of the tracks. This problem he solved by buying from the railways a very small earth-floored concrete shelter, only a few yards from his house but across the tracks on the wet side. From there he began selling wine in flagons to passing motorists. Great oaks from little acorns . . . New Zealand's wine industry was under way.

Mike's father, the child of settlers from County Armagh, taught English at a grammar school in the city. His mother, of longer-established but also Anglo-Irish stock, had trained as a teacher but had given that up to be a suburban wife and mother. They lived, in the region of upper Te Atatu Road, in a large weatherboard house on an acre of land adjoining the orchard and vineyard of a Dalmatian family, the Seleniches. Each day, walking down into Henderson on his way to school, Mike passed a sign on the Selenich gate which read LICENSED TO SELL TWO GALS. The unintended meaning was exactly right for a schoolboy's sense of humour, especially because the Selenich extended family included two dark-eyed, long-legged young women who would have been decidedly saleable. Remembering that sign all these years later, it's the other meaning, the intended one, that strikes him as funny. It was not the case, as a visitor ignorant of New Zealand's licensing laws of the time might have supposed, that the Selenich family were permitted to sell up to two gallons of their wine; it was that they were not permitted to sell less.

At first, and for a number of years, relations between the adult members of the two families were civil—they might almost have been described as friendly—without ever quite generating real warmth. This must have been partly because the Seleniches were Catholic; and in the Newall family distrust of 'Papists' (pronounced by the grandfather Pe-pists, with a very long e) had been brought out from Ulster along with loyalty to Crown and flag. It was a prejudice time and distance had diluted but not destroyed. Priests, and especially nuns in their black flowing robes, were faintly sinister. Catholic items and practices, summarised (again by Grandfather Zeb) as 'candles, confession and canonisation', had about them an aura of darkness.

There was also the barrier of language. The younger Dalmatian adults, recently arrived, struggled with English; their

parents spoke it hardly at all. And though the children were
fluent in the language, they went to the local Catholic school,
while the Newalls went to the State school, Henderson Primary.
The two school groups, when their paths crossed, sometimes
shouted juvenile insults at each other. At those times the Newall
and Selenich children behaved as if they didn't know one
another. But on their home territories, which lay side by side, or
back to back, divided only by a sagging wire fence, it would have
needed a parental embargo to prevent fraternisation. There was
no embargo. They played together, wandered in and out of one
another's houses, were invited to one another's birthday parties,
argued, as they grew older, about Papal infallibility and tran-
substantiation, and became part each of the other's lives and
landscape.

For Mike, getting to know the Dalmatian neighbours began
pre-school. There was at that time, parked at the edge of their
orchard, a derelict truck; and for what was probably a brief period
but seems in recollection a very long one, he went each day to
sit on its cracked shiny brown leather seat, behind its flat glass
windscreen, where he was joined by solemn, silent little Marica
(pronounced Maritsa), the Selenich child nearest to him in age.
There, with appropriate noises and sawing at the wheel, the two
infants motored stationary through many miles.

Then the truck was removed. One day it was there, the next
not. Soon after, the two began at their different schools. A lifetime later Professor M. F. Newall, Fellow of Bardolph's College,
Oxford, looking down on the fast-flowing river while eating cod
and chips with his amiable colleague Lord Winterstoke, is able
to remember little about the child Marica except that she was
always there, one of the Selenich clan. That was how she remained for him, part of the background, silent, round-eyed,
enigmatic, until their first year as university students when he fell
in love with her.

The war (also called, or so it seemed to the child, 'the
Duration') was the background to his early life. At first it
presented itself in the form of a long exciting narrative, of which
selected episodes (*Mrs Miniver*, *Brief Encounter*, *Casablanca*)
were shown on Saturday evenings at the local town hall which
served as Henderson's cinema, while others (Mr Churchill's

speeches, the voice of 'Herr Hitler', the BBC news crackling through static) came over the wireless. The fall of Paris, Dunkirk, the Battle of Britain, the campaigns in Greece and Crete and North Africa—these were events along the way; and the promised end of the story was to be the Victory V was for.

But it was all happening 'over there', where 'our boys' were being sent; and although in Henderson, as everywhere in New Zealand, there were blackouts and rationing and bomb shelters and school air-raid drills and signs saying DIG FOR VICTORY and (as Winterstoke also remembers, from his experience much nearer the heart of the matter) CARELESS TALK COSTS LIVES, none of these seemed quite serious. They were like acts of loyal imitation, a way of honouring the ones to whom the real war was happening really.

But when the Japanese raided Pearl Harbour and began their big push down through the Pacific, as if they intended to have it all and the last stop would be New Zealand, the very long story that was to end in V for Victory seemed not quite so brilliant, its V-end a whisker less than certain. There were shadows over it, and they were the shadow of a doubt, and the fainter shadow of fear. Singapore fell. Darwin was raided. A Japanese submarine was seen in Sydney Harbour. A ship called the *Niagara*, with a cargo of gold bullion, was sunk off the Hen and Chickens not far north of Auckland. Around the countryside, on roads coming up from likely landing places, 'tank-traps' appeared—the trunk of a large tree, one end pulled up on a steel cable, ready to be dropped down in the path of invaders. And then, pretty much putting the shadows to flight, the Americans came.

But before any of those shadows had begun to darken the picture, the war had brought Marica's cousin Frano into the neighbourhood, and into Mike Newall's life. Marica's aunt Ljuba was married to Joe Panapa, a Maori freezing worker from Northland, and Frano was their son. Early in the war Joe joined up with the Maori Battalion and went into training at Linton Camp near Palmerston North. So Ljuba returned to live with her family on the orchard. Frano was the same age as Mike. They met among the fruit trees, and in the way small boys do without adult introductions, after a few half-challenging approaches began to play together.

Joe wasn't Catholic, which might explain why, although Frano was baptised and went with the Selenich family to church on Sunday, he was allowed to go to the State school. It was probably a compromise agreed between the parents. So now Mike on his way to school each day went first through the orchard to the Selenich house where Frano was waiting. Together the two boys walked down the drive to the gate with its TWO GALS sign, and then on down the hill and across the main road to Henderson Primary.

There are two scenes Mike remembers clearly and now describes to Bertie Winterstoke. The first was the day Joe Panapa came to tell Ljuba that he was on final leave before posting overseas, and to say goodbye to her family. The two boys must have been playing in the orchard or the packing shed. Frano was called indoors, and Mike tagged along.

The Seleniches sat in an informal circle, Joe at the centre, almost silent, probably embarrassed to be getting so much attention, but dignified, handsome in his uniform, his black hair cut very short, glossy with Brylcreem. Ljuba and her sister-in-law Vica (Marica's mother) were looking sad, close to tears. The older Selenich men were solemn, speaking in low crackling voices, sometimes in Croatian, sometimes in their heavily accented English. Joe took Frano on his knee and held him there. He asked who Mike was, and pulled him close so the boy felt the sandpaper roughness of the khaki battledress. Joe had brought Frano presents. Now he reached into his jacket pocket and pulled out a clasp knife. That, he said, could be a present for Frano's friend.

Mike was too shy to say more than a murmured thank you; but he turned the knife over in his hand, pulling its blades out, hoping it would be apparent how pleased and grateful he was. And when Joe was leaving he found his voice and called loudly after him, 'Goodbye Joe. Good luck.' And then (imitating the Seleniches), 'Adio, Yoseph.'

Joe took Ljuba and Frano on his farewell visit to his family north of Auckland. In three or four days they were back. Then Ljuba went south in an attempt to see him off—first to the army camp just outside Palmerston North, and then to Wellington where the troopship sailed from.

Mike remembers Ljuba telling his mother in their kitchen how the men were not allowed out the night before they were to take the train to Wellington. The camp was surrounded by a high fence of corrugated iron topped with barbed wire. The men were inside the fence, and outside it were wives, parents, sisters and younger brothers, family members who had got wind of the fact that departure was close. So the men used their bayonets to punch holes in the iron, and soon, all along that stretch of the road, there were people murmuring into the gaps. 'It was like the Wailing Wall,' Ljuba said. 'And next morning the fence looked like a kitchen grater.'

Next day there was a race to get to Wellington and to the wharves, to see the ship sail out. Some must have picked up the night train from Auckland as it came through early in the morning. Some got lifts with the very few who owned cars. Some hitchhiked, and some didn't make it. But again the men and their families were to be kept apart. There was singing from the wharf, and from the ship, waving and cheering, faces blurring into distance. It was the last many were to see of their soldier son or husband or lover.

So now Joe was gone, and life went on as before. There were letters from him, headed 'Somewhere at Sea', but with Australian, and then South African postmarks. Weeks went by. At last he was in England, in training, doing long route marches, seeing something of London, experiencing the Blitz. Then he was 'At Sea' again; or as the top of another of his letters put it, 'Heading for Trouble'—and on these letters there were no postmarks. Sometimes parts of the letter had been inked out by the censor.

Frano and Mike played war. They did bayonet charges, dug and dived into foxholes, threw hand-grenades, shot a lot of Jerries. They also climbed trees, built huts, made bows and arrows out of bamboo.

Two streams run through Henderson, the Oratia just below the school, and the Oponuku on the other side of the village. At Tui Glen below Falls Park, the two join to become the Henderson Creek, which runs on down into the upper reaches of the Waitemata. The two boys spent hours together on the banks of those streams. As they grew, sometimes Mike's mother, sometimes Ljuba Panapa, would take them down Te Atatu Road to Bridge Avenue where they could swim off the boat ramp in the Whau Creek. Later, when they both had bicycles, they went unaccompanied.

They didn't quarrel much, but when they did Frano would sometimes glower and draw back into himself and hurl the word '*Pakeha!*' with a ferocity that made it an insult; and Mike would be reminded that his friend was Maori—or (as you were allowed to say in those days) part-Maori—and that it was something he didn't forget.

One day Mike was sitting in the classroom trying to hear the sound of the stream which ran under a bridge below the school grounds and which sometimes, especially after summer rain, when the sash windows were raised, he could just make out from his desk. He was straining to listen when he became aware that the teacher had said something that had produced, not just silence, but an unusual stillness. There was a moment in which he did hear the stream; and then the teacher began to speak again in the special hushed way, all breath and whistling sibilants, she reserved for things that were important.

Frano wasn't there (Had he not come to school that day? Had he been taken away before the announcement was made? Mike doesn't remember) and what she was saying was about him. Or rather, it was about his father, Private Joe Panapa, who had gone overseas with 'the famous Maori Battalion'.

There was a lot of palaver in what she said, a lot of beating about the bush—preparation, no doubt was how she saw it, for the shock she was about to deliver. But in the end she got it out. She told them. Frano's father was dead. He'd been killed fighting the Germans in Crete.

Some of the little girls cried. Some of the boys seemed excited. One jumped up as if he was going to run and do something; and then, looking embarrassed, he sat down again. Mike felt a shock that was not quite like anything he'd felt before, a jolt that was almost physical, curiously like pleasure, yet not pleasant at all.

That afternoon he made his way home up the hill, past the sign on the gate, and down the Selenich drive. He dragged himself past their house, not knowing what to do, not wanting to be seen, but curious to know what was happening in there. What did you do when your father was killed? How did you behave?

No sound came from within. He climbed the wire to the Newall side and hung about, playing with sticks, talking to himself. Once the back door opened and Marica's mother went along the verandah at the back, took something from the clothes-line and returned indoors. Mike went on to his own house. He told his mother the news and she wept, hugged him, made a telephone call to his father, wept some more, hugged him again. His sister Stella came home and there were more tears.

Later that afternoon Mike drifted back through the trees towards the Selenich house. And now, through open windows, came the sound he remembers so vividly he could almost imitate it, like a tune learned in childhood—the wild sounds of Ljuba Panapa's wailing and lamentation.

Very recently (Mike tells Bertie Winterstoke)—in fact on the trip to Croatia from which he has just returned—he heard that same sound again. He was staying in a village near to the Dalmatian coast and, with a woman friend, walked up to the cemetery that looked over the roofs of the village and down the long blue estuary that ran in from the sea. It was hot summer and they seemed to be alone there, walking slowly among the graves in the intermittent shade of cypresses, when all at once a wailing began that seemed to lift Mike out of himself and back to that day in his childhood. On a path below the one on which they were walking they saw a young woman shouting and throwing herself about in anguish, being restrained and comforted by two who were, Mike's Croatian friend told him, her parents.

Mike asked what she was saying.

Her husband, the friend explained, had been killed in the recent fighting, and she was shouting to him in his grave. 'My darling Tonci, why did you leave me like this? I loved you more than the whole world. How can I live without you? Why did you not take me with you?' And so it went on.

What was strange to Mike was that it was as if the words, the rhythm and sounds of this rolling lamentation, were identical to what he'd heard from the Selenich house that afternoon when the news came of Joe Panapa's death. He remembered it as if

Ljuba had been using English. He seemed to remember her shrieking the same declarations and the same questions. Joe, my darling, I loved you more than I love life. Why have you left me? How can I live without you?

Yet surely Ljuba would have been wailing in Croatian, as this woman was. And if that were so, how could he possibly have understood her? What he understood, he now supposes, was an emotion, not a language.

In the days and weeks following the news of Joe's death details about the circumstances were slowly assembled. The New Zealand Division had gone into battle, first in Greece, where, after a month of fighting, the Allies were driven out by the invading Germans, and then in Crete, where the New Zealanders had withdrawn, and which they were to help to defend. After a few quiet weeks the Germans attacked Crete from the air, bombing and strafing first, and then landing troops by parachute and glider; and although many hundreds, perhaps thousands, of them had been killed, they were successful in taking the airport at Maleme in the sector of the island which it was the New Zealanders' task to defend.

A night counter-attack was organised to recover the airport. Despite heroic efforts, this failed, and the Maori Battalion were ordered to form the rearguard covering a withdrawal. Some time during that action Joe Panapa had stepped on a mine and died.

The loss of that airfield meant the Germans now had a point of entry for more troops and weapons. A week later it was accepted that Crete could not be defended by an Allied force that lacked air cover. The surviving New Zealanders, together with British and Australian troops from other sectors of the island, conducted a fighting withdrawal to the southern coast, and from the fishing village of Sphakia most were rescued by the Royal Navy and ferried across the Mediterranean into Egypt.

Frano stayed away from school for a week, after which the Seleniches sent word that Mike should call for him as usual. Next morning he was there, waiting by the back steps, his tearful mother, Ljuba, standing on the verandah ready to wave goodbye.

As they went down the drive to the gate Mike felt he should say something about the death. He felt sorry for Frano; but there was also something like curiosity. He'd been thinking about Joe

Panapa's body, buried on the island of Crete in its wide black shiny boots and khaki battledress. How would it be to have thoughts like that about your father?

They walked along, silent, two small boys in outsize raincoats, until Mike managed to say, 'Your dad's been killed.'

Frano nodded. 'Yeah.'

'In the war,' Mike said, not wanting the subject to end there.

Frano confirmed this too. 'In Crete,' he said.

'Miss Glass told us.'

'What did she say?'

'She said your dad was killed. Fighting—you know—the Jerries.'

Frano nodded.

The silence went on. There was a question Mike was trying to frame but he couldn't find the right words. 'What's it like?' he asked.

Frano didn't understand. 'You know,' Mike said. 'I mean, when your dad's killed.'

Frano shrugged. 'It's OK.' But his eyes filled with tears.

In Mike's pocket was the knife Joe Panapa had given him. It was the first clasp knife he'd ever owned. He took it out and looked at it.

'Your dad gave it to me,' he said. And then (a moment of inspiration, because it wasn't true): 'Mum says I should give it to you.'

He pushed it into his friend's hand. Frano took it and, as they walked on, held it as if he wasn't sure he should accept. And then they stopped, because at the same moment they'd seen a rat running along between the rows of grapevines.

'Rat,' they both shouted, letting their schoolbags slide to the ground and looking around for stones. They let fly at the place where it had been, but it was gone.

When they took up their bags again there was no sign of the knife, and Mike supposed it had gone into Frano's pocket.

THREE
Take Your Own Loo Paper

'OH I SAY, THERE THEY ARE!'

It's the trout Winterstoke means, that can be seen now, swimming hard to stay in one place, heads pointing into the current as it rushes down from the weir. Mike stares too, down into the turbulence. The one at the front of the group holds its place for a time, as if leading them somewhere, then moves slightly to one side and drops back, as team cyclists do, letting another take over.

'When you were talking about the woman in the Croatian cemetery,' Winterstoke says, 'and your friend's mother, Ljuba . . . There were some lines of a poem in my head. I've just remembered. It's Coleridge, "Khubla Khan" . . .'

And he quotes,

'. . . As e'er beneath a waning moon was haunted
By woman wailing for her demon lover.'

Mike nods and smiles, recognising the lines. 'There is something demonic about that sort of lamentation. Maoris do it. And Israelis. It must be rather satisfying. Not a lot to be said for a stiff upper lip.'

Winterstoke is not so sure. 'It's not that I don't feel sad the blighter's gone, Michael. But I just can't see how it would have

29

helped if we'd all been wailing our heads off this morning.'

'For Donovan the demon lover?'

Winterstoke pulls a wry face. 'I suppose some of the women would have enjoyed a jolly good wail.'

He takes a long chip between finger and thumb and guides it into his mouth as if it were a stick of asparagus. 'What took you to Croatia, anyway?'

'In a roundabout way it was because of having been in love with Marica.'

'Marica.' Winterstoke has reached an age when names, even (or especially) those recently heard, go into the part of his brain he thinks of as the aged porridge. 'She was the girl next door.'

'That's the one.'

'So how . . . Explain, dear boy.'

'Well. This was two years ago—the first time I went. Things had gone badly wrong between me and Gillian. I could see our marriage was going to end. Hard to believe after so many years, but the writing was on the wall. She'd turned off the life-support. It's the sort of thing that makes you review your whole history. I talked to O'Dwyer. I was toying with the idea of going back to New Zealand.'

'To live?'

'I thought about it. If Gillian was going to ditch me it seemed there was no very good reason why I shouldn't.'

'And what did O'Dwyer think?'

'He probably thought it was bullshit. Too much water under too many bridges. But he liked talking about it. It was something he couldn't do, but why shouldn't I?—that was the line he took. At least I could have a crack at it. No harm done if I didn't like it . . .'

'You thought you and Marica might get back together?'

'I suppose, yes. That idea was lurking somewhere. Foolish, of course. It was all quite foolish.'

The eighty-year-old takes a pull on his beer, wipes his stiff upper lip, shakes his shaggy white mane. 'No going back. Never is. Doesn't happen.'

Mike nods, head down, looking at a pattern of small fish bones he's making on the rim of his plate. 'No.'

'Marica was unattached?'

'Divorced.'

'Of course. With old friends these days one must assume divorce unless there's word to the contrary. But Croatia—how does that . . .'

Mike explains. 'Stella—my sister in New Zealand—she's still friends with the Selenich family. She phoned me. Ljuba Panapa—Frano's mother—had gone back to live in Croatia. She'd been there quite a few years, resettled in Dalmatia, in the area the family came from. But now trouble was looming. Slovenia and Croatia declared independence. Belgrade was threatening. Ljuba was in a disputed area. The family heard from a relative in Zagreb that her house had been damaged in a bombardment—or possibly destroyed, they weren't sure. They were worried. My sister wanted to know whether I had any way of finding out what had happened. That put the idea into my head. I'd visit Croatia before going to New Zealand. I'd be the one bringing out news. Mainly of course for Marica. She was always close to her aunt.'

'You weren't scared?'

'I didn't know how serious it was.'

'Tut tut, young Newall. When is what happens in that region ever less than serious?'

Mike nods his acknowledgement. 'We learn, Bertie. We learn. In the days before I left I started to take more notice of what was happening, and obviously it wasn't good. I was beginning to think about cancelling when Seb Straw brought a banker friend to dinner in College. He was in and out of that part of the world . . .'

'Money laundering probably.'

'Restructuring debt, actually.'

'My dear, same thing.'

'I asked him what I should do. He said I should go. Of course. Absolutely. No sweat. Nothing to worry about. Safe as houses. Just be sure to take my own loo paper.'

'Your own loo paper!' Winterstoke's braying laugh is so loud people nearby stop talking for a moment and look in his direction.

❧

Mike knows he doesn't have to tell his friend that the slow

collapse of a long marriage can put either party, or both, into a state that feels like driving blind. It comes of an excess of subjectivity, a protracted and repetitive reviewing of one's life. So many of the certainties have vanished. Did I make a mistake somewhere? Did she? Am I responsible for her mistake? Is she responsible for mine? What is there to salvage from this wreck? How will the children react? Do I even want to go on living?

It's only later, when the panic and confusion have passed and a new life has been established, that the divorced begin to behave with the never-divorced as those who have been to the Cocos Keeling Islands, or the New Guinea Highlands, or the Antarctic continent, behave with those whose travel has never taken them outside the regular air-routes. Not marriage, it seems, but divorce becomes the truly significant life-experience.

'The only thing I miss about marriage,' Winterstoke likes to say, showing off to Newall the novice, 'is the adultery.' Mike has always smiled at this and said nothing, remembering the nervous ruin Bertie was when the melodrama of his marriage was reaching the end of Act Three.

It was when his own marriage was approaching its black-comedy ending that Mike took off for Zagreb—on his way (though Zagreb didn't seem on the way to anywhere—certainly not to the South Pacific) to New Zealand. Everything had been carefully planned. He would visit Ljuba, or make contact with her through her relatives in Zagreb, so he would have hard news of her for Marica when he reached New Zealand. Then he was to fly via Frankfurt to Dallas, where he would stop off for a few days and conduct seminars on Wittgenstein. After that it would be straight on to Los Angeles, and then a final twelve-hour flight to Auckland, where he would stay with his sister Stella and her husband Bruce.

Ljuba's half-sister Grozdana, the relative in Zagreb who kept in touch with New Zealand, appeared to him first as an elderly lady who spoke no English. When he presented himself at her door, having climbed five grim liftless flights from a grim grey street, they had a brief exchange in which he spoke English, she Croatian, and nothing was understood on either side. She seemed ready to push the door shut when he thought to write Ljuba Panapa's name on a slip of paper and hold it up to the narrowing gap. The door stopped moving, opened a little, and through it he could see her, clearly in need of her reading glasses, fiercely squinting at the paper. The door relented somewhat, and Mike quickly wrote Marica's name, and Vica's; and then the surname (corrected to its Croatian form) SELENIC, in large square caps.

Grozdana read the names, smiled, and said a sentence or two in which he recognised 'Novozelandsko'—to which he responded with smiles, a vigorous nodding of the head, and what seemed to be the password, 'New Zealand'.

Excited, she had turned indoors and was calling to someone. Now a second woman came to the door. She introduced herself as Ira and together the two welcomed him in.

Ira was younger—in her middle-to-late thirties. She might have been beautiful, except that at that moment in her life she looked, Mike thought, in some way crushed, as if she'd taken a beating, not physical, but of the soul. Her English was accented, but fluent and clear. Her body was elegant, she moved gracefully, but her shoulders and wrists were thin and there were dark hollows in her cheeks.

Mike felt that he noticed everything about her, including that she seemed to notice nothing about him. He was talking, he thought, to someone who was walking in her sleep. This, and everything about her, fascinated him.

Ira explained that they didn't know where Ljuba was. Her house down on the coast had been destroyed, they were sure of that. They'd been told that she survived unharmed—that she'd left the area before the Yugoslav army arrived. But where she'd gone they didn't know. She had two half-sisters in a village close to the town of Sibenik, and Ira thought Ljuba would have gone to them if she had means of getting there. For the moment phone lines were down and mail couldn't be relied on, but they were sure they would hear soon what had happened.

What was he to do? He asked whether he could hire a car and go looking for her. Ira assured him it wasn't possible—wasn't safe. Only a few weeks back she had tried to drive down to the coast by the direct route that would take her through the town of Karlovac, less than fifty kilometres south of Zagreb. Halfway there she'd heard on the car radio that Karlovac was being shelled, and she'd taken another route. A bridge had been destroyed, but a temporary pontoon crossing was in place, and she carried on. She was going to the funeral of a dear friend killed in the fighting, and that had made her determined to press on; but it had been foolhardy then, she said, and would be impossible now.

They invited him to stay and he accepted, intending to leave within forty-eight hours. But now, as the crisis worsened, international airlines cancelled all flights in and out of Zagreb. A Croatian service was still operating, but its flights out were full. So he found himself stranded in a country that was sliding into war.

Ira, a journalist, went to a newspaper office for some part of each day; and since Mike and Grozdana could only exchange hand signals and a few words of French, and the flat was cramped and austere in the manner of the Worker State, he spent many hours wandering about the city, drinking in its atmosphere of crisis which served as a distraction from his own. Everywhere he could feel there was a huge indignation, growing and hardening into hatred of Belgrade and the Yugoslav army. People outside shops stood staring in at television screens, unable to drag themselves away; or crouched over radios in the squares. And Mike, who felt that he hardly existed, that he was irrelevant, enjoyed the sense of being an invisible observer.

Zagreb itself was a strange mix, half imperial grandeur, half communist austerity. Its central streets and squares, its equestrian and literary statues, its museums and public buildings, elegant in the style of Vienna, generous in space, redolent of privilege, told one story; its broken pavements, dingy offices, and post-Second World War apartment buildings, grey and dirty and in need of every kind of repair, told another. The foreignness of the place, and the political and military drama of the moment, took him out of himself. He found himself interested, and not unhappy. But there were moments when he plunged back into the old wretchedness. Once, in a post office with a notice which said ZABRANJENO UNOSITI ORUZJE, and showed, like a 'no smoking', or 'no dogs' sign, a handgun in a red circle with a diagonal red line through it, he was suddenly invaded by thoughts of Gillian, their house in North Oxford, the little lopsided gate and the copper beech at the front, the lovely walled garden with its apple trees at the back, and was embarrassed by a tightening throat and prickling eyes.

But Ira, who had taken him there, didn't notice. She was always kind, patient and helpful; and yet always he felt that she was not entirely present, and that he was not quite real to her.

Almost everything about the growing crisis was coming to him through the filter of translation. But there was a moment when he felt caught up in the excitement. Croatian militia shot down two Yugoslav war planes, one after the other. It was the first time this had happened (this was the period when the Serbs still held most of the weaponry) and someone caught it on a video camera. It was shown on television, not once but many times. The Croatian soldiers could be heard shouting, 'Oba dva! Oba dva!'—'Both of them! Both of them!' And in the days that followed Mike heard that phrase on the street, saw the accompanying smiles, and felt a rush of pleasure as if he'd taken sides.

Sometimes he and Ira went to an American or a French movie together. He sat in cafés with her and drank coffee while she scribbled notes for her paper. He went with her to a camp for refugees who were beginning to come in from areas where the fighting was intense. Sometimes in the evening they drove to a park called Tuskanac on high ground looking over the city. There, despite the chill of the weather, they would have ice cream. It was the only food Ira would let him order for her; and even then she only stirred it around in its dish until it was half-melted, and licked small amounts off her spoon. Before long her cigarette would be alight (she was seldom without one), and the ice cream would be pushed across for him to finish.

Grozdana's flat consisted of two bedrooms, one she occupied, the other Ira's bedroom and study, the windows of both looking down on a central city street in which blue trams banged away all through the day and far into the night. There was a very small kitchen with a table just large enough for three to sit at, and with a balcony that looked down over an inner courtyard. The bathroom, with a curtain to protect the privacy of a person using the bath, was also the passageway to Ira's room. The only remaining space, apart from the entrance in which a refrigerator, a wardrobe, and the apartment's only full-length mirror were stationed, was a small room, hardly larger than a cupboard, with one bed and one window that opened on to the inner courtyard. It was here that Mike slept, listening to the voices of many families, every word foreign to him, yet all of it seeming intelligible and in some way—even the moments of distress and anger—reassuring.

Grozdana liked to cook, and when Ira was free to come back from her office in the middle of the day there was a full dinner for them—soup and a stew, usually, herb- and garlic-flavoured, with stuffed marrows and courgettes, potatoes and kale. In return for their hospitality Mike bought Grozdana flowers in the market, chocolates, and bottles of wine, and promised to send Ira books in English and CDs she wanted and couldn't get in Zagreb.

Often Mike and Ira sat together in a silence which was unembarrassed, companionable. When they talked it was as if they fell into designated roles. She, learning that he was a professor of philosophy, and what his special subject was, asked questions about Wittgenstein. He, who had come to Zagreb knowing less about the region than present events and past history suggested he ought to know, used her, the Croatian journalist, to correct his ignorance. Soon he had the map of the former Yugoslav federation clearly in his mind, the way its pieces related one to another, the ethnic mix in each, the balance of religious forces—Catholic, Orthodox, Muslim—and where these came from historically and went politically.

When it was his turn to be tutor he found himself engaged and challenged by Ira's questions. She was, he soon recognised, that famously formidable person the middle-European intellectual—intelligent, serious, knowing enough about any important subject at least to ask the right questions. There was still a lingering sense that she was not entirely present; but it was as if her intelligence worked even in her absence.

This intellectual give-and-take often took place at night in her room, with its clutter of books and papers, and with a low-volume background of taped jazz, at a time when the trams had almost stopped running and the street below was quiet. And always, as he lay awake afterwards thinking it over, it struck him that the flavour of these exchanges was something new in his experience, at the same time impersonal and intimate. There was a kind of closeness. But no feelings of any kind were expressed, or even signalled.

Word of Ljuba came at last, and a day later he heard that a seat for him was confirmed on a Croatian plane that would take him to Frankfurt. On the morning of his last day in Zagreb, Ljuba got through to them. The call had to be brief, but after talking to Grozdana and to Ira she found a moment to speak to the man who had been the little boy next door and the school-friend of her son.

'Tell them I'm OK,' she said. 'And safe. Pretty safe. Safe enough for an old lady.' As she said it he could hear the smile in that familiar voice he'd once heard wailing its grief at the loss of her beloved Joe. 'I'm moving to one of the islands for a while. Prvic.' And she spelled it for him. 'The family will know it—my mother's father came from there. Give my special love to Marica. Tell her I'm still waiting for her visit. And kiss Henderson for me, Micky. Do you remember when we used to call you Micky Savage?'

'Yes,' he said, but in truth he didn't remember.

'Come and visit me,' she said, 'when these stupid boys have stopped killing one another and blowing things up.'

She had a few commissions for him, things she would like him to do for her in New Zealand, if it wasn't too much trouble. He promised that he would do them, and that when the fighting was over he would visit her down on the coast.

'Bring me photographs,' she said. 'Come in the summer. You'll see why Dalmatians in New Zealand are sometimes homesick.'

'And you don't miss Henderson?' he asked.

'Oh yes, I miss it, certainly. And the people. But that Henderson, Micky—the place of your childhood with Frano and Marica and Stella—you'll find it's gone. It was going when I left. Your parents sold up and moved north, of course—I was sorry about that. And then when my brothers sold the orchard and the vineyard, I couldn't bear it. I'd lost too much by then, so I came home here. And now look. We have a war!'

Ira drove him to the airport, and there, as they sat side by side silently waiting for the call to board his flight, which was delayed, he recognised again, but more clearly, how close they'd grown. After a time he said, 'We haven't talked much about ourselves.'

She lit a cigarette and drew deep on it, looking around. 'Sometimes one says nothing because there's nothing to say.'

'Or too much.'

'Or too much, yes.'

'Have I told you the last sentence of Wittgenstein's *Tractatus*? "What we cannot speak about must be passed over in silence."'

She repeated it, smiling. 'Yes. It's good. I like it.'

Without looking at him, she put a hand over his, resting on his knee. 'While you've been here, I've been abstracted.' She looked at him. 'Abstracted. Is that the word?'

'That's the word,' he confirmed. 'And so have I.'

'So you didn't mind.'

No, he told her. He didn't mind at all.

He was surprised at the electricity that was flowing through his body from that unexpected touch.

She said, her hand still resting there, 'Three weeks before you came, the man in my life was killed.'

That was another, and very different, jolt. He turned to look at her. There was a resoluteness in her expression. It was the look he'd been aware of when he first saw her and thought it was as if she'd taken some kind of interior beating. There were no tears.

'Your husband?'

'Well . . .' (And he liked the way the W came out more or less as a V.) 'Not my husband exactly. He was someone else's husband. Her husband, my lover. We'd lived together for two years, on and off. He came and went.' She smiled. 'But he was mine. I felt I was married to him.'

This man, she explained, Josko, had worked for the state television service. He'd been in Dubrovnik on an assignment. The Yugoslav army had begun shelling from the hills, sending their fire straight down the main street.

'I've always loved that street,' she said. 'I was a student in Dubrovnik. Right now, if I could be there, I would—like the Pope, remember?—go down on my knees and kiss the stones. They were lobbing in fragmentation shells. Josko took a foolish risk. He left a piece of camera gear in the street and went back for it when the shelling started. He was killed outright.'

She had gone there for the funeral. The town couldn't be reached overland, so she had made her dash to the coast, and then had gone on by sea. As the ferry came into the port of Dubrovnik they could see the Yugoslav soldiers with their flags up on the hills. The captain told them to move to the far side of the ship, out of sight. Mostly those troops didn't fire on shipping, but he couldn't be sure an occasional bullet wouldn't come.

'I stayed where I was,' Ira said. 'They could kill me if they wanted—I didn't care. I wanted to be buried with Josko. It wasn't new for me, wanting to die. I'd felt it before. But for the first time I also wanted to kill. If I could have pulled a trigger and known the bullet would have gone straight into one of those murderers, I would have done it.'

Mike had pushed back again into his chair and was staring away through glass panels across the almost deserted airport. 'Why didn't you tell me?'

'Well, I have told you.'

'Vell,' he said, imitating her. 'But so late.'

'If I had told you, you would not have stayed with us.'

It was true; and he thought of the story of Alcestis whose husband, Admetus, instructs his servants to hide all signs of her recent death when their friend Herakles comes on a visit. But in that story the visitor, discovering the truth, goes down to the Underworld and wrestles with Death to win the dead one back to life.

When the call to board came they stood up, smiled at one another, and hugged, like very old friends. 'I think you will come back in better times,' she said. 'Ljuba wants you to visit, and so do I.'

'In that case,' he said, 'I'll come. You can count on it.'

FOUR

A Fat Brown Lady Chanting
in the Rain

MIKE NEWALL, STILL ENTERTAINING BERTIE WINTERSTOKE WITH WHAT is really O'Dwyer's story (Really? Perhaps really it's his own!) runs up against the unsatisfactoriness of memory—so vivid and complete one moment, so random and discontinuous the next. He can conjure up the marae of Frano's Maori family, and the meeting house, and the old kuia still with the faded purple moko on their chins, and the old men sitting in chairs on the porch leaning forward on their thick carved sticks. The marae and the local store were on a beach at the end of a long straight road, with a deep drain on one side choked with willow and edged with flax, and on the other a shelterbelt of pines. About half a mile up that road was the big old ramshackle house of Frano's grandparents; and it was there he and Frano stayed when they went 'up North' together on holiday—first with Ljuba, Frano's mother, later, when they were old enough, just the two boys together.

He remembers happy eternities spent walking down in morning shadow from the house to the marae and the store and the beach, and back to the house in the heat of middle day or late afternoon, stopping to inspect a dead animal or bird at the roadside, or to climb trees, lie in the grass, play under the pines.

They were children and no one up there ever asked them to hurry. Time was something there was always plenty of, as if the need to measure it, to parcel it out, belonged only to the city where anything might become scarce and everything had a price. Or was it that time belonged to the Pakeha, who made it, told it, sold it, and knew that it wasn't to be wasted, but who were consequently burdened with anxiety about it? It was up there in Northland that Mike first felt stirrings of rebellion (and they were never to be more than that) against his family of teachers and time-keepers.

The beach at the end of the road, beyond the marae, looked out across a very wide harbour which was also very long, very calm, and very blue, with black islands of rock that seemed to float at its edges or to reach out over it from the land like fingers stretched across a perfect surface. At either end of the bay were black, oyster-speckled rocks and above, green and brown promontories from which the pohutukawas leaned out so dangerously you might have thought of them as taking unnecessary risks, showing off, if they hadn't looked ancient and venerable. But since ancient and venerable is what those trees undoubtedly were, you had to accept that if they leaned out like that, craning to see past one another, up and down the inner coast as well as across to the opposite shore and even out through the gap, far away, that led to the open sea, there must be a reason for it: the pohutukawas were guardians. That is what the old people on the meeting house verandah said. Vigilance was something required of those trees, even if, as was quite possible, it was a duty they found irksome.

There was a legend to explain this, but Mike has forgotten it. All that remains is the memory that the trees were under some kind of spell which required them to keep watch whether they wanted to or not; and their shapes, gnarled and twisted, did seem to express weariness and reluctance.

Staring straight out from the marae, looking (unlike the pohutukawas) neither to left nor right, was the meeting house, not trim and spruce like the government-funded one Mike has seen there on his recent visit, but very much the worse for wear, some of its carving over the lintel broken, its coloured glass windows at the front cracked or with replacement panes that didn't match, and its corrugated iron roof paint-peeled and rusting; but with one authentic old carving upright on a pole, a red-painted, threatening, mad-tongued figure, half human, half supernatural, fierce enough to warn off an enemy or repay a child's apprehensive glance with several thoroughgoing night-mares.

And then, a mile or so along the shore from the marae, just yards from the beach and looking straight on to it, was the little house Frano's parents, Ljuba and Joe, had lived in before Joe had gone off to the war. It was still Ljuba's house, closed up when Joe left, and opened now only when she and Frano chose to go there. There was no road to it and it was reached on foot or on horseback at low tide—along the beach, around the rocks, along another beach, around another set of rocks, and there it was, hardly more than a bach or whare, three rooms, a water tank, an outhouse and a long-drop, on flat land beside a stream that ran leisurely through reeds and spilled out on to the beach.

How did Mike come to be in that place, staying with Frano? There must have been objections from his parents—in fact he's sure that there were, and that his mother worried. Would it be sanitary at the Panapa house? Would the children have sores, bare feet, torn shorts and runny noses? (Of course it wouldn't and of course they would. In those days, that's how it was. She knew all that, so why did she ask?) But how could the invitation be turned down? And Mike was keen to go.

In the end she must have relented because it was simpler and because Frano's mother would be there. Ljuba Panapa was a neighbour, almost a friend, Dalmatian-Catholic of course, but now a young war-widow, which somehow made her more accept-able than she'd seemed as the wife of a Maori freezing worker. Ljuba (and this was more to the point) could surely be relied on to see that the two boys were fed and kept out of trouble.

Mike and Frano did what boys, left mostly alone, will do in a place like that in summer. They swam, sometimes risking their lives, allowing themselves to be taken by the running tide and then battling to get out of it before it swept them out beyond their strength to swim back. They caught gurnard and kahawai from the wharf around in the next bay, and sometimes eels from the stream. At low tide they gathered mussels from the rocks, pipi and tuatua from the sand, made a fire, and boiled them in an old flame-blackened billy. They made and smoked roll-your-owns with tobacco and papers stolen from Frano's great-uncle's round tin labelled (on white sticking plaster) SMOKES. They rowed a small dinghy, not absolutely watertight, around the bay; and once took it right up into an estuary, deep green and still among mangroves at the full tide. They went into the bush alone and sometimes got lost and panicked and argued and calmed themselves before finding their way out. They made huts, climbed trees, played war and killed Jerries.

When they were hungry they ate and when they were tired they went to sleep. Depending on the point of view, their life in that place might have been described as idyllic, challenging, unsupervised, or running wild. Mike has more than once told English Gillian that it was there in New Zealand's warm north, among brown-skinned fellow-countrymen speaking two languages (possibly neither of them very well), that he first began to peel himself off from the collective identity of home-and-family and to become a person in his own right. But this is not something he will mention to Bertie Winterstoke, who might consider it sentimental, or extravagant, or meaningless, or fanciful. (Any or all of which it may be, Mike thinks. How is one to be sure?)

What he can tell his friend, however, is that it was there, at the marae of the Panapa whanau, he saw for the first time, and the only time in New Zealand, Captain Donovan O'Dwyer.

'Whanau,' Winterstoke amiably grumbles. 'Marae. Translate, dear boy. Translate.' And Mike does, before continuing.

'At first there was a welcome,' he goes on. 'A powhiri . . .'

And then, anticipating Winterstoke's objection, he pauses to explain how a visitor is welcomed on to a marae—the shouting of the women, the challenge by the guardian warrior, the slow advance of the visitor and his party, the careful picking up of the object put down on the ground. Did all of this happen? Mike thinks that it did, but after so many decades he can't be sure that he hasn't laid over the real event details from other and later ones. What he's fairly sure of is the karanga—the cry of the kuia—and the slow impressive dignified progress towards the meeting house of Donovan O'Dwyer, the decorated officer back from war, come to report to the Maori family how one of their brave sons, who was one of his men, had met death in battle.

O'Dwyer's was an overnight visit which began well and then went seriously wrong. At first the welcome was whole-hearted, sad and moving. There were tears and embraces—tears for the much loved Joe Panapa, embraces for the officer who had come such a long way to meet his family and tell them of his death. But later (as Mike recalls it) O'Dwyer went into close conference with the immediate family, and it was then the argument started. Ljuba was there as Joe's widow; but perhaps because she was Pakeha, or because of the protocols of the tribe, she seemed to have no authority, or anyway a lower status than Joe's parents, his brothers and sisters, even his aunt and uncle. And it was the latter couple, the aunt especially, known to everyone (and feared) as Auntie Pixie, who turned the quiet, sad, commemorative occasion, first into an argument, and finally a bitter dispute which, because so much of it was conducted between family members and in Maori, and because the two boys were sent away whenever they were seen to be drifting closer and trying to discover what was going on, Mike, at least, was not able to understand.

After the welcome on the marae the family moved up the road to the grandparents' house—a big old sprawling farmhouse with wood floors, brass bedsteads with lumpy mattresses, verandahs with occasional missing or rotten boards and balusters, and sacking hung up to replace broken panes in windows. There were four or five outhouses ranged in the lee of macrocarpas at the back, one of them the wash-house, one where things like saddles, bridles and gumboots were stored along with bins of grain and chaff, and the remainder serving as overnight shelter for visitors and guests.

A hangi had been put down in an area behind the house enclosed by a fence of manuka brush and stakes, much like an old-time Maori palisade; and although by the time the pit was uncovered and the steaming leaves folded back, the temperature of the argument had risen almost to match it, grace was sung in beautiful harmony and the meal was served. But before the pork and puha, the mussels and pipi and kumara and pumpkin, were out on plates, beer was being dispensed; and while the meal went on, and after it was eaten, the drinking continued. Soon feelings were threatening to run out of control, and not least Donovan

O'Dwyer's, whose capacity for alcohol even in those days was large, and whose fuse was correspondingly short.

So it was as a child that Mike Newall first saw one of those transformations O'Dwyer became known for in Oxford—so well-known, in fact, that mention of them, although oblique, was not entirely avoided in the stories told about him at today's funeral. The uniform that had looked so spruce during the marae welcome was pulled this way and that. The tie and hat were gone. The hair was dishevelled, the face red and angry, the voice loud and threatening. O'Dwyer was upset. More than upset, he was (and he shouted it) fucking angry.

For some reason he felt he'd been wronged by certain members of the Panapa family—that much was clear to the boys; and his reaction was so combative and strong, it was frowned on even by those (and they seemed to be a majority) who were taking his part. There was a sudden scuffle, fists flew, but in a moment O'Dwyer and the uncle, who had taken offence at something said about Auntie Pixie Panapa, were pulled apart.

While a certain amount of soothing and consoling went on, Mike and Frano were told by Ljuba that they must go to bed. With a show of compliance, the two boys made a quick escape down to the bay. By the time they got back it was dark, there were two kerosene lanterns burning on the verandah throwing light down on the gathering, and the two sides to the argument seemed to have been separated to opposite ends of the garden. Donovan O'Dwyer appeared now too drunk to fight, or even to argue. Joe's parents were distressed, as was Ljuba, who took the boys indoors, waved a damp flannel over each of them by way of a token wash, and put them to bed in a room at the front of the house away from the noise and action. For a time they talked of creeping out to see what the adults would do next; and then they were asleep.

Mike woke in the early hours of the morning to two sounds—a woman chanting in Maori, and rain falling. He was aware of the chanting first. It seemed to go on and on, something strange and sinister and interesting that pulled at his consciousness; but his body, weary from the day's, and many days', physical effort, resisted. The chant was gathered into a dream which prevented full waking.

The rain began gently at first, then heavier, until finally it was coming down with a sound that is, Mike tells Winterstoke, among the loveliest memories of a New Zealand childhood. It was summer, and day after day the weather had been hot and humid. Now the air seemed to have reached the point where the excess of moisture in the upper atmosphere simply sheds itself, cool and refreshing. On the iron roof of the old house, with no insulation in the ceilings to muffle it, the rain thundered. But still, against that all-out rain-on-roof drumming, the chant continued, the woman's voice rising, seeming determined not to be defeated by it. This was very different from the woman wailing for her demon lover. It was like a haka, loud, charged, purposeful—the voice as weapon.

When Mike woke himself sufficiently to get up and go to see what was happening he found Frano's bed empty. There were no lights, but in the dark of the big farm kitchen, which was the main living space, he bumped into one person, then another, soft bodies moving blindly about, murmuring in English and in Maori. Others were on the back verandah, and as he peered into the darkness he recognised the outlines of Frano and his mother standing together at the rail. Beside them were Frano's grand-parents with arms around one another's waists, and they were all staring out into the rain where the chanting was coming from.

It was now, looking where they looked, that Mike saw the naked figure of Auntie Pixie. In the dimness of what must have been the earliest pre-dawn light—the light before the light—he could make out the shape and shine of her fat smooth wet body and the black, almost oily glint of her hair flattened against her head and back as she marched up and down chanting in fluent, vibrant Maori. In one hand she held what Mike recognised was the peaked officer cap that belonged to O'Dwyer, and in the other a stick which she pointed at the small whitewashed out-house where the officer was sleeping but from which came no sound or sign of consciousness.

Mike sidled up close to Frano, and their exchange, as he is able to re-invent it now, went something like this:

'It's your Auntie Pixie.'

'Yeah.'

'She's got nothing on.'

'I know.'

'What's she doing?'

'Putting a makutu on the Captain.'

'A what?'

'A makutu. That's why she's taken her clothes off.'

'What's a makutu?'

'It's a curse.'

'Why? What's he done?'

'Dunno.'

'Ask your mum.'

'I did. She won't tell me.'

So their exchange continued, flat and basic, small boys' talk.

'Why's she got his hat?'

'It's got his wairua.'

'What's his wairua?'

'I dunno. Bits of his hair.'

'What does your mum think?'

'She doesn't like it.'

'Is she angry.'

'Yeah. And my tupuna.'

'Why don't they stop her?'

'They can't. No one can.'

'Why not?'

'They're too scared.'

And that, Mike recalls, was what he recognised even in the darkness—their fear. But he didn't feel it himself, because Auntie Pixie was naked and to him that made her seem harmless.

'What are they scared of?' he asked.

'Her. She might put one on them.'

'A makutu?'

'Yeah. She can do it to anyone.'

'Is she a witch?'

'Sort of. I think so.'

'What will happen to the Captain?'

'Dunno. He might die.'

But O'Dwyer didn't die. He slept the sleep, not of the blessed, but of the inebriated, and only learned in the morning that a curse had been put on him—not the worst Auntie Pixie was capable of, which the older Panapas believed would have meant a death almost as sure as an execution, but her second level of makutu. The chant she'd uttered while holding strands of his hair meant he must go for ever into banishment. In his home territory he would never prosper; and if he insisted on staying he would become weak, useless to himself and others, and would slowly sicken and die. If he wished to make a life for himself it would have to be elsewhere, part of the whanau-a-rere—the family of exiles. That's what Auntie Pixie said, and it's what the Panapas were disposed to believe. Donovan O'Dwyer was now destined to live as a foreigner, forever less than happy in some distant place.

Mike's recollection is that O'Dwyer behaved next morning like an officer and a gentleman. He emerged from his ablutions with the kind of gleaming, slightly wounded face that comes only from an old-fashioned blade shave, his army-cropped hair wet and brushed, his uniform clean and tidy, his boots polished. Even the cap Auntie Pixie had held in the rain (if it wasn't a spare kept in reserve for emergencies) seemed clean and almost dry. But no one, Mike observes to Winterstoke, should have expected otherwise. O'Dwyer was still, at that time, a serving officer. There must have been many harder nights from which he'd had to recover quickly and be ready for morning parade and inspection.

'He must have decided the whole visit had been a mistake,' Mike says. 'He'd behaved badly, and so had they—or he considered some of them had. I suspect all he wanted to do was get out of there fast and with the least fuss. He was polite and respectful to everyone without trying to be charming to anyone.'

The weather too had sorted itself out. The rain was gone, the air was emptied of its humidity, the sky was clear, the sea calm. The whole world glittered and shone, its colours vivid, its edges sharp.

Mid-morning O'Dwyer briefly addressed a small gathering down the road at the marae, telling them that as a Pakeha he'd been proud to serve for a time as an officer in the Maori Battalion —an arrangement meant only to last until enough Maori soldiers had been promoted and could take over the responsibilities of command. And he'd been especially proud during that time to be a comrade-in-arms of Joe Panapa, a man of great strength, courage, and calm acceptance.

'I salute Joe Panapa,' O'Dwyer told them. 'I salute his mother and father, his brothers and sisters, and especially I salute his wife, Ljuba, and his son, Frano. I regret his death, and your loss. I honour his memory. Beyond that, all I can say to you is that Joe Panapa lives with me, and will be with me always.'

Then, without waiting to see what else might be asked of him, he clapped his hat on, put his swagger stick under one arm, marched to the marae gate where a military car and driver were waiting, turned to salute the meeting house and its fierce carved guardian-figure, and was gone.

'A good exit,' Winterstoke remarks.

'I'm not sure that from their point of view it was good,' Mike says. 'What he said was OK. But to walk out like that . . . Maori don't like things to be cut short.'

'But what did he make of the curse? Did he take it seriously?'

Mike shakes his head, downing the last of his beer. 'I can't believe he did. Later, perhaps yes. But not then. He knew the Maori. He'd lived with them for two years or more. He'd travelled with them, fought beside them, seen them die. He knew how they like drama. Even in those days they lived in two worlds—liked to play one off against the other. And in any case, Don was a rationalist. He knew how much weight to give to a primitive curse. But later, you see, here in Oxford, his life seemed to bear it out. Or he thought it did. And by that time I think he rather liked the idea of it. I'm guessing, but I think it lent a bit of colour to his sense of failure.'

'It became an excuse.'

'Something like that. But there must also have been a lurking thought that he really was . . .'

'Cursed?'

'Yes. Even if he didn't believe in it; even if with his rational mind he rejected it as primitive mumbo-jumbo—nothing more than a fat brown lady chanting in the rain—still, here he was stuck in Oxford, not really wanting to be, or thinking he didn't want to be, drinking too much, getting into scrapes, not fulfilling his early promise, persuading himself that he would have been happier at home. It was pretty much what Auntie Pixie had predicted for him.'

'What a pity none of this was known, Michael. There was

so much more to be said.'

'At the funeral? There's always more isn't there? And could it have been said?'

'I suppose you're right. It couldn't.' Winterstoke reflects. 'And you two lads—you and Frano. You didn't really know what all the fuss was about.'

'No.'

'But now you do.'

'Now I do. Yes.'

'You said that Don . . . It was alleged he'd killed a man. One of his own soldiers.'

Mike smiles at the jurist's choice of words. 'Yes. That's what was alleged, Bertie. But that wasn't Auntie Pixie's reason for the makutu.'

'It wasn't?'

'No. She didn't like the way it was . . .' He checks himself and adopts his friend's formulation. 'The way it was alleged it was done.'

FIVE

Dog Save the King

IN THE COURSE OF HIS ACADEMIC CAREER MIKE NEWALL HAS OFTEN thought about stories of sudden and miraculous transformations—ugly ducklings that become swans, frogs that turn into princes when kissed, maids in rags and tatters whose foot is found to fit the golden slipper. In his own life Marica Selenich was such a case. Not that she was ever ugly—only unnoticed. She was, as he recalls her in those early years, a silence, a stillness, sometimes a smile, and always a pair of large round dark watchful eyes. She was background to some parts of his life with her cousin Frano Panapa; and for the rest, she was a space marked out for the future, one he paid little or no attention but would have missed if it hadn't been there.

As for Frano—he was Mike's companion in infancy, and his good (though not his only, or always his closest) friend right through their years at school, until . . .

Until what? And is it important? How has Mike wandered into this tangled thicket? He's not sure and perhaps it doesn't seem to matter, since Bertie Winterstoke, for whom these events are being reconstructed, is easygoing and appreciative, 'and not' (as he says by way of reassurance over their continuing lunch), 'or not especially, wedded to chronology as the only, or even the best, governor of sequence.'

'It's life one wants, isn't it?' he trumpets, standing suddenly to brush down the enormous number of crumbs his bread roll has shed over the lower part of his body, and causing the wooden table to lift and crash back down.

The lunchers at tables round about look up uncertainly, as if called upon to respond. What they see is a tall shaggy man in a suit who has at this moment (though this, of course, is not apparent to them) suddenly reminded his companion of Babar the Elephant.

Some minutes later, after Winterstoke's final call at the Trout's men's room ('Needless but precautionary, dear boy'), and as the two are making their way out to the road, he takes the point up again, as if there has been no break. 'And life,' he pronounces, like a verdict from the bench, 'is not, on the whole, or not usually, the shortest distance between two points. Am I wrong? Think of Homer. Think of the *Odyssey*.'

Mike, smiling and nodding as if the point is taken, tries and fails to think of Homer and the *Odyssey*.

They leave the Trout now and cross a stone bridge towards the entrance to the Port Meadow where they plan to follow the river past the ruins of Godstow Abbey, past the lock, and on until they come to another pub, the Perch. There, following the pattern of other afternoons together, they will settle to cool drinks, outdoors under trees, before making their return.

It's summer, an unusual one, as summers usually are these days while the globe warms and the century, and the millennium, amble towards an end. Day after day is warm-to-hot, hot-and-still, still-and-gravid. At the very least it feels to Mike like an Indian summer for life as he and Winterstoke have known it; and in response to this suggestion his friend quotes Enoch Powell: 'Every political career ends in failure.'

'But so does every life,' Bertie goes on; 'and every civilisation, and—the scientists now tell us—every planet and every star. Everything's always coming to an end.' He stops, leans on his stick, half closes his eyes and seems to sniff the heavens. 'It's called entropy. Rotten that it should be so. Rotten luck.'

'Our revels now are ended,' Mike quotes, and Winterstoke takes it up.

'These our actors, as I foretold you, were all spirits and are

. . . What are they, Michael? How does it go?'

'Melted into air,' Mike carries it on. 'Into thin air.'

But now, by way of contrast as they continue along the narrow road, they can see there are boys jumping from an outsize willow into a tranquil reach of the river. There are cattle coming down to drink. Two barges, decorated and summery, are approaching one another at their respective levels on either side of the lock. There are fishermen with all their absurd gear (the bag-ladies of England's rivers, Bertie calls them) ranged along the banks on one side, and on the other an academic procession of honking geese. As the meadows recede into the distance their pasture looks more gold than green. Somewhere away to the west the A34 hums and murmurs to itself, composing something potentially symphonic that never quite gets off the ground. Two jet trails go over, straight white pairs of lines turning wide and wobbly on a blue page. And to the south, or just east of south, as the two men go through gates and down on to the turf of the meadow, the dreaming spires are doing their famous old-fashioned finger-pointing at the place where God used to be—on High.

But He is no longer there, having been replaced by Nothing, or Albert Einstein, or $E = MC^2$; and that blue page, even on such a day as this, is smudged at its edges with faint grime, a small part of which must be smoke and gases from this morning's burn-up at the Oxford Crematorium, Donovan O'Dwyer's last contribution to the pollution of Britain and to global warming. 'Melted into air, into thin air'—the man who survived the German onslaught on Greece and Crete, the pounding battles of the Western Desert, the long remorseless winter slog up the Italian peninsula, and even and finally, Auntie Pixie Panapa's brown-bodied chant in the rain with its consequences (if that's what they were) of exile, booze and disgrace.

'I should have died at home,' were Don's last grumpy words, which the ever-patient and often-wronged Camille answered by telling him that's where he was, darling. At home.

'He just glared at me,' she told Mike and Bertie, half-laughing this morning in the crematorium courtyard, her eyes filling with tears. 'And then he died.'

'Typical of O'Dwyer,' Mike remarks now, as they make their

way along the path to the lock, 'that his last act should have been to glare at someone.'

'Oh yes and especially,' Winterstoke agrees, 'that it should have been at the one who warmed his declining years with inexhaustible coals of fire.'

'Not fair, not fair,' Mike protests. But he too is laughing. And unlike Camille and Bertie, he knows what O'Dwyer meant when he said he should have died 'at home'. Auntie Pixie's makutu had not been forgotten.

༨ৡ৻

Telling Winterstoke how mysteriously absent Marica Selenich was from his childhood Mike surprises himself by demonstrating the sense in which she was present. He remembers that she was, briefly, something called a Child of Mary. He remembers her running about in the orchard, tripping and falling and staining the white dress for her first communion. He remembers 'doubling' her on his bike down to Bridge Avenue for a swim, her black hair in his mouth.

He remembers that he taught her to play tennis, and then table tennis, and finally chess; that she could read two pages of a book in the time it took him to read one and one third; and that she could play on the piano 'Für Elise', and 'In a Monastery Garden', and 'Rondo alla Turka', and 'La Paloma', and 'Polonaise in A', and 'Humoresque', and 'Traumerei', all with ease and fluency, when he was still struggling with the 'Sailor's Hornpipe'; but on the other hand that it was said he had perfect pitch and she did not.

He remembers her in the summer shadow of the packing shed lifting her shirt to show him her sprouting nipples, and then pulling down her pants to let him see the new dark shadow of pubic fuzz; and he recalls especially that although it was the nipples she was proud of, and keen to show off, it was the new hair, and the new look it gave to what it surrounded, that excited him more.

And then for a time she was really absent. The Selenich orchard and vineyard were doing well, the wine was beginning to be known, the family was prospering, and Marica, already dux of her local convent school, was sent to a rather superior Catholic boarding college in the city where she would get a good academic preparation for a religious order in the event that she should discover a vocation, or for Teachers' College or university if she did not. What would be done with, or for, or about, the emerging equipment she'd shown Mike in the packing shed was a puzzle; but he supposed it was a development that would somehow be put on hold.

She was home for holidays, and sometimes at weekends, but for almost five years the paths of the two Ms, Mike and Marica, crossed only now and then, and never significantly.

Frano and Mike went to Mt Albert Grammar, travelling in each day on the train from Henderson station, along the back of the Waikumete Cemetery, through New Lynn, past the eastern corner of the Avondale Racecourse, getting off at Mt Albert station and walking from there to the school. Frano had a strong hand-some face, with his father's brown skin. His hair was thick, shiny-black and curly, and began the day stuck down hard and fast, dividing like symbolic bow waves on either side of a dead-straight parting; but as the hours passed it rose in slow-motion rebellion until, by the time of their journey home late in the afternoon, it had become the mop of iron curls God (who didn't exist, and whom the two boys referred to as Dog) always meant it to be.

The Dog joke began at Henderson Primary where a clergy-man came each week to 'take them for Bible'. One day, after he had finished his homely chat and departed, a truculent little boy with blond hair, whose parents had given him the forenames Karl Marx, said that god was only dog spelled backwards; and although Mike had pretended to share in the shock and distress which the class perhaps pretended to feel at this outrage, secretly he was excited by what, much later, he came to think of as one of his earliest pre-Wittgenstein recognitions—that even a word as socially well connected as 'god' might in fact signify nothing at all; that indeed such a word, for all the great respect paid to it, and the ease with which it rolled off confident, or reverent, or glib tongues, might in a very real sense be meaningless; and that such force as it had lay in its consequent adaptability. Since it meant nothing, it could mean whatever you liked. The only rule (and it was a social rule, not a supernatural one) was that you should treat it with respect.

These stumbling thoughts were his own; and although Frano didn't understand them quite as Mike wanted him to, none the less he was then, and always, in a state somewhere between protest against, and rejection of, the Selenich family religion. So together they began, when Christian observances were required of them, to pray or sing unobtrusively to Dog, watching to see whether it made any difference to anything; even challenging the Almighty Silence up there to give some sign of his almighty displeasure. He never did, and was, they concluded, if not absent or nonexistent, at the very least indifferent or lazy. As they sang 'Dog save our gracious King', or 'Dog defend New Zealand', or prayed to Dog to protect them from every kind of trouble now and in the hereafter, the heavens didn't open to strike them down, nor the earth to swallow them up. Dog's head was never so much as lifted from the eternal hearthrug. The schoolboy joke never seemed to wear thin, and they never felt worse for their blasphemy. Rather, they felt enlivened by it. It was an act of inner rebellion and it made them cheerful.

Frano played league and boxed, Mike played soccer and tennis, but from time to time they used to travel to watch one another's games. Frano's boxing style was all his own, and strange. He bounded up and down on the balls of his feet, as if on springs, making it hard for his opponents to know where to aim their blows. In his third year at the school, however, after successes in early bouts of the annual championships, he was knocked out cold in the final of his weight. He'd been doing well, bounding about, landing punches and eluding his opponent's gloves until, late in the second round, seeming to run out of puff, he stopped jumping and dropped his gloves to his sides as if taking a brief rest. In that moment his opponent, unskilled but strong, swung a desperate stiff-elbowed haymaker in a great arc at the side of his head, and felled him.

Frano was carried from the ring and laid out on the floor, still unconscious. Minutes later he was still groggy, and was taken away in a car by one of the schoolmasters—whether home to Henderson, or to hospital, Mike no longer remembers. He was said to have suffered a significant concussion, although so far as Mike can recall not much was done about it. Frano's playing league was stopped for a time, and he was told that he shouldn't box any more.

After that his behaviour changed. He claimed to have blackouts during which, although he didn't faint or fall down, he had no notion of what he was doing and no recollection of it afterwards. When this happened (and the episodes lasted only seconds) Mike could never quite decide whether Frano had really been, as he claimed, unconscious, or merely pretending to be. They might be on their bikes, going side by side along a suburban street, talking, sitting back on their saddles riding 'no hands', when all at once, mid-sentence and without cause or warning, Frano would reach down to the grips, stand on his pedals, and accelerate away, often straight at a stone wall or at an oncoming car. What made Mike doubt Frano's later protestations that he'd acted unconsciously and had no memory of it, was that at the last second he would always swerve away, just missing the wall or tree or car or person, escaping the collision.

Once when this happened—a downhill plunge taking him straight at an outcrop of volcanic rock from which he veered away at the last moment, ending arse-over-kite in a grass-filled ditch—Mike chose, in answer to Frano's 'What happened? What did I do?' to say only 'You rode into the ditch.'

'But before that?' Frano said.

'Before it—what?'

'What did I do?'

'You were riding along with me.'

'And then what happened?'

'You rode into the ditch.'

There was a long silence between them, an air of tension, a feeling of Frano's suppressed anger, almost a threat of violence. Mike understood then, or thought he did, that he was not required to believe completely in Frano's blackouts—only to pretend that he did. And still he was not sure that the episodes weren't at least half-real.

Since they were small boys they had always wrestled in the orchard. Over the years Frano had grown to be the stronger, but only just, and they were fairly evenly matched. They would come home from the pictures and without any preliminary word would go up through the trees to an open space lit by moon or stars and go at it like a pair of gladiators, silent except for the grunting of the effort and an occasional cry of pain. Wrestling was never done in anger. It was a pleasure, even the pain of it, engaged in like a Zen exercise, or like sex. On the rare times when a quarrel between them turned to a fight it was fists they used, and it never lasted more than a few seconds.

Frano was observant, sensitive, quick-tongued—clever in his way, but not academic, and the two boys took different courses at the school. After the fifth form Frano left to become an apprentice motor mechanic; Mike stayed on a further two years. But still on the home turf only a wire fence divided them; and when Frano abandoned his push-bike in favour of a second-hand Norton, the two took to the roads together, riding at weekends all over the Auckland isthmus and beyond.

They liked to go out on the bike late when there was little or no traffic and to race full throttle along Great North Road, down the strip of concrete known as Waikumete Hill and up the other side; or, further afield, to take the machine at top speed the length of what was called the Dominion Road Extension, where two parallel strips of concrete roadway were divided by a no-man's land intended for tram tracks, all the way to Waikowhai on the Manukau Harbour. The tramway had never been built, so for the length of that strip it wasn't possible to meet other traffic coming head-on.

There were no crash-helmets in those days, little traffic, no speed- or alcohol-checks, only power, noise, and thrust; only danger, fear and excitement. And associated with the bike and its power went the quest, its endless optimism endlessly dis-appointed, for 'girls'.

Together Mike and Frano went to dances. They enjoyed the dancing, but the real purpose, the serious, the important one, was to persuade a girl—any girl—outside the dance hall. The girls were taken up the hill, down on to the beach, out into the lupins, the long grass, the bush, the scrub. In those days a bit of the natural world, a fragment of wilderness, was never far away; but wherever the male, boldly going where every male went before, led her, for the female, social constraints, moral prohibitions, and fear went also. There was a great deal of lip work, tongue work, hand and finger work; nipples were encouraged to stand out; vulva was explored; penises achieved a rigidity so remarkable it seemed to put them in danger of breaking off; there was sometimes orgasm. But for Mike at least, and probably for Frano too, penetration was never accomplished.

'Two years of my life,' Mike tells Winterstoke, 'more than two, passed in intellectual stimulation, physical exhaustion, and sexual frustration. And then I started at university and so did Marica. Suddenly there we were side by side again, as we'd been all those years before, driving the big old dead truck in the long grass at the edge of the orchard. But now—or pretty soon—I was in love.'

At first, knowing Marica so well was an obstacle. If he paid attention to her, sought her out in crowds, went about with her, which in another young man would have signalled a special interest, in his case it meant nothing more than that they were old friends. He might as easily have been a brother as a potential lover. And shyness kept him from making the grand declarations he thought up in the night.

Sometimes she looked hard at him, as if asking herself, and in a way asking him, what was going on in his head. He thought she knew the answer; but he was sure she wouldn't ask. Black-haired, round-eyed, red-lipped Marica: she was beautiful, intelligent, quick-witted, funny; but she was also timid. If a move was to be made, he would have to make it. If something was to be said, he would have to say it.

Once he came close to telling Frano that he was in love with her. They'd ridden the Norton late at night out to Waikowhai and were half-lying, half-sitting on a steep grassy bank looking down through trees at the sand of the bay, shiny-dark at low tide under whatever light came from night sky and surrounding houses. Mike was making awkward approaches to the subject of his new feelings for Marica when he felt a threatening stillness in the air between them. After a moment Frano said—growled it, as if embarrassed but at the same time compelled—'You should stay away from Marica.'

'Why?'

'Because she's not yours, that's all. She's none of your business. And anyway,' he added, 'she's a bitch.'

Mike was on new strange ground here—dangerous ground, it seemed, though he didn't know why. 'What do you mean she's not mine? Whose is she then?'

Frano didn't answer. He was standing up now, hitching his trousers, unfastening and fastening his leather belt. 'Let's go,' he said. 'I don't like this crappy place.'

Mike asked, 'You think she's yours?'

Frano threw his leg over the bike and fired up the engine, revving it. 'You fucking coming?' he shouted above the noise.

The ride home that night was breakneck. Mike knew it was a challenge. Frano wanted to scare him, wanted to make him shout, 'For Christ's sake slow down!' Mike was scared, but he clung on, his arms tight around Frano's waist, and kept his mouth shut.

Back at Te Atatu Road they parked the bike, went silently to their usual place in the orchard, its long brown grass flattened by many previous bouts, and wrestled. But this time it was different. It went on too long, too relentlessly, and there was no pleasure in it—only pain, exhaustion, and something dark, like anger, or hate.

SIX

Sex and Death

AT THE TIME WHEN MIKE WAS PLANNING THE VISIT TO NEW ZEALAND that was to include a stop-off in Croatia in search of Ljuba Panapa, he and Gillian were still living—an agreed together-and-apart arrangement—in the same house. He had the study he'd always had, looking out over the front garden towards the road. Gillian had as her study one of the upstairs bedrooms, looking down on the walled garden which opened from a lane at the back. They had a double bedroom each, and often found themselves, since their habits remained pretty much unchanged, saying a faintly embarrassed goodnight from their respective doors. To avoid overlap in the bathroom it was agreed that she should use the one upstairs, he the down. The dining room went unused—there were no longer any sociable suppers or dutiful dinners with their friends and associates. So far so good! But there was still the kitchen to be shared, and the kitchen table; and to a lesser extent the main living room and television.

The problem was not, or not at once, that they quarrelled, but that they got on, as they mostly had in the past, rather well. It would have been difficult, sharing like that, not to exchange a word now and then about the news, the weather, the flowers in the front garden and fruit at the back; and the squirrels, thrushes, magpies, robins that could be seen coming and going, mainly in pairs, reminders of the Flood and the Ark and How Things Were Meant To Be.

They were polite, as they had always been, but rather more so now, Mike careful, as he would not always have been during their marriage, not to claim, without thought or question, first read of the paper, first choice of programmes on radio and television, first call on the car. And since it made little sense to have two people cooking separate meals in the same kitchen, they sometimes took turns to cook for each other. So on the nights when Mike didn't dine at the College (and he liked to ration his use of that too-calorific resource) meals were often shared—and wine, and conversation—as if they had been still a pair. There may even have been moments (Winterstoke is given this impression, but doesn't like to ask the question) when they found themselves back together in the same bed.

'All of which probably sounds,' Mike concedes, 'like a recipe for marriage repair. The end of the end and the beginning of a new beginning.'

'But clearly it wasn't,' Winterstoke responds.

'No. It looked promising. But really it was just a short-cut back to the battleground.'

'A pity, Michael. A great shame.'

'We'd always shared everything, got on well, been good company for one another. None of that had saved us.'

'Is it foolish to ask why?'

'It was a philosophical difference.'

'But not one you were able to be philosophical about.'

Mike smiles.

'When we thought of ourselves as separate we were civil to one another. As soon as it seemed we were back together, it broke out again.'

He looks into the far distance, beyond the dreaming spires, where the sky (or so he thinks, feeling a moment's nostalgia for things domestic) appears to have hung small washed fleeces along an invisible wire.

'So you planned your return to New Zealand,' his friend prompts.

'It was a nonsense, Bertie. But I was in a bad state. The ship was on the rocks. I was looking for a lifeboat.'

'No going back,' Winterstoke repeats. 'Second law of thermodynamics. Entropy rules.'

They've stopped and are leaning together on a rail watching iron gates open and water surging in to fill the lock while a barge waits to come through. A man in a white sailor suit and peaked cap, the controller of the flow, asks them to please step back from the edge.

'But my friend wants to jump,' Winterstoke says.

※

At the university Marica was taking science courses while Mike's were in Arts. He no longer remembers how he went about explaining to her why, despite their differing timetables, he always managed to be waiting for her outside lectures, travelling with her on the same bus, having lunch at the same hour. What she had to be made to understand was that these concurrences had nothing to do with neighbourliness and everything to do with his new passion, his discovery of what 'being in love' really meant. But the very intensity of his feeling for her, the surprise of it, the suddenness, made him clumsy, inarticulate and fearful of mistakes. He'd had no practice in this kind of thing, and no one gave lessons. So he wrote her letters which weren't sent, and composed, in his head in the night, absurdly romantic declarations which the cold light of day was kind enough to turn thumbs down on.

It was in the dark of the downstairs deck of a ferry during a night ride across the harbour that he managed to make it clear to her what he was feeling; and although there was from her no matching declaration, she did seem to accept his as a generous gift, and to welcome it without reserve. It was as if she was falling into step with him on a long road. In the breezy dark of the lower deck, drumming over the star-lit harbour, they kissed, and then kissed more seriously—and that, the kiss, he remembers still, when so many events in his life, more important, more remarkable, have slipped from memory. He was now her boyfriend, she his girlfriend; and the courtship ritual of the 1950s, a long, sometimes painful, hesitation at the border between innocence and experience, had begun.

Soon afterwards, a Saturday, they were going through the

orchard, holding hands, when they heard Frano crooning somewhere up ahead among the trees. At once Marica let go his hand
and moved to put a space between them. That same night they
walked down into Henderson village and on the way back found
a grassy bank among trees where they could lie down together.
They hadn't been there long when the sound of a motorbike
coming up the hill made Marica roll away from him and sit up.
The bike's light swept over and past them, and went on without
seeming to lose speed; but now she was nervous, not wanting to
be kissed, keen to get home.

'It's Frano,' Mike said. 'You're afraid of him.'

She said she wasn't; then that maybe she was, sort of but
not really; then fell silent and wouldn't talk about it. All next
day she avoided him.

One evening they were lounging in the back seats of a
picture theatre before the lights went down when Mike, one arm
over her shoulder, felt her jerk forward and upright, pulling away
from him.

He looked where she was looking. A young man going down
the centre aisle had dark curly hair and the same build as Frano.
As he turned into one of the rows they could see him in profile.
It wasn't Frano, and Marica relaxed.

Mike said, 'You thought it was him.'

She bit into her ice cream. 'I wasn't sure.'

'What are you scared of?'

She put a finger on his lips. 'Shush, Mikie.'

Again he let it pass, but it was unavoidable. She was watchful,
distant with him if her cousin was near. Mike grew impatient;
irritable. He was wanting sex, real sex as distinct from the everything short of it which was what they had. There were quarrels;
but there was also serious talk. Did Marica's Catholicism stand
in the way? It was supposed to, she said, but she didn't feel that
it did. There was her fear of pregnancy—but he was ready with
condoms and promises of marriage if she would have him. So
what was the obstacle? Did she not want him?

It seemed she wanted him very much. But she didn't want
it to happen unintentionally. It should not, she said, as if she
might know what she was talking about, be 'just a bad end to a
skirmish'. She wanted to decide.

Then decide, he urged; and she did. They would do it. She had even decided when and where.

The following Sunday afternoon they set off on foot from the orchard to a place on the far side of the cemetery where the pines were almost a forest, spreading up over the tops of low hills and down into the valley on the other side. Mike still remembers that late shedding of his virginity—the first-time, blind sensation of it, the pushing at what it seemed would never allow passage, and then did.

And while they were still recovering on the lovely tan-coloured and comfortable bed of needles, rain began to fall, summer rain. Still too pleased with themselves to get up or put on clothes, they lay there watching the long slow curving lines of it coming through and down at them, silver against the pines' pale green tops and darker flanks.

After that day they couldn't stay away from one another, had always to be touching, one touch leading to a second that led to a third, until they were back, unless interrupted, or in some place that put it totally out of the question, in one or another of the classic textbook postures.

On that return visit to New Zealand, Mike tells Winterstoke, he was astonished by the number of places in which he found himself remembering that there, vertical or horizontal, on some dark night, or even in broad daylight, he and Marica had contrived, often in the five minutes before a bus departed, or in the back seat of a small car, or in almost perfect silence because someone was on the other side of a wall, to obey the orders coming down to them from the genes. With typical human deviousness, however, they were also managing to do this, their first duty as planetary creatures, while avoiding the consequences the genes intended.

He remembers crossing the harbour with her by ferry to the Chelsea sugar works in sunny humid weather, walking up the road there from the wharf with trees closing right over, so full of cicadas and the cicadas so loud they had to shout above the noise; and from there hitchhiking around the top of the harbour, all the way (the long way, the wrong way) home to Henderson, stopping between rides to fuck in the fields. It's a memory that seems to stand for many memories. It was the best of times—a summer without end.

Henderson in warm weather offered them any number of places; but it was also where Frano came and went, and Marica didn't now deny her fear, if not of him, at least of his knowing they were lovers. 'I've always thought of him as a brother,' she said.

'And he thinks of you . . .'

'Not as a sister.'

'So he should be told.'

'No.' She was emphatic. 'I don't want that.'

'Tell him. Then he'll know where he stands.'

'He thinks he knows that already.'

'What does that mean?'

'Unwanted.'

'Well he is, isn't he?'

'He feels shut out, Mike. He thinks it's because . . .'

She stopped, and Mike repeated it as a question: 'Because?'

'Because he's Maori.'

'How could he think that?'

'He does think it.'

'He's part of your family, for Christ's sake. You're first cousins.'

Once again she did that thing she'd done before, putting a finger over his lips and saying 'Mikie, please. Shush.' It ought not to have silenced him, but it did.

The risk-takers took one risk too many and Frano caught them at it in the packing shed. They were doing it quickly, standing, Marica up on a little box with her back against something that might have been a hay bale, Mike's trousers around his ankles, her skirt held up in her teeth, hanging on to one another as if they were on a promontory buffeted by a strong wind.

Frano stopped, stared hard into the dusty striped lines of light as if to take in the detail, thickness of shaft, smoothness of thigh; and then, as her teeth let go the skirt and it dropped down like a curtain over the ancient scene of Welcome to the Tall Stranger, he turned and was gone. A moment later he was riding away down the long drive, letting his Norton be the one to utter the angry roar.

That was the end of that. There was to be no finishing,

though Mike, if he'd been permitted, would have carried right on. And now as they pulled their clothes up and shook themselves, like straw men, back into shape, the argument began. Sooner or later, Mike insisted, this was going to happen, so why not now? Frano had done nothing, said nothing—and after all, what could he do or say? They should forget it, shrug it off, behave as if nothing had happened.

But Marica was upset. 'Didn't you see his eyes?' she asked; and she wept—and went on weeping at intervals, it seemed to Mike, for the next couple of days, even though there were no consequences, nothing said by Frano, no sign that anyone else among the Selenich clan knew what had happened.

Three nights later Mike was walking home alone from the bus, down Te Atatu Road, when he heard the Norton. Frano ranged up alongside him, slowed, went ahead, turned in at a driveway and waited, the engine idling. Light rain was beginning to fall and Mike could see it drifting in the beam of the headlight.

Frano put out a hand and grabbed his shoulder. 'Get on,' he said.

Mike looked at him, trying to read in his face what mood he was in. Did there have to be another fight, a worse one this time? Mike didn't want to run away from it. He knew Frano well, or thought he did, but there was a tinge of fear. He said, 'It's starting to rain, Frano.'

'Get on.'

Mike put his leg over the seat and his arms around his oldest friend. At once the bike curved away into the road, turning back the way it had come. Without any warning from Frano there was the kind of acceleration that had always seemed thrilling but now seemed dangerous, threatening.

They went down into the village and up the valley road, Mike shouting, 'Where are we going?' and Frano not replying.

Soon they were up in the hills, on the Scenic Drive, then off on the unsealed road to Piha. No longer shouting questions into the wind, knowing there was no getting off until Frano decided to let him, Mike held tight, leaned with the bike as it swung into bends, and wondered, as the rain grew heavier, how long the tyres would keep them upright on this unsafe surface at this unsafe speed, and whether Dog had at last chosen the moment to show his immemorial hand.

They must have gone three, perhaps four miles along the Piha road before Frano pulled over on to the grass verge, and stopped. There was nothing on this road, no lights, no habitation, just the bush stretching away on either side. With the bike's engine and lights switched off they were all at once in complete darkness and a silence that seemed total except for the faint swish of rain on leaves.

Mike tried to get used to it, tried to make out the shapes of Frano, the bike, the road, but all he could see was the two lines of treetops, marking the road edges, against a sky that was clouded over and offered next to no light. The silence went on and on as he waited for the first blow to be struck; but it didn't come.

'What are we doing, Frano?' he asked. The tone was conciliatory, was meant to be, but no more than that. It wouldn't help to plead; and even this small sign of mateship might only make things worse.

Frano didn't reply. Mike's eyes, growing used to the dark, still saw nothing but shadow-shapes and outlines, black on blacker. Frano was no longer astride the bike. He had propped it and was sitting, back-on to it and to Mike, arms folded, legs stretched towards the roadway, staring up at the heavy sky.

The bastard was enjoying his moment of control. Mike remembers that recognition, and the surge of anger that went with it. He wanted to shout, 'Marica's not yours, you stupid prick. She doesn't want you. She wants me.' But he hadn't forgotten what she'd said about Frano, and that checked him. Best to do nothing, say nothing, wait.

Quite suddenly the rain got heavier, then very heavy; became what they used to think of as a Waitakere downpour—great clean buckets of the stuff dragged in by winds that have twelve hundred miles of the Tasman Sea in which to gather it together. In seconds Mike's clothes were sodden, hanging heavy and cold.

Frano, his jacket managing to gleam as if there was in fact light up there to be caught and reflected, put a leg over the bike and looked at Mike, reaching towards him. 'Give's a hand.'

The voice was cold, hard. This wasn't a gesture of friendship, of reconciliation; but Mike took the hand that was held out to him. Instantly he felt his own brutally squeezed. It was the old schoolboy competition of the handshake, which Frano had always won. Mike managed to get the kind of grip (gap between thumb and forefinger pushed hard against the opponent's matching gap) that was some protection against superior strength. It helped, but still, as the pressure increased, he was forced inch by inch down until he was on his knees. With pain came anger and something close to panic; but he resisted the impulse to swing in with the left fist, which would have made a fight of it. Better this way, if he could stand it. Let it happen. Suffer it. Somehow the rain, the scale of the deluge, made that easier.

Through clenched teeth he asked, 'What's this, Frano?'

'It's goodbye,' Frano said.

Mike tried to ask another question but the pain was too great. 'Jesus Christ,' he croaked. 'Frano, please . . .'

The rain pelted down on them, drumming on the leather jacket. 'Say goodbye,' Frano said.

'Goodbye.'

'Say it nicely. Say, Goodbye Frano darling.'

'Goodbye . . . Oh shit.'

'Say it.'

He said it through gritted teeth. 'Goodbye Frano . . .'

'Darling.'

'Darling.'

Frano laughed, pushing hard and letting him go so he fell backward into the grass at the roadside, already so wet that his elbows and one knee sank into it.

'Fucking queen,' Frano said. 'Fucking Pakeha.' And then in a moment he was gone, roaring away full throttle into the dark.

Mike set off walking. At first he thought Frano would come back for him; or that he would be waiting around the next bend, or the next. Then he realised that of course he wouldn't.

There were no cars on that road; no one was going to or from Piha that night. And even back on the Scenic Drive, when he reached it, and down the steep bush roads into the Henderson Valley, the few cars going his way, towards town, wouldn't stop for the sodden figure in the continuing downpour. It was two in the morning before Mike reached home. By that time he had passed from anger, through a sense of the absurd, almost of pleasure, and into the neutrality of sheer exhaustion.

Next morning, still in bed, he heard the phone ring at the front of the house. His father took the call, spoke for some time in a deep, concerned rumble, and then went into the kitchen which was not far from Mike's bedroom. His parents spoke together in low voices, not meant for Mike's ear, so they could decide first how to break the news to him. But he heard. It was as if he knew already, had known, but hadn't allowed himself to know. Frano was dead—killed last night. He'd been riding through Titirangi at high speed, his bike apparently holding the road well enough, when all at once he veered off and drove straight at a wall, not braking, seeming even to accelerate. A young couple coming home late in their car had seen it happen. They said they found it inexplicable.

There were head injuries and loss of blood. He hadn't died instantly, but in the ambulance on the way to the hospital.

SEVEN

Joe's Year of War

MIKE HAS BEEN DESCRIBING JOE PANAPA'S DEPARTURE FROM NEW
Zealand—the troop train journeying south from Palmerston
North with windows shuttered and doors guarded for security;
and at the Wellington wharves, the battalion filing up narrow
gangways, laden with gear, and Joe Panapa's friend Boy Keratu
baaing like a sheep, setting them all off pretending to be on their
way to shearing or slaughter. But the train had gone all the way
on to the wharf with everything closed down, and the wharf was
closed to friends and family, many of whom, against orders, had
been warned of the departure and had come to Wellington to
see them off but were shut outside the wharf gates. Some had
been outside that corrugated iron fence around the army camp
the night before, talking to their men through holes punched
with bayonets, and had managed to get down to Wellington in
the intervening hours.

On board, the soldiers lined the rails hoping to see familiar
faces, but all they saw were Ngati Poneke women singing farewell
songs from the wharf while the ropes were released and tugs
moved their ship out into the stream. Only then, from that
distance, they saw the big gates open and the crowd streaming
in. Joe hung over the rail searching the crowd for Ljuba, as she,
in the crowd, was searching for him, both thinking they could

see the loved face but uncertain whether it was really the one.

It was to be the last these two would see of each other—no more than a blur in a crowd; but then the people on the wharf joined the Ngati Poneke group singing traditional songs—'Meha manu rere', and 'He putiputi'; and back across the water came the men's voices singing in reply 'Po atarau'—Now is the hour. They couldn't see one another's faces any more, but they could hear the tears in the voices.

All this is perhaps a touch too intense, too florid, for Winterstoke, who interrupts to ask, as if from the bench, how Mike can possibly know so much about a man dead half a century, killed in Crete on 23 May, 1941 when the New Zealanders, including the battalion that was always designated '28 (Maori)', tried, and in a gallant action failed, to retake Maleme Airport.

'What's surprising about it,' Mike says, returning to a more level tone, 'is just how much there was to discover about Joe Panapa.'

'It's not that I doubt you,' Winterstoke says. 'I just wondered about evidence—and how it survived.'

'It's simple, Bertie. Joe wrote—letters of course. But there was also a notebook. Ljuba gave it to him on that final leave, so there'd be some kind of record.'

'And you've seen these things?'

'I have.'

Winterstoke relaxes back in his chair. 'Not that stories have to satisfy the rules of evidence. Still, it's of interest, isn't it? Provenance is of interest.'

'It was O'Dwyer brought the notebook back from the war,' Mike explains. 'He meant to hand it over when he visited the family. But things went wrong and he forgot. And then later, when he remembered, he thought bugger them. He hadn't really wanted to hand the notebook back. He had his own special reason for wanting to keep it—so that's what he did. Kept it all these years, along with a few other precious mementoes of the war. And then, just a couple of weeks ago he heard I was going to make my second visit to Croatia to look for Joe's widow. Don was dying. There were things in his life he wanted tidied up. So he gave it to me to pass on to Ljuba. And while I was there she let me read Joe's letters.'

The two fellows of Bardolph's College, lawyer and philosopher, have been settled some time now, outdoors at a wooden table under trees at the Perch, the Trout's matching pub downriver on the other side. This is not a place Mike enjoys as much as the tables at the Trout, because it lacks the other's outlook on the water rushing from the weir; but it's pleasant enough and gives them a place to rest and recover before making their return to the carpark.

Joe's notes, Mike explains, were pretty basic, but often vivid. This was a man of only primary school education; but he wrote well enough, and he was travelling for the first time in his life.

'This was a whole army on the move,' Mike says. 'By the time the New Zealand contingent had been joined by ships in Sydney and Melbourne it must have been a massive convoy. The *Aquitania*—that was the one the Maori Battalion was on. The *Empress of Britain*, *Empress of Canada*, *Empress of Japan*, the *Mauritania*, the *Queen Mary* . . .'

'Grand old ships,' Winterstoke (himself a naval man) murmurs. 'And very large.' His hearing aid emits a faint whistle, as if piping someone on board.

'And there was a posse of warships guarding them. Joe puts it all down—the ships ranged out in formation. The darkness of the ocean-colour once there's no land in sight. Big seas in the Great Australian Bight, and bigger after Fremantle when they were going head-on into the Roaring Forties. He describes looking down the line of ships, watching them lift right out of the water and then smack down into the troughs. It's all there. But then he gets used to it, and bored as the weather starts to improve, and the notes are more sporadic.'

There were days, and sometimes weeks, when Joe wrote nothing much more than a word or two, or a sentence. But the life of the troopship went on, and he was part of it. There were inspections, PE, weapons training, lifeboat drill. There were concert parties. There was housie which was legal, and crown and anchor which wasn't.

Food figured often in his notes and letters, and not just the official food of the mess. Between Wellington and Sydney there

were mutton-birds smuggled on board by Maori from the south
and hidden in lockers to be eaten at unofficial feasts, until grease
melting and running out on to the floor drew attention to them,
and an officer who had turned a blind eye insisted the remainder
must be confiscated. After a brief shore leave in Capetown there
were watermelons and corn cobs brought back by the men; and,
for a few lucky ones, crayfish, caught or bought Joe didn't know
where, but secretly kept alive by two of his comrades in the salt-
water bath in their cabin, and boiled in the galley, two per day,
to be shared among friends. Off Freetown there was tropical
fruit, traded for anything the soldiers could lay hands on that
the people down in the boats would accept.

Also on the Freetown stop Joe recorded a win at crown and
anchor, and a fine for disorderly behaviour, the one cancelling
out the other. It was here that the two who were his closest
friends right up to the moment of his death got special mention
in a letter to Ljuba. Their names were Boy Keratu and Tu
Shilling. They came from Joe's district, he'd been to school with
them, and Ljuba had met them and possibly hadn't altogether
approved of them, because Joe went out of his way to assure her
they were his best mates, the two he could count on. He told
her he knew people saw Tu as 'Tu tough, Tu big and Tu angry',
but he was 'really a kind-hearted give-you-anything sort of joker'.
Boy Keratu was 'still the smiler', someone who could make them
laugh even when they were hungry and tired and everything was
going wrong. 'I'm the solid fella,' he told her. The three together
were known in A company as 'the front row'.

As they pushed on up the coast of Africa beyond the Canary
Islands and the Azores, the war came nearer. More battleships,
almost a fleet of them it seemed to Joe, including an aircraft
carrier, met the convoy and shepherded it into European waters.
There were practice alarms calling the crew to battle stations, and
discipline became more rigid. Off the coast of Portugal they
passed a half-submerged wreck, its superstructure blackened with
fire, and another ship abandoned and ablaze; and from the areas
where the warships patrolled came, at intervals, the dark thud
and shudder of depth charges.

At last they came into their final port, small and remote on
one of the Scottish lochs. They were disembarked, breakfasted,

marched to a railhead, and loaded on to a train. The journey that followed was long and slow—a day and a night, with many hours spent in sidings going nowhere, until they reached what was to be their base, at Aldershot.

Now Joe had his chance to see real England, as distinct from what he called 'the England in his head'; and it did seem, he said, like the place he'd imagined it to be, 'only more so'. There was something about red pillar-boxes and double-decker buses and London taxis and bowler hats and London bobbies and Piccadilly Circus and the Underground, that took him by surprise. They were so familiar; but it seemed wrong, he said, or puzzling, that they should be so real.

'These things make us laugh and behave like kids,' Joe wrote to Ljuba. 'We're supposed to be Maori, and we are Maori, so what's going on? It must be the Pakeha bits of us jumping up and saying, "Hey fella, we know this place."'

And so the bombing of London, of which he saw a lot, made him feel something that had only been vague before—that this really was his war too. Now, he wrote, he was 'busting to have a crack at the bastards that were doing all this damage'.

He saw the English countryside too, many miles of it, like the pages of a book, because so much of the battalion's training consisted of long route marches through country lanes.

The rumour was that they would soon be sent to Egypt. Then it changed: they were being kept, along with other forces, in readiness for a German invasion expected at any moment. It was summer, and their camp was visited by King George—'quite a shy little bloke', Joe wrote, 'but still, he knows he's the King of England, and we know he is, and one day I'll tell our mokopuna I met him and he asked me how I was getting on.'

The raids on London got worse. Orders came to pack their gear and their tents. Late that same afternoon they were loaded into lorries and driven all through the night, headlights dimmed. At dawn they were in the Kent countryside. During the next few days they set up a new camp among apple orchards and oast-houses, stopping from time to time to watch and cheer dogfights overhead, duels to the death, Spitfires against Messerschmitts.

Summer drifted into autumn and towards winter. Marching and training went on, but the idea that an invasion would soon give them their first 'crack at Jerry' faded. The heat seemed to be going out of their war, and as leaves showered down and fields turned brown and began to show signs of early frosts, Joe wrote that he felt homesick and that his mates were feeling it too. They talked a lot about home, what a great place it was, and about the food there, and the fishing, and made plans for what they would do when they got back. Joe was missing Ljuba and missing his little son. In one letter he mentioned a photo she'd sent of Frano with 'the Newall boy' in the Selenich orchard. He had it pinned up on the tent pole.

Christmas came, and each of the Maori companies was given permission to put down a hangi. And then a few days afterwards came unmistakable preparations for another departure.

They were glad of it; and as they marched at night, heavily laden, to the train that would take them to the coast, the old excitement stirred again, the camaraderie and the sense of drama, local people coming to the doors of their blacked-out houses to call, 'Good luck'; while in the distance could be heard the crump of bombs and the responding fire of anti-aircraft guns.

Early in January they were at sea, at first accompanied by the bristling might of the Royal Navy, with RAF cover, and even the merchantman crew of their own ship, the *Athlone Castle*, practising with Brens and AA. But as days and miles passed, the escort ships dropped away. Life-jackets and steel helmets were no longer compulsory on deck. The now familiar routine of shipboard life, more relaxed than the officers wanted it to be, but inevitable as big seas subsided into an oily calm and temperatures rose, settled over them all. The crown and anchor board, really a cloth that could be pocketed when an officer came by, was laid out on deck and bets went down on it. The dice rattled with a strange, hollow, muffled echo inside two leather shakers as the soldier who ran the school called, 'Any more for the more', and players and watchers pressed in close to ensure that no official eye could see what was going on, and that anyone who tried to push into the centre couldn't reach it before everything had disappeared from sight.

Still they had no official announcement about where they were headed, only rumour, the most persistent that they were headed for Greece, which the Italians had invaded. But, unbelievably to these men who had come so far to fight and had yet to shoot at an enemy, they seemed to be going back the way they'd come—the Bay of Biscay, the coast of Portugal, the Canary Islands, Freetown, the crossing of the equator (but north to south this time), Capetown, where they stopped for five days, and where a route march each morning didn't prevent carousing ashore in the evenings.

And while the newsreel of their lives as soldiers seemed to be slowly playing them backwards around the continent of Africa, Joe read English murder mysteries by Agatha Christie and Ngaio Marsh, and for the first time saw the London he read about as a real city, with real streets and buildings, not just a place in a book or a movie.

It was in Capetown he bought an atlas and began to work through and beyond rumour, plotting their course, which took them now up the east coast of Africa, through the Mozambique Channel, past Zanzibar, on into the Gulf of Aden and through the Red Sea to Suez, where they left the ship.

From Suez they went through Cairo to a camp in the desert, not far from Alexandria. Now they were truly in the war zone— had simply reached it by going the long way around—and the sound of distant bombardment became a familiar background. Yet still it was the boredom of route marches and inspections that made up their day—the preparations for a war that seemed to come so close and never to arrive.

A month went by. There was leave in Alexandria. There was wind, heat, grit, glare and flies, but no fighting, despite the distant bombardments. Joe had discovered reading was the best way of passing time that otherwise dragged. Books were hard to find, but he read anything that came his way. He wrote long letters to Ljuba, and scribbled in his notebook.

It was 25 March, 1941 when, with his comrades, he gathered his full kit together and boarded the train to Alexandria. They were there in one hour. In another they had boarded what Joe described as 'a big ugly rusty old tub', which set sail that evening and for two days and three nights fought its way through stormy seas towards Greece. To every man of NZ Div was now relayed a message from their commanding officer. At last, General Freyberg told them, they would have their chance to strike a blow at Hitler's army, which had followed the Italians into Greece; and it was appropriate that this should happen in defence of 'the cradle of civilisation'. They would find the work hard, but he was sure they would live up to the proud tradition of New Zealand fighting men.

Having read this message, their battalion commander added a short speech of his own, telling them they were going into Greece at Mr Churchill's request and that should be reason enough to satisfy them all, since they'd spent some months in the Old Country and knew what a great war leader he was. What was being asked of them wouldn't be easy. They would need cool heads and brave hearts. 'I know what we're capable of,' he concluded. 'Now let's get in there and show it to the world.'

These messages received, they landed in Piraeus and marched into Athens.

War, Joe Panapa was discovering, is seldom what you suppose. He'd heard of a hero's welcome. But to earn this, wasn't it necessary to do your fighting first, to do brave deeds, win battles? Here were the people of Athens cheering, weeping, throwing flowers. Joe enjoyed it—it was exciting—but he felt half-ashamed, as if they were being paid in advance for work not yet done.

That was at the end of March. Not much more than three weeks later these same soldiers, or most of them, would pass again through the city, in retreat this time, the streets empty, the windows shuttered, the people indoors, silent, obeying a curfew, though a few, tearful young women mostly, would run out quickly to give a soldier a flower and to wish them luck. The battles, such as there had been, had taken place in sight of, and in retreat from, Mt Olympus; the evacuation they were heading for would be at Marathon. As their CO had said they must, the battalion had kept cool heads and proved they had brave hearts; but little or nothing about their first venture into real war had matched the glory of those ancient names.

It had consisted mostly in preparing defensive positions on difficult and rocky slopes and then retreating from them long before the fight to defend them could be said to have been lost— sometimes without any fight at all. Weapons pits were dug, ammunition brought in by mule, wire laid down, tracks cut through scrub and oleander, lines of fire cleared. Hours and

sometimes whole days were spent on this, often in rain, sometimes in hail or sleet; and then as reconnaissance planes discovered their positions and fighter planes strafed them, and as
the first enemy troops began to appear, the order came to
withdraw—the position was not to be defended. And while this
went on up the mountain slopes and along the ridges and down
in the gullies, on the roads could be seen civilian refugees,
sometimes with deserters from the Greek army hidden among
them, making their way south to escape from the invaders.

There were artillery and mortar duels. There were serious
engagements with rifle, Bren and grenade, and occasionally with
the bayonet. Acts of bravery were performed. Men on both sides
were killed, wounded, captured. But even when there were
successes, the order never came to follow them up, to go in
pursuit. The Luftwaffe's fighters and bombers ruled the skies—
swept suddenly down from a great height or swooped over ridges
and along roadways, making every hour of daylight dangerous
and unpredictable. It was hard to see how they could have fought
effectively on the ground without matching air cover from the
RAF, which was always lacking. But even so, it seemed to Joe
they must have been sent into this battle zone only to put on
some kind of show and then, almost at once, to be withdrawn.
What were the men who made the decisions—the generals, the
politicians, the statesmen—intending? Why had the great Mr
Churchill sent them there? What was the point of soldiers dying
if they were not there to win the battle—not there even to try?

Some of the withdrawals were made in almost complete
darkness, in strong winds and driving rain, the steep slopes
and mule-tracks alternately rocky and muddy, the men carrying
full packs, slipping and falling and cursing, each with a hand on
the shoulder, or holding the bayonet scabbard, of the man in
front. In this way it could take one long night to cover ten miles.
And the morning would bring German planes, strafing and
bombing.

There was a time when Joe's platoon took up positions in
and around an abandoned house on a flat wooded shelf beyond
which the land dropped steeply to a valley that mixed the grey-
green of olives, the black of cypresses, and the mauve of the judas
tree. The rain stopped, the planes stayed away, and there was a

whole day in which to look up at the mountains high over them, and down at the river winding through the pass, and even to notice wildflowers—violets, pansies, mountain lilies—coming out, signalling spring. And then the strafing began again, the grey uniforms of their enemies appeared among the trees and on the ridges above them, and the order came to continue the fighting withdrawal.

After that moment of rest Joe's notes became scrappy. It was clear now a decision had been made to cut and run, to get as many out as possible while still defending their rear. They were instructed that each man was to keep his personal gear and that once they reached the coast all the rest, vehicles and artillery pieces, even mortars and Brens, were to be destroyed or abandoned.

Loaded into trucks, they set out along the road at night. For some of the journey Joe sat up front beside a driver, helping to keep him awake. It was a long convoy, they had more than a hundred miles to cover before first light, and speed, meant to be kept at a constant fifteen to twenty miles per hour, in fact veered between five and fifty as circumstances changed and the long line stretched and closed like a concertina. At times the truck in front was lost and their driver had to put his foot down to catch up. Other times there were nose-to-tail collisions. One truck ran off the road and burned. Another broke down on a straight stretch where the convoy had picked up speed. The soldiers from that truck tried to wave down others, but no one was willing to stop for them. All this was going on in near total darkness. What was out there in the countryside to left and right, nobody knew or cared. In effect they were a defeated army and they were making a run for it.

So they approached Athens in the grey light of dawn and, as the sun rose, made their way into its deserted outskirts and out again towards the place on the coast from which the evacuation was to take place. There, in a pine forest close to Marathon, the battalion rested, ate, slept, waited. In the late afternoon they moved out to the beaches. Truck tyres were slashed, crankcases drained and engines run until they seized. Soon after dark the first small craft came in to ferry them to transports which took them to waiting ships.

It was 25 April, 1941, a month since they'd set off from Alexandria, almost a year since they'd sailed from New Zealand. It was also Anzac Day.

EIGHT

Symmetry

MIKE REMEMBERS LOOKING DOWN ON THE DEAD FACE OF HIS FRIEND, asleep in his coffin in the Selenich house. That's how it looked— a young man asleep. There was no damage to the face, none at all, and this was Frano. But not asleep, because his stillness was so absolute. And it wasn't Frano.

Mike had never seen a dead body before. That it should be his friend, and that he might himself have been in some way to blame, made it all the more a shock. Discreetly watched by family members, Mike couldn't weep. He had wept, and would again. But at this moment it was something worse.

Thinking back to it, struggling, as the memory becomes clearer, to find an analogy that might convey to Bertie Winterstoke how he felt at that moment, Mike says it was like trying to vomit when you can't, and at the same time trying not to when you must. And what he was struggling to bring up, or to keep down, was the sense of a contradiction. This was Frano, and it was not. He was there, in the box, and he wasn't. You could touch him—and Mike did that, reached out, made himself put a hand on the stone-cold brow. But Frano was gone; and even 'gone' was a wrong way of putting it, because that suggested he was somewhere else. Frano wasn't anywhere. He didn't exist. He was history.

'It was one of those awful moments,' Mike says, 'when you discover that your bent is towards philosophy. But I don't think I knew that at the time. I just knew I was tied in a knot. Thinking gets you into it, and you think that thinking will get you out. It takes a whole lifetime to unlearn that, and by then, it's too late. Philosophy's your trade, and you have nowhere else to go.'

The Seleniches knew nothing of what had happened between Mike and Marica. And no one, not even Marica, knew of the night ride and the long walk back in dark and rain. Mike had come in quietly, long after his parents and sister were asleep. Next morning Frano was dead.

For days he would be on the brink of telling someone—his mother, his sister Stella, one of his friends—about what had happened that night; and then he would stop, uncertain whether it would make him responsible, and wondering how he could describe the event while keeping secret its cause.

And there was another thought that checked him: did he want to tell something that might suggest to the Seleniches, and to the world, that their beloved boy had killed himself? Even Marica he didn't tell, though he meant to, and would have if she hadn't been avoiding him.

The inquest came and he wasn't called as a witness. The young couple who had seen the crash described it and said it was as if the bike had been driven straight at the wall, deliberately. But everyone who spoke of Frano said that he had always seemed quiet, self-contained, and cheerful; that he'd been popular at school and then at the garage where he worked as an apprentice; that he had never been depressive—certainly not suicidal. There was the shadow over his early life of his father's death in the war, but that had been minimised by his mother's return to the Selenich fold where older male family members had served as father figures. There was no reason why he should have killed himself.

But he'd bought that powerful motorbike, a Norton, and liked to take it out late at night when the roads were empty and he could enjoy the thrill of high speed, powerful acceleration and loud noise. There lay the cause—no more than youthful high spirits in fatal and familiar conjunction with bad weather and bad luck. It had been an accident, a lapse of attention late at night when he was tired.

The finding was accidental death.

In his own mind Mike went over and over this question. He knew it was possible that Frano had killed himself. He might even have taken Mike with him that night intending to kill them both, and then changed his mind; might have been weighing it up as the rain fell on them in the dark of the Piha road.

Then Mike would remember the strange episodes in the years after Frano's concussion. How much will, and how much that was beyond the will, had determined those sudden mad impulses to hurl himself towards a wall or a ditch? Perhaps he had not, after all, killed himself, but was a victim of that earlier brain damage in the boxing ring. Or perhaps the inquest finding was correct—it was just an accident.

The day after the death Mike walked all the way to Bridge Avenue, and sat where he and Frano had gone so often to swim. As he walked down Te Atatu Road, and as he sat alone watching the tide flow into the estuary, he was saying the word 'dead' silently to himself, over and over, slowly, like a funeral march. Sometimes it took on its full painful meaning; at other times it became only a sound, an utterance, from which meaning vanished.

He wondered why there were so few words meaning dead. He could think only of deceased. But that was only dead with the addition of a c, an e, an s and another e. Remove those and you were back to the same old monosyllable.

He thought of defunct. And done for. And dead as a door-nail, and dead as a dodo. And donged. And dropped. And destroyed. What was it about the letter d?

He let his mind roam more freely. Kaput. Killed. Corpsed. Felled. Finished. Fucked. Smashed. Wiped out. Expunged.

The morning sun glanced off the water of the incoming tide and lit upon the patch of white sand opposite, as upon a new idea. He changed the word. 'Loss' brought constriction to the throat. They had swum here together, he and Frano, as little boys, as bigger boys, as young men. Loss . . . loss . . . Repeated, the meaning at first swelled and became huge and tearful, and then shrank away.

Experiencing his own feelings, attempting to control them, there was an interest beyond the feelings themselves—something that had to do with language, with the meanings of words. He was unhappy, but not too unhappy to go in pursuit of the workings of his own mind. He was sad, even at moments intensely sad; but there was a kind of pleasure in that. He thought this was pain he was feeling, and it was; but the real pain was yet to come.

During the days and weeks that followed Mike looked constantly to Marica for aid and comfort, and was constantly rejected. She avoided being alone with him; and when being alone was unavoidable, she refused to talk about Frano, and resisted physical contact. At first he thought it was because she was afraid the family would discover their relationship and its connexion—if there was one—with Frano's death. Then he began to recognise that it was something more. Perhaps she blamed Mike for what had happened. But much more deeply, she blamed herself. The guilt Mike felt wasn't superficial; but hers, he could see, was much more agonising and disabling. So their being lovers, which had seemed to both of them innocent, natural, wholesome, had taken on for her the colour of sin. She had been to confession, had taken communion, had been instructed by the priest, and none of this, Mike guessed, had made any difference. She was not at heart a believer, and so her guilt was unrelieved. She blamed herself for her cousin's death, and that cast a shadow over her relations with Mike.

Recognising all this, still he didn't at once understand how profound the feeling was—or didn't foresee how durable it was going to be. To himself he prescribed patience. Time would bring her back to him. Meanwhile he would try to hide his frustrations.

But Frano's death, which was making Marica avoid him, made him want her all the more. When he found it impossible to be alone with her, he phoned. When she wouldn't come to the phone, or wouldn't say more than a few words, he wrote her letters. He trapped her on the bus, and cornered her in the university cloisters, trying, against his own better judgment, to reason her back into loving him. He knew that pestering her only made her resistance greater, but he couldn't stop, couldn't leave her alone.

This was a phase of his life when Mike saw himself from the

outside, recognised that he was behaving badly, and couldn't change. There had been moments during the first few days after the accident when he'd felt his grief so intensely he thought he was the only person grieving at all. Reason, and his own eyes, soon told him this was absurd. For Ljuba Panapa, Frano's death was a tragedy beyond measure. She hadn't married again. In the ten years since Joe's death all her love for him had been invested in their child. There was no wailing from her this time, no overt display of her grief. She was crushed into a silence, a heaviness of limb and dullness of eye that would make it seem to anyone observing her that her life was over.

But knowing this, and recognising that Marica was also— and inevitably—more deeply disturbed than he was, still Mike couldn't make himself behave consistently, considerately, patiently. It was as if he was pushing himself forward where he had no right to be. Catching Marica once after a lecture, walking beside her in the half-light of the cloisters, he told her, 'I'm a mess. I need help.' When she didn't respond, he pulled at her elbow so she was forced to stop, to turn towards him and meet his eye.

'Please, Marica,' he begged. 'Say something. Help me.'

And for just a moment she softened. He saw that she looked at him with concern, even with love. She gave him a half hug, and said, 'You'll be OK, Mikie. You'll survive.' They walked on together, and the moment was gone.

Marica was arranging to have the units she'd passed towards a Bachelor of Science degree converted into what was called in those days Medical Intermediate. That would mean at the beginning of the following year she could go to Otago, the only university that offered a degree in Medicine.

'I think I've always been a slow learner,' Mike tells Winterstoke. 'Even then I didn't see that it was the writing on the wall. She was leaving me. Frano had won the last round.'

Those days and weeks after Frano's death were like a terrible emotional storm, but one which he knew—or thought he knew—would pass. Under all the turmoil of it he believed nothing had changed. He was in love with Marica, and believed she was in love with him. They would have the next year, and however many years it took to complete her degree, studying at opposite ends of the country; but in the long summer vacations they would be together in Henderson; and afterwards, he was sure (thinking like a man of his time) they would be married, would spend the rest of their lives together. He would be a schoolteacher like his father; Marica would be a mother, as his mother had been—a doctor too, if that was what she wanted, but principally a mother.

Three years later, the announcement just made of the scholarship that would take him to Oxford, Mike attended Marica's wedding. It was in the Henderson Catholic church, followed by the traditional 'breakfast', held out of doors in the Selenich orchard. Marica in her white satin appeared to Mike more beautiful than ever; but what struck him especially was that the groom, Barry, or Gary (to Bertie Winterstoke he pretends— or perhaps it's true—that after all these years he can't remember the man's name) looked so like Frano. He had Frano's build, Frano's swarthy skin, Frano's dark eyes and tight curly black hair.

Was this her subconscious way of making amends? More than ever it seemed to Mike that Frano, his friend who had become his enemy, had defeated him; that here, in the orchard where the wrestling matches of their childhood and youth had taken place, the last bout was only now being concluded. Despite the three years that had gone by, Mike's love for Marica hadn't changed or faltered. He felt bruised to the soul by her marriage —wretched, bitter—and had come to the wedding only because to stay away would have signalled the sense of defeat he felt, a defeat pride wouldn't allow him to acknowledge.

He tried to behave like a man who didn't care, and probably (he now reflects) looked more than ever like a man who cared too much.

There were lanterns in the apple trees, the packing shed had been cleared for dancing, there was traditional Dalmatian music, and late, when he'd had enough to drink (how much was enough?) Mike danced with the bride. But to have an arm around her, and her hair close to his cheek, was too much. They were both tense, and danced without speaking. As the dance was ending Mike said, 'He looks like Frano.'

She looked up and then, recognising what he meant, didn't reply. Anger, or despair, surged up in him. Talking now to Winterstoke, Mike can't remember exactly what he said next, or doesn't want to repeat it, but it was something heavy-handed, not even clever, implying that she'd married her dead cousin.

She remained silent, tight-lipped. He had the faint satisfaction of having stirred some feeling in her, but that was all. She didn't speak to him again. A few months later he was on the high seas, on his way to Oxford.

❧

Someone in the Classics Department at Auckland University College gave Mike Donovan O'Dwyer's address—or perhaps it was the name of the pub where he could be found most evenings. O'Dwyer was well known as a New Zealander who, after distinguished war service, had made a name and a place for himself in Oxford, and who acted as mentor to a select few young New Zealanders, teaching them the basics of survival there. It wasn't long before Mike found him in the Eagle and Child, where, at that time, O'Dwyer had his own chair and held court in one of its small cosy rooms.

O'Dwyer liked him—well enough, anyway, to put him on trial. Not that this was said, or would ever have been admitted; but it was how it felt. If Mike played his cards right he would become one of 'OD company', as Don's small troop of acolytes was sometimes called. OD stood, of course, for O'Dwyer; but the joke was that it could stand equally for overdraft and overdose.

At their first meeting O'Dwyer offered some useful advice about how Mike, already a graduate, should deal with his College and his tutor. Soon after, he invited Mike to his house for supper.

There is a memory comes to Mike sometimes when he walks along Parks Road past the university's natural history museum. It is of trying to find his way from his College to O'Dwyer's house, which was in a small square, really an enclosed oval, off Banbury Road, with tall terrace houses looking out on the trees and garden to which they had access. It was evening, early summer, the weather unusually dry and warm, and having made several wrong turnings he decided he would stop and study his map of the town. He went on to the lawn in front of the museum, put his bag down on the grass and sat on it, leaning his back against a low brick wall. For a moment he held the map unopened, closed his eyes, and felt a great wave of regret wash over him, sweeping away the sense of excitement that had buoyed him up through the weeks of the voyage and of his first experiences of London and Oxford. It was homesickness he was feeling, and there was to be a lot of that during his first year away; but its focus at that moment was Marica. He was still in love with her; felt that he would be always, and that this new life was only something pasted over a reality that was black and empty.

Sitting there outside the museum while the life of Oxford went on up and down Parks Road, he was invaded by the memory of the wedding, and of his last dance with her in the packing shed where, three years before, Frano had discovered them.

Mike could see the lanterns in the apple trees, could hear the stringed instruments and the accordion, could smell Marica's hair close to his face, and feel her body moving with his to the music. It all went together, the woman, the orchard, the music, the summer night. The regret he felt seemed huge, insurmountable.

The mood was so strong he was not able to fight it off, carried it with him up Banbury Road to the O'Dwyer house, and so, as it seemed to him, was much less talkative and interesting that evening than he had been on the occasion of their first meeting.

O'Dwyer, who sometimes admitted that he couldn't bear to be alone, and that any company was better than his own, was always quick to recognise the signs of depression in friends and associates, and knew how to help them over or through or around the bad times. Helping them was a way he helped himself. That evening they ate together with the family and then removed to the pub, where the usual crowd gathered around the great man. But at closing time, as they stood at the corner where they would go separate ways, O'Dwyer, who must have observed Mike's mood, asked was he finding his first weeks in Oxford heavy going; and Mike, having drunk much more than he was yet able to cope with, responded with immediate and reckless confidences.

'I spilled the beans,' he tells Winterstoke. 'The whole sad story.'

O'Dwyer was thoughtful. He suggested a turn around the

block. He seemed to like Mike much better for his sadness than for any cleverness he might have displayed. He was generous, patient, comforting; and he left the younger man with an open invitation: 'When things get too tough for you, come to us. Don't hesitate. Don't ask. Just come.'

And Mike did. The O'Dwyer house was usually full of action; and when it wasn't, that meant only that the action had transferred to the pub. The talk was quick, intelligent, educated, mostly serious, always sharp and witty, sometimes cruel. The drinking was measured (generous measure) and continuous. There was a formidable and intelligent wife, Camille; there was a brilliant daughter and two brilliant sons; there were sometimes house guests and often a young research student in a spare attic room; there were male colleagues from St Antony's, and women friends, one or two of whom were said to be, or to have been, mistresses.

Mike is not now sure whether he knew before arriving in Oxford that O'Dwyer was the officer he'd seen all those years before with the Panapa whanau, the object of Auntie Pixie's makutu, or whether he made the connexion only after their first meeting in Oxford; but certainly some months passed before he mentioned it. He felt it was something that might help to cement their bond as New Zealanders, and he didn't want to speak of it until he had O'Dwyer's undisturbed attention.

The chance came after closing time one night when the rest of OD company had dispersed and Mike was walking alone with O'Dwyer to the corner where they took their different paths home. In a tone that mocked himself, Mike asked whether Don remembered the sad story he'd told about himself that evening of his first visit.

Yes, the older man said. He thought he remembered it—the death of Mike's friend who was his girlfriend's brother . . .

Cousin, Mike corrected; but yes that was it.

'And the girl blamed you and married someone else, I think—is that right? And you hadn't got over it. Still haven't, I should think.'

'Still haven't.'

'And won't for a very long time,' O'Dwyer said. 'Because that's the nature of first love. But we can carry a few battle scars.

None the worse for it. Everyone has them.'

'There was something I didn't tell you,' Mike said. 'The friend who was killed on his motorbike—Frano—he was the son of one of your soldiers. He was Frano Panapa. His father was Joe. Joe was killed in Crete.'

O'Dwyer had stopped. He stood quite still, staring down at his feet. When he moved it was only to reach out and put a hand on the lamppost at the corner. It was not as if he needed to steady himself, but just to touch something near and solid and present. 'Joe Panapa,' he repeated.

The silence went on. It was as if, head down, O'Dwyer was at prayer. Disconcerted, Mike waited; then decided it might be best just to go on with what he'd begun to say. 'Frano and I were there when you visited the Panapa whanau. The night Auntie Pixie put the makutu on you.'

Now O'Dwyer looked up, his hand still touching the lamppost. In the light of the street lamp his expression was serious, pained. 'And you know, do you, why that makutu was put on me?'

Mike shook his head. 'We were just kids. They wouldn't tell us.'

'You never heard later on?'

'I didn't. And if Frano did, he didn't say.'

O'Dwyer straightened up and began to move forward, but slowly, thoughtfully, head down. 'Then I'll tell you. But I want first,' he said, 'your solemn promise of silence. About the makutu, and about its reason.'

He had stopped again, and looked for Mike's response. Mike met his eye. 'You can trust me,' he said, and meant it.

O'Dwyer nodded, believing him. 'The makutu was put on me,' he said, speaking clearly, measuring his words, 'because I killed your friend's father.'

'Joe Panapa?'

'Joe Panapa.'

'How?' Mike asked. 'I mean what . . .' He didn't know how to frame the question.

'What happened?' O'Dwyer was leaning forward again, thinking, remembering. At last he looked up. 'One day when we're alone together, Newall, when there's time, and I'm feeling stronger than I feel at this moment, I'll explain. I'll tell you the story of my worst twenty-four hours of war.'

They continued walking, not speaking now, not noticing where they were going, or that their path was taking neither of them home. As they went, Mike's mind was wrestling with the thought that there was something here that was like a symmetry. He couldn't yet know exactly what O'Dwyer meant when he used the word 'killed'. But he couldn't believe it meant, literally, killing—murder. It must mean, surely, that he'd made some dire mistake, or perhaps taken a tough tactical decision, given an order in the heat of the battle, which had led to Joe's death.

But wasn't that the sense in which it could be said that he, Mike Newall, had 'killed' Frano? And Joe and Frano were father and son.

He was pushing the facts into a more perfect pattern than the muddiness and confusions of reality were likely to confirm— he knew that. But he was excited by it; and not put out, or put off, by the further thought, which came to him now, that if one could believe in the efficacy of the makutu, then perhaps its power, and its effects, would extend also to him.

NINE

'Hamlet's My Middle Name'

WHEN MIKE NEWALL AND BERTIE WINTERSTOKE COME OUT THROUGH
the trees that close over the path to the Perch there's
the question of which way to turn. 'We could go on through
the meadow,' Bertie says. 'That would take us to Southmoor
Road.'

Winterstoke lives there in a tall dampish brown-brick house
with a rather nice back garden that runs down to the canal, and
with long views from its upper windows over the railway line and
the river, right across the meadows to where the A34 hums in
the distance.

'We could have supper, if you're of a mind . . .'

'Let's do it.' Mike says it quickly, noticing his friend tailing
off, worried, no doubt, about whether the kind of meal he can
throw together will be acceptable.

'But there's your car . . .'

'I'll go back for it later. By bus. Or a cab. Or if you look
after me too well, Bertie, I might have to walk it off.'

So they make their way forward again along the river,
threading through a herd of cattle which stop chewing, eyeing
them, but deciding, those lying down, not to get up, and those
standing only to move a step or two out of the way. Soon the
two men are surrounded by the steaming, soft-eyed beasts. Mike

pats flanks, left and right, enjoying the cow smell and the feel of bristled hides.

'Did you read in the paper about the woman trampled to death?' Winterstoke asks. 'Somewhere in the Cotswolds. She was walking through a field and a herd of cows went for her.'

Mike says there must have been something odd about her.

'Or about them,' Winterstoke suggests. 'Mad cows. British beef on the rampage again?'

'No, Bertie. Mad cows just go wobbly and fall down.'

Mike rubs hard with his knuckles between the mounds where a heifer's horns have been removed. It tosses its head but then submits to the sensation. The poplars rustle—almost, in a surge of the breeze, rattle—overhead, and Bertie reminds him, not for the first time, that Gerard Manley Hopkins wrote a poem about the Binsey poplars being cut down, but here they are, a century later, huge and healthy as if they'd never been touched.

'When you've lived a long time it's not just the human capacity for destruction that surprises. It's the world's capacity for recovery.' He stops, staring into the sky where another gleaming speck draws a double jet trail out behind. 'You didn't see Germany at the end of the war?' He glances at Mike. 'No, of course you didn't. Too young. It was unbelievable. The cities were shattered. You couldn't imagine they'd recover in several lifetimes.'

They have gone on in silence past the Boat Club and across the Rainbow Bridge before he stops again and asks Mike whether he has contradicted himself. 'Entropy and renewal. Is that a contradiction?' And then, answering his own question, 'No, because in the bigger picture the renewal's short-lived.'

He repeats the word renewal. 'It must be why your surname always seemed cheerful, Mike. Newall. It's the sound, isn't it? Not an entropy sort of name. Quite the reverse.'

'At school it was Know-all.'

'As in opinionated? Of course you were. Bright boys are, aren't they? I was. Mine were.'

On the path out towards the road the older man shows signs of exhaustion, stopping to lean forward, both hands on his stick, and seeming to gasp for air. Mike thinks it best to stand by, saying nothing while he recovers.

But the sight of the big new housing development along the canal revives him. How could it happen? How could it have been allowed? The meadow-space is finite and when it's gone it's gone. It should have been inviolate . . .

And so on—each new burst of indignation seeming to pump the old man up further, bringing the blood back into his cheeks. Soon they're in Southmoor Road.

Winterstoke lets them in, points to the bathroom, which Mike declines, and withdraws there himself.

Together they prepare the meal. It consists of thick slices of cold meat—some ham, some pressed tongue, some corned beef—with small boiled potatoes, boiled peas, and a green salad for which Winterstoke makes, Mike considers, quite a respectable dressing, mixing a generous spill of olive oil with a much smaller one of white wine vinegar and a squeeze of lemon, and then (as he puts it) 'spicing it up' with dobs of French mustard and some flicks of a very good, though bought, mayonnaise—all of this stirred and shaken together in a jar with salt and pepper.

In honour of Mike's joining him Winterstoke, who keeps a cellar, hunts out a New Zealand white. 'Not Cloudy Bay,' he explains, 'which has become something of a cliché in this country. This is a chardonnay from . . .' He looks at the label. 'Waiheke Island.'

He pronounces it Why-heek and Mike doesn't correct him.

He hands it to Mike, with the corkscrew. 'Go to work on it, laddie. I'll do the other. I know you have a preference for those leggy southern hemisphere reds, but you won't say no to this one. Côtes de Beaune. And there'll be a bachelor pudding.'

'Bachelor pudding?' Mike's cork makes an excellent cloop.

'It means you have a choice. Ice cream. Or tinned peaches. Or tinned peaches with ice cream.'

And they've reached that choice with surprisingly little talk (both have the tinned peaches with ice cream) before Winterstoke reminds Mike of what he said back at the Perch about discovering himself to be a philosopher. 'Is it really any different if one discovers oneself to be, for example, a lawyer, a judge, a person whose job is to stand back, to weigh up . . .'

'But to take sides,' Mike says, cutting in. 'The lawyer argues a case. The judge rules on it.'

'And the philosopher?'

'He asks what it means to make the choice. Philosophers are not good at coming down on one side or the other of a question. Lawyers and judges have to.'

'Your man Wittgenstein made choices.'

'In his life he did, that's true. Dramatic ones. He was slightly mad, of course. All three of his brothers committed suicide. When he was young he was one of the richest men in Europe. He fought for Germany in the First World War, and at the end of it he gave away his whole fortune. Wanted to be a simple artisan. He used to wash his dishes in the bath.'

'In the bath. I see,' Winterstoke says. And then, 'Why?'

'He was very strong on cleanliness. Hot water and lots of soap. He seemed to think the bath was better than the sink.'

'Very bad for the back.'

'Terrible.' Mike takes a spoonful of the ice cream and closes on it, enjoying the sensation of the meltdown. 'I've never been a man of action. Never had the capacity to be, or had it forced on me by circumstance. Hamlet's my middle name. Even when action's clearly called for, I reflect, I weigh up, I ask myself what it means to say I want to do this or do that . . .'

'Don't we all, dear boy?'

'Do we all? I suppose so. But for some there's an outcome. For me there only ever seems to be further thought.'

'Nonsense,' Winterstoke murmurs. 'I'd put you into my OCTU without a moment's hesitation.'

'Kind of you Bertie. And you might be right. Trouble in my case is that it didn't happen, so one doesn't know.'

'Seems to me, Michael, you've been decisive enough about this divorce. Too much so, if you'll allow me . . .'

'Oh, but I think that was Gilly, wasn't it?'

'Was it? It's a puzzle to me, dear boy.'

'And to me, Bertie.' Mike thinks about it. His mind goes all over the place, and then settles into another anecdote.

'When our girls were very small I got the only full sabbatical year of my whole career. I think Jane would have been three and Emily five. Or four and six. We went as a family to a small town in New Jersey. Woodlake. There was a College there, quite well endowed. The professor of philosophy was a Wittgenstein man.

He persuaded his superiors to invite me as what they called their Distinguished Visitor. It was a nice open woodsy campus. Plenty of space. And only an hour's drive from Princeton. This was the period right at the end of the '60s when the universities were in a state of uproar—the height of Vietnam, and everything that went with it. Flower power. Tuning in and dropping out. Kent State.'

'Make love not war,' Bertie murmurs.

'Make love not war, yes. And Ho Ho Ho Chi Minh.'

⁊ℓ

It wasn't until he got there and settled to his tasks that Mike quite recognised how strange a thing it was to be a teacher in an Oxford college which admitted only male undergraduates. He'd got so used to it he'd forgotten his own university beginnings. To be back suddenly, at this moment in history, in a co-educational college was a surprise. The social revolution, the political revolution, the sexual revolution, were all happening at once, each linked, all concentrated in the universities.

Gillian, who was happy there, involved in good works, used to quote lines by Wordsworth about the French Revolution—

> Bliss was it in that dawn to be alive,
> But to be young was very heaven.

For Mike, aware that he was on the downward slope towards forty, it was never going to be 'very heaven'; and though there was a sense of history in the making, what he felt was more the keen interest of the observer than the bliss of the participant. His intellect was excited and his emotions engaged—up to a point; but something always held him back. He would not go out into the streets; he would not carry placards and chant slogans. He admired, and even envied, those who did, but he knew that for him to do it would be alien to his own nature.

Gillian's faith had always been of the liberal kind. To her the war in Vietnam was an outrage and now, in America, it seemed possible to work against it. She joined the students in the streets, helped to organise protests, even encouraged the burning of draft cards and the escape to Canada of young men called up for service.

Mike shared her view of the war. The distortions of truth and fact by which it was justified distressed him as a philosopher; and its cruelty distressed him as a human being. But wasn't this just the awful ongoing story of the human race? Wasn't that how it had always been, and would always be? His study of philosophy had taught him to view things *sub specie aeternitatis*—from the perspective of eternity. The human animal was territorial, tribal, and a killer. If you found yourself in the firing line of history it was bad luck. If you didn't, you should thank your stars—without, however, making the mistake of believing that there were any stars that were yours, or that they had anything to do with your luck. That the universe seemed beautiful to our human eyes shouldn't be allowed to conceal that it was also arbitrary, violent and cruel, that it had been around for a very long time, and that it would continue after we, along with our planet and our sun, had been expunged.

These, he would tell Gillian, were the hard truths which, every day, science was confirming. To go out with protest banners and songs and chants might relieve the feelings; it wouldn't alter the facts.

The difference between them on this score only slowly became clear; and came to a head on the issue of whether or not they should go to Washington to join a protest rally. Gillian was determined they should. At first he used the little girls as an obstacle, an excuse; but she said Jane and Emily should come too, and that if it seemed the event might be dangerous, one parent would stay with them in a hotel, or at some safe place, while the other marched. She had new friends and fellow workers who were going and she wanted to be with them.

He has a very clear memory of standing at a window looking out from the campus house that had been provided for them. Leaves were beginning to fall and drift around an artificial lake on one side of which a white marble Virgin looked with benign interest across to a neo-classical pagan figure, also marble, of a naked boy who stared down into the water, showing no reciprocal interest. The trees were a mix of green and gold, the sky clear blue, and there was only as yet a hint of autumn in the shadows. And while he was taking all this in Mike was listening to Gillian who was suggesting that his reluctance to join these protest marches was just an inhibition, a fear of seeming foolish; or worse (her voice, not rising exactly, but becoming tense), that it was really anxiety about letting his American colleagues, some of whom would disapprove, know what his convictions were.

They had usually been patient and considerate with one another, treading carefully around the areas of intellectual difference; but now, as Gillian became more involved in the protests, they were getting nearer to frankness, and even to open conflict.

'I've never tried to stop you doing these things . . .' he began, meaning to go on to suggest that she, on the other hand, should not pressure him to take part, but she interrupted him.

'Not directly, you haven't. But you don't encourage me.'

'You don't need encouragement. You're so convinced you're right . . .'

'But you pretend to agree.'

'I don't pretend. On the subject of the war, I do agree.'

'What's the use of agreeing in your head? If it's immoral it should be opposed.'

His tone remained patient, reasonable. 'Is it our business, though? We're visitors here.'

'It's happening in Vietnam, Mike. Out there in the world.'

'A lot of things are happening out there in the world, a very high proportion of them bad. Are you sure you're not casting yourself in the role of . . .'

'Yes?' she said, when he hesitated. 'In the role of?'

'A sort of moral busybody?'

'Are you sure you're not a coward?'

After a moment's thought he said, 'No, I'm not sure. But I'm not going to Washington just so I can test my courage.'

'Mike . . .' Her tone was one of appeal. 'I feel this thing very deeply.'

But he'd been offended by the word coward. 'What you feel,' he said, 'is indignation. You want to relieve your feelings.'

'My feelings are strong, but I'm not ruled by them. I pray, because I don't always trust them. I ask God to confirm them.'

'And of course he does.'

Her face flushed at his tone of near-contempt.

'When I was a child,' he told her, 'there was an old Maori

man down in the village who wanted to go and live up north on the Hokianga Harbour where he'd come from originally. His wife didn't want to go. She liked Henderson. They were very religious, so he said he'd ask God to direct them. He prayed for a few days, and then back came the reply. God said they were to move to the Hokianga.'

Gillian's silence lasted several cool seconds before she said, 'You've told me that story before, Michael.'

'That would be, I suppose, because it makes a point.'

When she didn't answer he said, 'Prayer is propitiation. It's the science that failed.'

She wouldn't argue. He had always disliked her unyielding silences, but his response to this one took him by surprise. He felt himself surge into a diatribe, a direct frontal assault on her faith. It didn't last long, but while it did he was carried along by it, even able to enjoy it, as he might have enjoyed driving a fast car. The engine was logic, but the fuel was a passionate feeling that had been pent up—concealed from her, and even from himself.

When children had an imaginary friend, he told her, it was usual to be tolerant, but not to encourage the game beyond a certain point of reason. With adults, on the other hand, if they said the friend's name was God, and especially if they conducted conversations with him and called it prayer, we were supposed to be respectful, even reverent, even join in.

It wasn't that God did or didn't exist. It was that the word had no meaning: 'God' (and he remembered the old joke)—dog spelled backwards—the vacuous monosyllable, the great vacancy of sense, a sort of gas-inflated noun-balloon designed to make empty minds feel as if they were filled with something, and flying.

Did she know (she'd turned away and the question was directed at the back of her head) that the nearest star—the nearest!—to our sun was twenty-three million million miles away? That astronomers were detecting what amounted to thousands of millions of galaxies out there, each with thousands of millions of stars. Could she get her head around those numbers? *They* were the mystery. God was not the mystery. God was the evasion of the mystery. God was the three-letter quick-fix for those who couldn't even begin to face the realities of time and space.

And then (he went on) to live by the fiction that death wasn't an end; that there was something else, and a code by which you could access it; a self to be preserved and somewhere for it to 'go': it was frivolous. Where did the flame of the candle 'go' when it went out? Did it go back to the big flame in the skies from which it came, in whose image it had been created? What would she think of him if he told her he believed that it did? She'd think he was childish, intellectually puerile, and she'd be right.

Still she didn't reply. He said, 'Let me give you the history of the Church of the Spiritual Bowser. It was established two thousand years ago when an angel came down and said there was a gas station on the back of the moon.'

'Two thousand years ago?' she interrupted. 'A gas station?'

'Don't get hung up on the detail,' he said. 'Just listen. What the angel said was that when you died you could go there and fill up on the holy spirit and live for ever. But you had to believe in it first, or that was the end of you. No faith, no gas. You were done for. Finished, fucked, kaput.

'The word spread, until . . . I don't know. Let's say half . . . Half the world believed in the spiritual bowser. They prayed to it, made images of it, sang hymns to it, celebrated its birthday, wore hair shirts to be worthy of its promise, starved themselves, ate fish on Fridays, went on pilgrimages. Then an argument blew up between those who said the pump of the holy spirit was blue and those who said it was red. The reddists made war on the blueists. The blueists tortured reddists, branded them with hot irons, stretched them on the rack to make them change what they believed, and burned them at the stake if they wouldn't. Millions died defending the doctrine that the pump was red, and millions more died because they knew it was blue. Finally, about now, humankind made a rocket and got around to the back of the moon, landed, and looked about. There was nothing there. No pump. No spiritual gas. What did the priests say? They said, "Of course not. You can't see it if you're alive. You have to be dead."'

'That seems reasonable,' Gillian said. There was a faint smile. After a moment she said, 'If you expressed yourself like that more often, Mike, you might be a happier man.'

He kept a straight bat. 'You'd like that, would you?'

'Well, at least I'd be entertained.'

He absorbed that in silence.

She said, 'Maybe you're not really a logician at all.'

It occurred to him that the iron had entered her soul at the moment when she'd called him a coward; but it had entered his at that moment too. He shifted ground. 'D'you know why I stopped coming to church with you?'

'You said it was because you couldn't think for all the noise that went on.'

'I must have been trying to entertain you.'

'No doubt.' She tidied some objects on the table.

But he wasn't going to be stopped now. 'The last time I went with you,' he said, 'they sang "All things bright and beautiful".'

He sang a verse in a light, silly-silky voice, like a crooner of the 1920s:

> 'All things bright and beautiful
> All creatures great and small
> All things wise and wonderful
> The Lord God made them all.'

'Yes,' she said, 'I do know the words, Mike. And the tune.'

'I looked around the church and there were all these intent faces singing about God the great Santa Claus in his eternal workshop, making lovely things for us, and I thought suddenly, What the fuck am I doing? This is an intellectual slum and I don't want to be here.'

She said, 'But you used to sing the hymns so lustily.'

He felt himself smiling. 'Well, at least I bark in tune.'

'Shall we give this subject a rest?'

'Yes, I think we must.'

'But you have to understand, Mike, I'm going to Washington. I'll go alone.'

He sighed. 'We'll go together. All four of us.'

He knew she wouldn't accept this, would insist that he wasn't to come. Having asked to be excused he would now have to spend several days proving that he wanted, that he was determined, to accompany her. It was another example of how Dog moved in mysterious ways.

TEN

Kalí Méra, Kia Ora

JOE PANAPA THOUGHT IT MUST HAVE BEEN CLOSE TO MIDNIGHT BEFORE his platoon was ferried out to a Royal Navy ship waiting off the beach of Porto Rafti close to Marathon and not far from Athens. On board, they were given cigarettes, hot cocoa, hunks of buttered bread, and a blanket, and told to find themselves space in which to rest, leaving passageways clear for the crew. By the time the ship had its full load, every corner, even on the decks, was taken up. Joe, with his mates Boy Keratu and Tu Shilling, was wedged into a corner of the foredeck under one of the guns. As they left the coast of mainland Greece behind he felt the ship begin to vibrate, the engines rising to full power, driving into the swells of the open sea.

Lulled by the movement, he slept. Now and then, when someone got up or rolled too far, causing a wave of restlessness and grumbling to pass through the mass of sleeping men, Joe half woke, looked at the stars of the northern sky, listened to the swish of sea past bows, and slept again. In the early hours of daylight he caught his first sight of mountains in the far distance, but the exhaustion of the past days, and the relief to be out of it, was stronger than curiosity, and he slept again. The sun was well above the horizon before the men were all awake and standing about, watching the rocky shoreline as it came closer.

'Where are we, Tu?' Joe asked, leaning on the rail beside his mate.

'Crete. That's what the Navy jokers say.'

'Never heard of it.'

'It's an island. Belongs to Greece.'

'I thought we were heading back to Egypt.'

'Hundred miles long, they reckon.'

'Why're we going there?'

'Holiday, I think.' Tu's laugh was like an unoiled door.

The ship was close in now. It sailed past a small island topped with a fort, made its way through a double-boom and on into what they would come to know as Suda Bay, with the barren heights of the Akrotiri Peninsula to the right, and to the left a view of olive groves, woodlands, small farms, pale flat-roofed houses among trees, and in the far distance, the looming mountains, their peaks snow-capped.

The morning sun was beginning to be warm; the harbour was full of shipping, large and small. There were two flying boats, one with its propellers turning.

'Looks nice,' Joe said.

'But Jerry's been here.'

There were smouldering fires from air attacks, and one large cruiser burned out and sunk in shallow water, its superstructure above the surface.

'We need another crack at the bastards.'

'You reckon? I need a feed first.'

'Well yeah. A feed, and a few days' rest, and then another crack at them. It'll be better next time.'

Lighters and other small craft took them ashore to a stone wharf where officers bleated and bellowed among the milling khaki crowds, not always able to find all their men or call them to order. Queues formed and were kept moving—away from the central wharf area which might at any time receive another visit from the Luftwaffe. Any Brens, machine-guns or mortars the men had brought from the mainland were to be handed in as they left.

Like many in the battalion, Boy Keratu had ignored the order that Brens were to be left behind at Marathon. 'Bugger that,' he'd said to Joe. 'I'm keeping mine.'

An English officer wearing a red tab was trying to keep watch as they filed by. Seeing Boy still with his Bren he pointed back towards the growing pile. 'Back there with it, laddie.'

A New Zealand officer turned back and spoke in an undertone. 'That order made no sense, sir. These men were right to keep their weapons.'

'There'll be a distribution later, Captain,' he was told. 'They'll get their proper share then.' And turning to Boy, 'Put it down, private.'

Boy added his Bren to the growing pile, and a moment later, as the English officer moved away, picked it up again. The New Zealand captain looked at the sky and said nothing.

Away from the wharf area they sorted themselves into their proper units. Joe was aware of a rip in his tunic and holes in a trouser leg; but when he looked at the men forming up he saw what a ragged lot they'd become. And their faces, he thought, matched their uniforms. They were unshaven and looked tired. But it wasn't just scruffiness and exhaustion. They looked different around the eyes, like the losing team coming off the rugby field.

Soon they were marching at ease along a dusty winding road, and he began to feel better. The road took them through olive groves and stands of oak and pine and poplar, past scattered clusters of houses where women and girls came out to greet them with flowers and oranges, and old men in cafés called to them offering drinks of the local wine. On the outskirts of the town of Hania they were stopped by the Welsh Regiment handing out chocolate and oranges, cigarettes and mugs of tea.

Joe's first night on the island was spent in a transit area, a flat tree-covered space south-west of Hania. They were fed tinned bully beef, biscuits and tea. Each man was given a blanket and told to bed down as best he could. Some went hunting for wine shops. Joe and his mates wanted only to sleep, and not even the damp chill that came down from the hills as soon as the sun was gone could keep them from it; but it was a shivering, tossing half-sleep on the hard ground.

In the morning their cook got them ready a breakfast of eggs, bought or scrounged from round about and boiled in cut-down petrol cans over fires of bamboo and olive twigs. The sun rose in the sky and before long they were shedding their battle-dress tunics, lying about under the trees smoking and talking, borrowing shaving gear, queuing for water, wandering from one unit to the next asking for news of missing comrades, exchanging stories of the retreat, of the thrashing they'd taken, not from the forces on the ground but from the remorseless hardware hurled at them from the skies.

What had happened on the mainland had been a bad episode, best put behind them; but the habits learned there remained. When a plane went over, fear came back. They stopped talking and listened; watched until it was gone. If it came on them suddenly at low altitude they threw themselves to the ground, getting up grinning, embarrassed, when it was gone.

A day or so later Joe's company moved off along the road that ran parallel to the coast from Hania towards the airstrip at Maleme. They whistled, sang, and kept in step with their own music, swinging along in the spring sunshine, feeling rested and in better spirits. The road was white, dusty, unsealed, beaten flat with ragged edges. To the right, the land sloped down to where they could see beaches only two or three hundred yards away, some pebble-coloured grey and orange-white, others sandy. There were painted wooden fishing boats pulled clear of the water. The sea was a heavy blue—calm, but not mirror-flat. There was an island offshore. Beyond and to the right of it was the high hazy curve of the Akrotiri Peninsula; and then nothing—only a blur where sea became sky. Somewhere out there was the Greek mainland they had been hounded out of. Somewhere out there was the enemy, and the Stukas and Messerschmitts of the enemy airforce.

Left of the road the land went on rising gently. There were olive groves, citrus orchards and, at intervals, tall stands of reedy-looking bamboo, or bamboo-looking reeds, closing in on the road and blocking the view. Seen at a distance the citrus trees were glinting dark-green masses speckled with bright dots of orange, and women and children could be seen, up ladders and on the paths between, gathering the ripe fruit in big sacks. In the vineyards not much was happening, but here and there an old peasant woman in black could be seen trimming vines of excess leafage.

The houses were grouped in clusters, not large enough, most of them, to be called villages. At the centre of one of these there was a well, and women drawing water and carrying it away on their shoulders in earthenware jars. Round about the houses were vegetable gardens, hens ranging free or in wire enclosures, tethered goats, beehives. As the soldiers marched by the women put down their jars to watch and wave, or stood with them gracefully poised on one shoulder.

The men they saw along the road were mostly old. They had fiercely curling moustaches, and most wore knee boots and baggy trousers with a sash at the waist. Many carried guns; all wore knives.

Now and then a man or woman would appear along the road on the back of a donkey bearing a load of sticks or bags of citrus fruit or goat's cheeses. Everyone welcomed them, called out, '*Kalí méra*', which Boy Keratu, with his huge grin, answered in Maori.

'Kia ora,' he called back. 'Tena koe.' When a little boy handed him an orange he rolled his eyes at it and said, 'Ka pai, e hoa.'

'I reckon it sounds like Greek,' he told his mates.

Joe's company made their camp in an olive grove on the landward side of the road not far from a cleft where a river ran, clean and fast over shingle and stones. Although it was an elevated position, trees enclosed it and there were only now and then long views down to the sea. But there was good shade, and cover against surveillance from the air; and they'd learned on the mainland that a slit trench under an old olive tree was protection against anything the Luftwaffe could throw at them unless there was a direct hit from a bomb. Standing at full height under the trees you couldn't see far; but at ground level, squatting, or from a trench, there were good lines of sight for men with rifles.

The soil, a lovely reddish colour, was dry underfoot. There were places where the ground was bare, and others covered in a thick close carpet of grasses and flowers. As a breeze from the sea blew, just faintly audible through the olives, their leaf-faces switched from dull to bright to dull again.

Joe noticed daisies a darker blue than any he'd seen before, mauve-coloured flowering thistles, oleanders, and what he thought of as Anzac poppies. There were green lizards and bright-coloured butterflies and moths. Close to where he and his two mates had hollowed out their beds was a little iron shrine, like a home-made letter-box on legs, painted deep blue. Joe stretched out beside it, his head propped on a tree root, smoked a cigarette, listened to the cicadas buzzing in Greek and the breath of the wind through trees, stared at the sky and thought of writing some of these things down in his notebook. There was something familiar and comfortable about this place, and he thought he must tell Ljuba, in the letter he would write her, not to worry about him, that he felt at home here and knew he would be safe.

For some few days they were all engaged in housekeeping—being issued with equipment, cleaning weapons, finding replacements for gear lost in the retreat (dixies, cutlery, digging tools), washing themselves and their clothes in the cold clean water of the stream, and doing whatever repairs were possible.

Discipline and order were re-established. Sentries were posted. There were platoon parades, inspections, weapons training, strategy talks, bayonet practice; there were night patrols to make them familiar with the terrain which by now they knew it would be their job to defend. The food improved, though it wasn't good and there wasn't enough of it.

They bought honey and cheese in the villages, and sat outdoors in cafés listening to music on the radio, or to the BBC, drinking with the locals, teaching one another words in English and Greek, in Greek and Maori. At Platanias, Joe and his friends sang Maori waiata and were taught a song in Greek about Mussolini and how the men of Crete would kill him when they caught him—the last line of each verse accompanied by a flat hand drawn across the throat. Now and then, given leave for the night, they walked and hitchhiked the eight miles into Hania where they sat drinking, talking and singing on the seafront, looking out on the little enclosed harbour with its Turkish mosque and its Venetian breakwater and lighthouse, the water so still and glass-like and the night sky so clear, you could look up or down and see the same stars.

In the later part of most afternoons there was a march, west usually, between the hill left of the road, designated 107, where some of 22 Battalion were dug in, and the airstrip on the right, where the Bofors anti-aircraft guns on flat ground stuck out of their sandbagged positions looking (someone said) like tucker for the dogs they were supposed to keep out.

Along that road were three or four big expensive-looking villas, with terraces facing the sea and iron gates enclosing gardens of magnolias and bougainvillea, and the men would sometimes be invited in for cooling drinks. On the return march, with the sun on their backs, there was usually time for a stop at the beach near Platanias where the men swam and lay in the sun.

'This isn't a war,' Boy said one afternoon as the three lay drying on the sand under tamarisks too feathery to cast real shade. 'It's a fucking holiday.'

Joe sat up to look again at the big black ants, at least half an inch long, that sped in amazing bursts, rear ends lifted, over the hot sand and stones, stopping to shelter under a pebble or a leaf before rushing on. As he'd done on previous afternoons, he chose a victim and began shelling it with pebbles, small ones at first, then larger. Now and then he scored what looked like a direct hit and the ant was buried under a shower of loose sand; but always it emerged after a time and raced away again.

'You giving those ants a hard time?' Boy said. He was flat on his back, eyes closed.

'I'm giving them a fucking holiday,' Joe said. 'Bombing the shit out of them.'

A plane was a distant drone, a black spot coming straight down the shoreline from Hania. The days when any aircraft meant enemy and danger seemed to be behind them. But now Joe recognised the shape, and the yellow and black of the Messerschmitt. So did others on the beach. The shout went up and there was a scatter into sand dunes where they dived, lay flat and still, trying to find natural hollows or press themselves into the ground.

In a moment came the familiar sound of the plane's guns, like the tearing of a huge piece of cloth. Bullets rattled the pebbles, the plane banked, climbed, and was gone, out over the sea.

It had been a random burst, more like a declaration of intent than a serious attack, and no one was hit. But it brought back the feeling of raw nerves that had gripped them on the mainland.

Joe remembered how they'd been strafed once by a whole squadron of Messerschmitts high up in the mountains near Olympus, and had all survived in their trenches. Then, when the attack seemed to be over and they'd emerged and were standing about talking and lighting cigarettes, a lone plane had come up from below, appearing suddenly over a ridge, and fired a single burst which killed three men—blew them apart, limbs and guts and brains scattered over the rocks.

It was towards the end of the second week of May when the pattern of air attacks changed. From the first there had been raids on Suda Bay, and on the airfield; but now nowhere was safe during the hours of daylight. The RAF planes stationed at Maleme put up a fight, but they were hopelessly outnumbered. On a practice manoeuvre one afternoon on a plateau thickly covered with scrub and trees, Joe's platoon heard the sounds of a dogfight and found an area of open ground they were able to watch from. Two Hurricanes were fighting it out with half a dozen Messerschmitts, while Bofors guns on the airfield perimeter joined in. Three German planes went down before the first of the Hurricanes was hit; then another Messerschmitt; then the other Hurricane. A day or so later the last of the RAF planes was withdrawn to Egypt. From that moment on, the skies over Crete were undefended.

It was about the middle of the month they were put on full alert. Word went around the battalion that the invasion would come in three or four days' time, from the air first. Seaborne landings would be attempted a day or so later, but the Royal Navy would be out there to cut them off.

How so much was known made the men doubt these predictions, but the officers seemed confident they were right and should be acted on. Every man was to have his hundred rounds and a rifle in good working order. Unless given a task, they were to stay under cover during the hours of daylight. No one was to take shots at low-flying planes. They were a waste of ammunition, and gave away the presence of defenders and their positions. It was believed the Germans didn't know the numbers of fighting men waiting for them, and this was an ignorance that should be preserved to the last moment.

Every day now the bombers came soon after first light. They

gave the areas east and west of the Maori Battalion most attention, but nothing was exempt, nowhere safe.

On the morning of the 20th they arrived earlier than usual and in greater numbers. At first Joe and his mates behaved as if this was just another day; but by the time they were having breakfast the noise had become immense. Sitting with his back to a tree, Joe felt the earth under him and the tree-trunk shudder with the impact of bombs dropped far away, bigger than anything unleashed on them before.

With Boy and Tu he climbed to higher ground where a few days before they had cut their special 'slittie'—in the shape of a V to give them two lines of fire. Others followed, and from up there they could see that the airfield at Maleme away to the west, and the hill overlooking it, were taking a furious pounding. So were the heights of Galatas to the east. The Bofors guns around the airport could be heard, for the first time all firing together, but how long could they last, exposed as they were? And how could the men dug in on the heights survive? Huge bombs whistled down in clusters, crumping into the landscape, making the ground shake, throwing up showers of red earth and clouds of white dust. Cannon and machine-gun fire were raking roads and hillsides. The German planes were stacked in threes out over the sea, waiting their turn to come in and deliver another load.

So it went on, formidable, remorseless, until around 8 am when it eased off and, in the area occupied by the Maori Battalion, stopped altogether. Not a shot, now, from the air; not a bomb falling—a change which made the continuing drone of aero engines seem like a kind of silence.

'Gliders,' someone called; and as the recognition spread, bursts of fire began to come up from disparate points, some near, some far distant—from olive groves and citrus orchards, from positions concealed in stands of bamboo, from scrub-covered hillsides like the one they were standing on, and from those heights east and west of the Maori Battalion where it had seemed no one could have survived the bombardment. Some of these silent aircraft, towed by bombers and released just short of the shoreline, could be seen finding even ground and landing safely, grey figures running from them and disappearing into the trees. Others came down in flames or broke up on landing. Some landed intact, but so riddled with bullets from the ground not a single soldier emerged.

Now, in behind the gliders, lumbered huge dark troop carriers, Junkers 55s, their engines throbbing, and from these, paratroopers emerged, dark shapes, arms high like divers, flinging themselves out in long lines, falling away behind, out and down, their chutes pulling free, canopies opening.

Behind the paratroopers, or among them, came their canisters of equipment and heavy weapons, the men's chutes white, the others red, brown and green to signify what the canister contained. It was as if the whole sky was breaking into flower, and as this went on the firing from rifles, Brens, and machine-guns on the ground redoubled. Some of the paratroopers were finding unoccupied places and landing safely. Many were falling directly on New Zealand positions and must be dead or seriously wounded before reaching the ground. Even at this distance Joe saw a black dot, that must be a weapon, dropping away under one of the parachutes as fire came up from below; then another, and a third.

'Why don't they drop some of the bastards on us?' Boy Keratu grumbled. 'When do we get our crack at them?'

Captain O'Dwyer, who had climbed with them to get a view of the action, was staring westward towards Maleme, his revolver in his hand. Awkwardly, as if embarrassed to find it there, he pushed the weapon, more a symbol of status than a serious piece of fighting equipment, back into its holster.

'Plenty more where they came from, private. We'll get our share.'

ELEVEN

Swimming to Nowhere

MIKE REMEMBERS THAT THEY HIRED A CAR AND MADE, FIRST, A LONG slow trek down what was called the Jersey Shore, that long stretch of coast running south from New York, where all the towns are named, but where the end of one and the beginning of the next is never clear. He remembers the big wooden houses, all turned seaward, the boardwalks and piers, and the long stretches of sandy beach. Then somewhere short of Atlantic City they turned west, finding the sea again, or the sea finding them, at the inland waterway of Chesapeake Bay. Later came the brilliant autumn colours of the Maryland woods; and finally Washington itself, smaller, more compact than he'd expected, with its white monuments and buildings, each one a public declaration of high and noble purpose, of stainless morality and honour, of the belief that the United States was the nation most favoured by the gods because its folk were the most deserving.

At first they went about as tourists, looked at the White House, the Capitol, the Washington Monument, the Lincoln Memorial; visited the Smithsonian, where they were chilled at the shameless presentation of 'Enola Gay', the plane that had dropped 'Little Boy' on Hiroshima; visited Arlington Cemetery and the grave of President Kennedy who, they believed, or tried to believe, would not have allowed this terrible war in Vietnam to happen.

But all the time in their minds they were preparing themselves, as the whole city was, for the march that was to put a symbolic ring of protest around the evil enclosure of the Pentagon. Protesters were flooding in by bus and train, and so were the forces of law and order—extra police, federal marshals, state troopers, units of the marines and of the army—so many, and so conspicuously armed, it was obvious the President meant business, and the business was intimidation.

As the day approached, Mike and Gillian became solemn. It was all more dramatic, more real, than either had expected. Now Mike too wanted to march. As the momentum gathered, his doubt about himself and his part in all this was abandoned, like something left on a wharf or a railway station as boat or train departs. He felt himself shedding his habit of analysis, slipping out of it as out of an old coat. There was a sense of being gathered up into a larger, collective will, of being 'lived by history'. He belonged to one side in this battle, and at last the wish to fight was strong.

But the little girls had to be kept safe, there was no one they could be handed over to in this place, and it was Gillian who had come to protest and who had friends and fellow-workers to meet and march with. One parent had to stay with the children, and clearly it had to be him.

So Mike watched it all on television—the huge crowd coming, endlessly it seemed, out of the woods around the reflecting pool that runs most of the half-mile between the Washington Monument and the Lincoln Memorial—gathering, pushing in towards the centre, more and more of them, fifty thousand, then a hundred, below the steep marble steps that ran up to the grandiose statue of the man credited with saving the Union; hearing speeches from the famous, the infamous, the anonymous, before surging out in a great powerful inspired mass over the Arlington Memorial Bridge and along the highway towards the nation's battle headquarters, grim and heavily guarded.

While Jane and Emily were played with, read to, fed, encouraged to entertain themselves, taken for a walk, fed again, Mike kept returning to the set, flipping from channel to channel, keeping track of the march as it moved, was stalled, pressed forward, was checked again, and as the atmosphere among the marchers grew more determined, more exalted, while that among the defenders of the symbolic five-sided citadel became grimmer, threatening, dangerous. As the day wore on there were more and more scuffles, arrests, moments of violence; more tear gas and riot shields and batons; more shouting and screaming.

Once, by an extraordinary chance, he caught a glimpse of Gillian in the midst of a pack of protesters that seemed to move, or to be moved, by larger forces outside the frame of the screen —hurled forward like a wave of the sea against a black-helmeted line, swung sideways, driven back. There was something white on her head that might have been a bandage. Her face white, her expression grim but resolute, she was shouting something to those around her and trying to link arms. And then, before he could fit this into the larger picture, or see the outcome, the restless camera was elsewhere.

It was midnight before she got back to the hotel room, by which time his anxiety had grown so huge his first response was not to welcome her but to berate her for taking risks; after which he bathed her head wound, checked her bruises, fed her hamburgers and coffee, followed later by more hamburgers and more coffee, and listened, on into the night, while she wound down, telling him, step by step and blow by blow, of the day's events . . .

✢

The bachelor pudding has been eaten, but there's some left in their second bottle, the Côtes de Beaune.

Mike stops talking, and Winterstoke, whose eyes are closed, opens them to ask (as if wanting to prove that old men can both sleep and listen) why Gillian's accusation of cowardice should have been such a sore point.

Mike tells him, 'I grew up thinking there would be a war for me. Of course I should be pleased that there hasn't been. Am pleased.'

He stops to reflect—is he pleased?—then gives it up and continues: 'But growing up when the big one was being fought—and at that time there was an older generation who'd fought in the one before—it had an effect on one's notions of manhood. And then later, when I came to Oxford, there were people like O'Dwyer, and yourself—all my teachers, in fact—you all had your battle scars and your war stories. At the very least you'd experienced the Blitz.'

'Hardly your fault, dear boy, if you were too young to be called up.'

'But I'd like to have been challenged. Pitched into something that was life-and-death. It's not that I especially want to think well of myself. It's more that I'd like to know.'

Winterstoke pulls a long comic-reflective face. He has clearly been refreshed by his doze. 'I don't think my war proved anything to me about myself, one way or the other.'

'You were in a ship that went down.'

'Yes, but that doesn't make one a hero, Michael. It just happens. Down the bloody thing goes, and you go with it.'

Mike remembers now that this, too, was part of the battle for Crete. It was something that had given Winterstoke and O'Dwyer common ground, even though they didn't meet until after the war.

'Off Heraklion,' Winterstoke confirms. 'The wrong coast for an easy getaway because Jerry was strongest there. The ships to the south got away to Egypt. We'd done some good work a week or so earlier under the cover of night. Wiped out the Axis sea invasion. But when we had to get men off from that north-eastern sector we didn't manage to get clear before daylight. Took a most frightful pounding from the Luftwaffe. They sank our ship and then they strafed us in the water.'

'And you survived.'

'God knows how. It was like swimming in oil. The smell of it, the taste of it. Ghastly. Everyone around me was dead.' He stares wild-eyed about the room as if seeing them there.

'Shooting men in the water doesn't seem . . .'

'Cricket, no,' Bertie agrees. 'It doesn't. It wasn't. The Italians picked up survivors—some say because we'd done the same for them. The Germans shot us to pieces. It might have been because on Crete our side shot at their paratroopers before they hit the ground. Wasn't what they'd expected.'

He takes a sip of the red and takes his time savouring it.

'So much of the war was boredom and bungling. Never been so bored in my whole life; and never seen such monumental blunders. But then the moments of action suddenly burst on you, and you were either drunk with excitement, or pissing yourself with fear, wanting the boredom to come back.'

He refills Mike's glass. 'But there was courage,' he admits. 'Mysterious thing, courage. Never felt it in myself, but saw it. Often. Lots of it. Mostly from men who'd say they had no choice. They did, of course—they could have chosen not to do what they did. But that's not how it seemed to them at the time.'

'And you don't regret your war.'

Winterstoke sweeps back the grey locks that are falling around his face. 'I regret the dead mates. And this,' he adds, tapping his ears. 'The deafness. But not the experience. No.' There's a silence, and then a rumble from the old man which seems to reverberate in his ear-machine, and which Mike unscrambles as, 'Wouldn't have missed it for the world.'

The deafness was caused, as Mike knows, by damage done when a winter supply convoy, which the Royal Navy was escorting through arctic waters to Russia, came under German attack. The destroyer the young Bertie was sailing in as a rating took a direct hit close to the bow but above the water-line. Fires were burning and the ship had taken water and was tending to list. Winterstoke was given a hose and a mask, pushed into the for'ard part of the ship, below decks, and told to fight the fire there. Once in, the steel doors were shut on him.

The hole in the ship's skin was not far from where he stood. Spray shot through it in sharp loud bursts, and as the bow dipped into the troughs, icy water sloshed in. As the ship rolled and plunged, turning this way and that to avoid the incoming shells, the water in the hold washed back and forth from ankle-deep sometimes all the way to his thighs. Up ahead of him, in the bow, the fire went on burning, and his work with the hose seemed to make no great impression on it. Around him the bodies of four men killed by the explosion floated and rolled, turning face up, face down, their hair spreading around their heads.

'They were all men I knew,' Bertie says, recalling it again. 'Sometimes they nudged me. Floated up, nudged me, and floated off again. I could only see them by the light of the fire I was supposed to be putting out. And a bit of daylight through the shell hole. I stayed sane by thinking they were alive. Or that

I was already dead. I knew I had no chance of surviving. This was it. The next hit for'ard would flood that section of the ship. That's what the steel doors were for. I was shut in with the dead. I was dead and this was going to be our tomb.'

'But you weren't and it wasn't.'

'No.'

But worse than the claustrophobia, Bertie says, worse even than the cold of that arctic seawater, was the noise—not just the roar of the guns overhead, the loud dark heavy beat of the engines, and the throb of the pumps, but the hissing scream of a safety valve releasing steam, a sound so piercing and continuous he remembers it still as the worst pain he ever had to suffer.

'No industrial earmuffs in those days,' he says. 'No pro-tection. If I could have run away from it, I would have. It wasn't courage kept me there. Or dooty, as L. J. Silver calls it. It was the steel doors.'

When the attacking German ships were at last driven off and Bertie was released, he could hear nothing. Slowly over many days his hearing came back, but never completely; and slowly over many years it went again.

⁂

Walking back late to Wolvercote where his car is parked, Mike reflects that the worst moments of Winterstoke's life, or equally of Donovan O'Dwyer's, could be represented pictorially and vividly—a man among dead men fighting a fire below decks in a stricken ship; a man with a revolver in one hand and a grenade in the other leading bayonet-charging infantry through the olive groves of Crete. In his own case, on the other hand, the worst moments might be represented by a man standing in a street in Woodlake, New Jersey, staring down at his feet and frowning; or a man sitting at a desk in Oxford, head in hands in a posture of despair. In the first picture he would be inwardly admitting to himself that he was losing either the ability or (it came to the same thing) the will to follow to their utmost limit the most com-plex of Wittgenstein's logical arguments. In the second he would be reflecting on this or that morning's quarrel with Gillian, so wracked with guilt and anger, so depressed, puzzled and depleted, that he couldn't find the energy even to pick up his pen.

Still thinking of that American year he puts it to himself: if there's no God (and there is none), and if the story of human consciousness is so unsatisfactory and destined to end so bleakly (and that's how he sees it, and saw it then), why should it have mattered so much that the intellectual energies of his youth were beginning to fail, or that the appetite for logical challenges on which his academic success had been built was diminishing? And why should stupid meaningless bad-habit quarrels between two specks of consciousness in the vastness of time and space have been upsetting?

But matter it did, and upsetting they were.

Wouldn't it have been easier, he asks himself, to deal with the simple demons of war—the fires, the explosions, the enemy with a weapon in his hand and fear or hatred in his heart—than with interior and domestic ones? Who was the famous thinker— was it Keats perhaps?—who wrote, 'O for a life of sensations rather than of thought!'

Wittgenstein, Mike knew, said that the propositions set out in his first book were like a ladder. Once used, you could kick it away and forget it. After that you were up where you needed to be, in the realm of pure philosophy. You could now dispense with propositions, forget theory, and get on with the practical business of being a philosopher—which meant inspecting the meaning of every statement, searching for subtleties, undertones, contra-dictions, ambiguities, all ultimately (it must be supposed) in the interests of exactitude and truth.

The kicking away of the ladder has always seemed to Mike a lovely, liberating idea. But what if you should find that you've gone up the ladder with a bag on your back, and in the bag are most of the fears, fads and fancies which clear thought and logical practice are supposed to rescue you from? That, he has come to think, is his own case; but he now believes it also to have been Wittgenstein's.

He stops under a street lamp and stares at the crumbling red bricks of a wall, seeing and not seeing. There is, simply, no escape from one's self, one's childhood, one's community, one's history —not in thought, not in logic, which are only another kind of exile; but probably no escape in action either, unless the end should be death.

Turning into Woodstock Road, Mike looks up and sees, through the leaves of the huge copper beech, that there's a light in Gillian's bedroom. He wonders whether she's reading late, or has dropped off to sleep with the light on. He wishes he could talk to her about the things he has rehearsed with Winterstoke during this long day of O'Dwyer's funeral. Or just climb the stairs and get into bed with her, not for sex (but why not that too?)—just for the comfort of proximity, the confidence and ease of being together.

His eyes are watering, whether with exhaustion or sadness he can't be sure.

The street lights, the comfortable houses of North Oxford, the tall trees, the church tower with its clock that is never less than five minutes wrong in sounding the hour, swim and shake.

Mike finds his car, solitary in the carpark over the road from the Trout. He has completed the circle on foot, and though it's late and he's physically tired, he feels pleased to have walked. There's something restorative about one's own company and the night.

He unlocks the car, gets in, gets out again—walks to the stone bridge, leans on the parapet, and looks down on the water rushing over the weir. In the pub all lights are out. The peacocks are silent, shadowy and still in the garden and on the roofs of outhouses, their long showy tails folded away for the night. Under a light that shines down on the river from the path outside the pub door he can make out the dark shapes of trout, keeping up their endless swimming against the flow of the river.

He thinks of Gillian and their life-long argument, often seeming to be about Dog, but perhaps not really about anything at all.

He remembers Winterstoke saying once, when he confided about their domestic conflicts, 'She's trying to stay afloat, Michael. So are you, of course. Nobody's fault, dear boy. It's called matrimony.'

That's Bertie—fair-minded behind the mask of misogyny. An 'our's-not-to-reason-why' man; an 'England-expects' man; a 'hearts-of-oak' man—but with good sense and unfailing humour. How could transportation to the other-and-under side of the world, and a few generations of solitary confinement, have made such a difference to the stock? Or have they done nothing of the sort? Are the differences an illusion? 'Same race, same face,' as the Greeks say to the Italians.

He drives back through Wolvercote, up the hill (where he once saw a hit-and-run driver kill a red fox), around the round-about and down Woodstock Road, conscious as he goes of a light-headedness, a sense that he is outside himself, that nothing matters, that his own absurdity is only a reflection of the world's.

Is something happening that he should know about—a heart attack, for example? A stroke? But no, he decides. It's just that his brain is still flapping in the butterfly net of Bertie Winter-stoke's well-chosen wines. He has noticed these days it some-times happens that way: for a long time there's no effect, and then, after the drinking is over, the brain remembers to reel.

As he approaches the house again he sees that Gillian's light is still on. She must be asleep in there, propped among pillows, her book fallen to the floor. If he still had a key he would go in, remove her spectacles and settle her down in the bed. He did that once and she didn't wake enough to object—only remem-bered it in the morning, and was angry. It was then she changed the locks.

The little red-brick terrace house in Saint Bernard's Road which he now rents from the College greets him as he enters with a reminder that he burned his breakfast toast before leaving for O'Dwyer's funeral. All that long time ago—seventeen hours? eighteen?—and the smell lingers. Or could it be that this is a house that always smells of burned toast?

And as he considers this, and rejects it, the fact that O'Dwyer is dead comes home to him; strikes him for the first time as a reality, like a sandbag swung on a rope. Upright and steady in his little parlour, he is, metaphysically, felled by it, like the Zen pupil felled by satori. It isn't grief that strikes, though there is something of that. It's the stone wall of the fact of it, as unavoidable as burned toast: Donovan is dead, his body burned to a cinder, his flame gone from its small corner back to the big Candle in the skies.

In the kitchen he makes himself tea and a slice of bread and butter with a hunk of cheddar. The mug is purple and bears the name, crest and motto of the University of Oxford—£2.99 at Bargain Books in the Cornmarket. He has four of them, bought as a sign to himself of bachelorhood, of being reduced to basics, even perhaps of justifying an occasional bout of self-pity. On one of them, the one he uses most, some of the lettering has rubbed off and it reads Univers of Ox .

The motto DOMINUS ILLUMINATIO MEA is inside the three-crowned crest, as if printed on an open book, so the eye is tempted to misread across the page, reminding him that when he and Gillian first got to know one another, he a graduate student, she an undergraduate, it was one of their jokes that the university's motto was

DOMI MINA
NUS TIO
ILLU MEA

He goes upstairs intending to get himself into bed, but drifts instead to the big desk in the little study and switches on lamp and laptop. He puts the bread on one side of the laptop, the mug of tea on the other, and goes on with the one currently on the file 'Letters to Gilly'.

At my worst times I wanted to say to my students, 'Don't do philosophy. Do something useful, or something beautiful. Philosophy is neither.' But I never had the courage, the ruthlessness, the certainty that that was truly what I believed and that it was right—and I'm glad I didn't. What's odd, though, is that if I'd had that certainty, and had said such things, I would have been following once again in the steps of the Master. Wittgenstein had that conviction, and said so—told his best students they should become mechanics or artisans. Yet he didn't follow his own advice—or never for long.

It's hard, after all, for an old god to learn new tricks. But I think of modern philosophers now as people who never get to really use the language because they're too busy pulling it apart—like someone whose powerful car never comes out of the garage because the bonnet is always up and the engine dismantled. Or who is always revving the engine without engaging the gears. That's how I'd begun to feel about myself—the engine of my mind was endlessly revving and going nowhere. I wanted more from language—as I wanted more from life— because, after all, in a very real sense language is our life.

At the Trout tonight I was looking into the river and I could see the fish under the light, heading into the flow. Think of the energy they have to expend, night and day for a lifetime, just to stay in one place! The phrase that came to me was Swimming to Nowhere. I thought of it as an image of life. One's job is not to arrive anywhere. It's to keep swimming.

I'm more relaxed these days—still 'doing' philosophy, but differently, with less effort, less stress. Do you remember how, when we were young, I used to concentrate on adding up the cheques and reconciling them with our bank statements and I was always getting it wrong? And then I discovered that if I did the arithmetic very fast, without trying, I got it right. That's not unlike the way I now do my philosophical thinking— in a state that feels like floating, or gliding. No strain. No tension. When I look down into the well and there's only darkness, that's what I report—and I wait for it to get light. And then it comes—illumination! Or it doesn't, in which case I have nothing to say. I don't try, I don't worry, I just wait.

And it's how I do my day-to-day living. No more pushing myself. Living alone I've had to discover the Zen of getting up and shaving and having breakfast and listening to the news and making my bed and glancing through the *Guardian* and gathering up my books and papers and walking to the College—and so on through all the normal things of a normal day, until it's time to go to bed and sleep. This is my version of Swimming to Nowhere. It requires discipline; but not the discipline of 'trying hard'. The discipline is to do but not to strive; or to strive without effort.

There's a teasing story by Borges about a man who wrote the whole of *Don Quixote*, word for word the same as Cervantes wrote it, not so much as a comma changed, but entirely different, because it was written by another man at another time and place. That's what my new life is like. Word for word the same, and entirely different.

I think back to the bad times before we agreed to separate, when you were tired of me and I was tired of myself. Such mammoth rows we had; such shouting and havoc! It would blow in like a storm, and when it had blown over I would try to remember what it had been about, how it had started, what on earth was at issue— and mostly I couldn't! But I do remember once that the subject of Donovan O'Dwyer came up, and you said you knew I envied him. I can still hear it shouted after me as I went up the stairs: 'I know you envy that drunken failure with his campaign medals and his string of mistresses.' And the more loudly I condemned him, you said, the more I gave myself away.

I shouted my routine denials back down the stairs, but of course you were right. I did envy him; because Donovan had (in that quaint old phrase used this morning at his send-off) 'lived his life to the full', and I, it could be said, have not. But I've come to terms with that now. I can say it. I am not Donovan O'Dwyer and I am glad not to have been. But it's true I envied him.

So now—I am I, Michael Francis Newall, and you are you, Gillian Florence Gately, and the twain have met, have spent a large part of their lives together, mostly with pleasure and profit, and have parted. That is all.

Is it all? For the moment it seems that it is.

Keep swimming, my dear Gilly (and remember to turn off your light).

Yours (truly)

Mike

PS: I've spent the whole day and half the night with Winterstoke. We're meeting again on Thursday for dinner at Gee's—that's the one on Banbury Road—looks like a conservatory, with rattan and cane and psalms— sorry, palms!

As he gets up and goes to the window his knees don't hold up well, and he staggers. Down in the grey pre-dawn street he sees the squat figure of the College senior porter wearing a baseball cap and taking his dog for a walk. A baseball cap? It seems out of character for the senior porter of an Oxford College. But, after all, he has seen the Bardolph's butler, quite a young man, riding a push-bike along this street with a pink plastic haversack on his shoulders.

The world is leaving me behind, Mike thinks, and finds himself back at the laptop.

> PS: Will you forgive me, dear G, for reverting to the subject of Wittgenstein one more time? He is still the Master and I love him as an intellectual father, a father with a compulsion, like alcoholism, or gambling, which is terrible but is also the very thing that makes him special, extraordinary, 'out of this world'. He says somewhere, 'If a lion could speak we would not understand him.' I think this is often taken to mean that the lion would have its own language; but I prefer to think of it as meaning that if the lion spoke our language, still we would not understand him. The lion's use of language would express his lion-ness, his lion ways, his lion society, all so alien that, despite understanding the words, we would not understand *him*. What I also take this to mean (without his meaning to mean it) is that he, Wittgenstein, is the lion. He can speak our language, and does, but we, not being lions, cannot understand him—which is another way of saying that he is for me no longer the master of logic but the Master of my Zen.
>
> What I now look to Wittgenstein for is not answers but questions, not logic but exercise, not wisdom but entertainment. To live is the business of living, and that is what I try to make of the discipline traditionally called Philosophy.

The early morning light is coming into the room now. He wants bed, sleep—or is it breakfast he wants? He decides he will have both ('Why not have it all?' whispers the ghost of Donovan O'Dwyer), first one, then the other.

Downstairs in the kitchen he's careful not to burn the toast.

He has a banana with his muesli—and more tea. He thinks of Wittgenstein telling a friend, 'It doesn't matter what you eat so long as it's always the same.'

A squirrel, who would agree with Wittgenstein, is at work out in Mike's tiny wall-enclosed garden.

Two squirrels. Two squirrels and a magpie.

Life's not bad, Mike tells himself. Not all bad. Not at all bad. Keep swimming. Always eat the same.

His eyes are falling shut against the invading light as he climbs the stairs and at last puts himself to bed.

TWELVE

Staying with Stella and Bruce

WINTERSTOKE HAS TURNED HIS EAR-MACHINE ON AND MIKE IS TELLING him, with quite long intervals of silence while they simply attend to what's on their plates, about his visit to New Zealand. They are in Gee's Restaurant on Banbury Road among the palms which, in his latest letter to Gillian, Mike first rendered as psalms.

Why can't I stop scratching that itch? he asks himself, during one of their silences. Why can't I leave the poor woman in peace with her imaginary Friend?

But the psalms joke, like the one about her imaginary Friend, amuses him all over again. If he should ever send that letter she would recognise it at once, like his handwriting, his voice-print, his intellectual DNA—possibly his true distinguishing quality, the one that charmed her most at their best times, and distressed her most at their worst. All this he knows. Even living apart, he can still have their quarrels in his head, and imagines that she can too.

Childish, she would say of the psalms joke; and child-like would be as near as he would go to conceding a point.

Another example of his compulsion to demean and belittle her faith, she would call it. A quiet registration of their ongoing difference, he would reply.

She would ask him why old wounds had to be opened; he

would ask why did she pretend they had ever closed.

She would say there was a failure of generosity in that kind of teasing; he would say there was a failure of humour in her response to it.

She would ask who fails when no one laughs—the comedian or the audience?—and he would be hard put to find an answer.

No, of course there's no need to send the letter. It's as if in the very act of writing it he has been reading it over her shoulder, registering her responses. Even in divorce they are married. Until death do us part—it's true. Comfortably true. Uncomfortably true. Like saying Heaven for all eternity—and *no escape!*

As he entertains himself with these thoughts he's noticing that there is kidney in his goulash. He wonders whether there should be—would be in the classic recipe—but is glad of it, and celebrates the discovery with a long-held and slowly swallowed taste of the Chateau Mouton Cadet Winterstoke has ordered.

'Not quite up to the mark,' Bertie has said, swirling, sniffing, tasting and nodding a qualified approval. 'But a capable wine.'

Strange to be able to turn the world on and off with a switch at the ear. For Mike, seeing it done is like a confirmation that his story is welcome. Sometimes in the past day or so he has asked himself whether he's shamelessly using Bertie, battening on him to relieve himself of a burden. But this opening of the ears—at once a motion of the will, and a symbolic act—puts the anxiety to rest. Bertie wants to hear, and wants it to last. They are using one another—and isn't that the way human beings get on together, by quid pro quos? When on either side there's something to be taken and something to be given, then there is what's called these days 'a relationship'.

Bertie and I, Mike thinks, have a relationship—and that too amuses him.

The world is so full of cant, it's a relief to be with this man who, half a century before, was afloat in his life-jacket in the waters of the Aegean, fired on by Stukas and Messerschmitts, all his comrades around him dying and dead.

Mike remembers Winterstoke's wild look as he told that story, the look of a man who has passed a lifetime with the puzzle, the randomness, the injustice, of his own survival—the miracle of it. These days he would be 'counselled'; but how could that conceivably have helped? With such a memory, how could you ever afterwards quite fall back into the ways of the world, with its invitations to pretence and pious observance, its shabby accommodations?

'I want a large steak,' Bertie has fearlessly barked, smiling at the waitress while his ear thing gave her a secret whistle. 'Medium rare. And no salad thank you.' And now he's sawing into it, eating with relish, washing it down with the Mouton Cadet and slapping his mouth with Gee's finely laundered white napkin.

'Excellent, excellent,' he says. 'I do like meat you know, Michael. It's what I remember most about my visit to Argentina. You grow great beasts down in your part of the world, and the portions are so generous.'

By 'your part' Mike assumes he must mean the southern hemisphere; and this is confirmed a moment later when he says, 'The Southern Cross was a surprise, though. Never thought it would be hanging down like that. It looked . . .'

He hesitates, and Mike suggests, 'Dislodged?'

'Dislodged, exactly. Hanging out of the sky at a rakish angle. Very odd. Now tell me about little Marica. How did you find her when you made your visit?'

Mike is pleased at the form of this question. 'Little Marica.' She's not really little, she was always of medium height, but he doesn't say so. Perhaps Bertie is thinking of her with infant Mike in their pre-school days, driving the derelict truck on the edge of the orchard. In any case it suggests the people in Mike's story have some kind of life in Bertie's imagination.

'I found her . . .' he begins—and discovers he's not sure what to say. He turns his head away from the table and looks out into the street, where the evening light of June is fading and a shower is falling. 'You know your Dickens, Bertie. You remember Flora in *Little Dorrit*?'

'Flora.' Winterstoke stops chewing while he considers. 'She's the one who chatters. Gets everything she wants to say mixed in a frightful tangle.'

'That's the one. Arthur Clennam comes back from years away in China and meets her again. In youth they've been on the brink of marriage and then parents intervened. She's now a widow, and he's unmarried. She makes it clear she hopes they'll get together again . . .'

'And Clennam's appalled. Yes, I remember. She's a total sausage. Amiable, good-natured, but a sausage. It was based on something in Dickens' own life.'

'Was it? I didn't know that.'

His friend puts down his knife and fork. 'But you're not going to tell me that Marica . . .'

'No, not at all. It's just that when I was leaving for New Zealand, and Gillian knew I'd be seeing her again, she made a joke about it. She said that Marica might turn out to be my Flora Finching. Who was Flora Finching? I had no idea. She told me it was a character in *Little Dorrit*, but that was all she'd say—so I had to read the novel to find out. I suppose it was her revenge for something or other. But it put a new thought into my head—a warning. People do change. I was going out there with romantic memories of Marica. What would I find?'

'And what did you find?'

'Not a Flora Finching. I wasn't disappointed—not in that way. I was . . .' Again he stops, feeling for the right word. 'I suppose I was intimidated.'

'Ah yes.' Winterstoke nods, helping himself to more of the hot English mustard. 'Women over fifty should be approached with caution.' This is evidently a preoccupation of Bertie's, the outcome of some undeclared but significant life lesson. 'In fact,' he goes on, 'safer to say they shouldn't be approached at all.'

❧

When (as he now explains) Mike flew from Zagreb to Frankfurt, from Frankfurt to Dallas, where he gave a lecture on 'Wittgenstein and Colour', and from there to Auckland, he carried with him a few commissions from his telephone conversation with Ljuba. One was that he should assure Marica that her aunt was safe. Another was that he would visit Frano's grave and see that it was tidy. 'Take a photograph,' Ljuba said. 'Will you do that for me, Mike? And bring it when you come to see me. Promise?'

He was met at Auckland airport by his sister Stella, and was to stay with her and her husband Bruce in Remuera, close to the bowling club where, now retired, they seemed to spend most of their days.

'So you've been lecturing in Dallas,' Stella said, as they drove away from the airport. 'What was that all about, then?'

'The usual,' Mike replied. And then, recognising this was an inadequate, even an ungenerous, response, he added, 'Wittgenstein,' and felt he hadn't added very much.

'Wittgenstein!' Stella turned her head from the road. Her white teeth flashed a moment like small memorial tablets through the scarlet wreath her lips made. 'And you still haven't run out of things to say about him.'

'Not quite, no. I don't think . . .' And then, faintly resentful, 'No I haven't, as a matter of fact.'

There was a silence, and Mike was reminded now how even Stella's silences could be bright and enquiring. It was something to do with the way she held her head, like a caged bird with a crest in the form of a question mark, and he felt compelled to go on. 'It was a lecture about Wittgenstein and colour.'

'Colour!' Stella affected, or perhaps felt, great surprise. 'I didn't know he was interested in . . . in that.'

Mike wanted to say, No of course you didn't. You don't know anything about him, and there's no reason at all why you should, any more than, if I happened to be a veterinarian, you should know about varieties of bacteria in the gut of a sheep.

What he said was: 'Oh yes. Colour was a great preoccupation —in his later years especially.'

When she began to say something about the anniversary of Martin Luther King's death he saw that they were, as usual, at cross-purposes. But jet-lag, and the difficulty of explaining, as she would want him to, just why, and in what way, Wittgenstein was interested in colours and how the human mind dealt with the perception of their differences—this and the knowledge that his explanation would be unintelligible to her and would make her irritable, caused his courage to fail, and he changed the subject. So when they arrived at the house and she called over her shoulder to Bruce that Mike had been lecturing in Dallas on 'What's-his-name and the colour bar', he let that pass too.

Late that afternoon, after a middle-day sleep that felled him like an ox and from which he woke to a few minutes' total and distressing amnesia, he made the effort to call Marica. She, after all, was the one he wanted to see; but because of the past with its residue of unspent feeling, something like shyness afflicted him. When he got through to her, his voice sounded strange to him. But contact was made. Words, whole sentences, went back and forth and sense was made of them. She said he should come and see her. And she added, 'Of course. You must.'

The 'of course' and the 'must' were meant to add warmth, enthusiasm; but they suggested, unintentionally he felt sure, something different—that given their past, a meeting was unavoidable. They must see one another 'of course', even if it wasn't altogether a welcome prospect.

He had come a long way for this meeting; but the why of it was now less than clear to him. It was easy to invent reasons—even good ones—and he had done that. Marica was a part of his emotional past, an important part, made more so by his severance from Gillian. But he'd begun to be aware that there was something else—something unworthy that had to do with ego, with hurt pride. This was the woman who had rejected him, at a time when youth and sensitivity made rejection terrible. Had he come all this way only to assert himself?

A day or two after his arrival Marica, accompanied by a small grey dog, some kind of over-excited terrier, greeted him at her door with a handshake that was allowed to merge into a French —or was it just Anglo-middle-class?—cheek-kissing. The cheek was full and firm and smooth—he liked the feel of it at once, and the smell of her hair. She was ample, not the slim woman she'd once been, but she carried it well. Her face was handsome now, no longer just pretty, with good features, keen intelligent eyes, confident lines.

'A long time,' they murmured back and forth, not managing to avoid the unavoidable.

'Too long,' he added. She smiled, as if enough had been said about the passage of time, and led him indoors.

The terrier was still leaping around them. Mike bent down to pat it and it cringed, half-snarled, and let out a warning yap, while at the same time its spine was pulled into a curve as if unable to hold itself straight against the electric force of a tail determined to wag.

'He's confused,' Marica explained. 'He knows he has to drive away the bad people and welcome the good people, but he doesn't know which is which, so for a first visit you get a bit of each.'

'Of course,' Mike said, crouching and patting the animal that had now rolled on to its shoulder, face-up and seeming to smile.

Marica was living alone in a roomy Mt Eden villa with polished kauri floors, fine rugs, comfortable furniture, many books and, on the walls, paintings by local artists whose names, new to Mike, she gave him as he looked around, and whose colours and forms, he couldn't help noticing, had a striking freedom and freshness.

The sun was shining and she had chairs ready beside a low table on which were set out glasses, cheeses, crackers, a bottle of wine and one of sparkling water—all this on a deck that opened from her living room and looked over a spacious green lawn and flower- and shrub-filled garden. It was as if one of the least abstract among her paintings had been projected outward in three dimensions, and would have seemed, Mike reflected, altogether charming if it hadn't been so perfect. Was she, too, fighting within herself the urge to make an impression, to prove something?

He gave her Ljuba's message. He'd thought of it as something significant he was bringing her, something, almost, that he'd travelled to Croatia to get for her; but there it was, given and received ('Ljuba wants you to know she's safe.' 'Oh good, I'm so glad, I've been terribly anxious about her—this war's so terrible.') and then what? A chasm opened again between them.

Feeling inept, then reckless, he took a daring route as they settled into their chairs, and asked straight out about her marriage; but she dealt with that in one sentence accompanied by a shrug. Her marriage, she said, had run its course. He replied, closing off inadvertently the parallel conversational track they might have taken, that the same was true of his.

He was impressed by her self-sufficiency—admired but didn't warm to it, because it seemed to shut him out; made him feel his visit was of no consequence. He wanted to impress her and knew better than to try.

She gave him the bottle to uncork, a sauvignon blanc from

the Selenich winery which had long since moved from Henderson to Hawkes Bay, and some minutes passed tasting and approving while she explained how big the business had grown, how exports to England and Europe were increasing, and which of her siblings and cousins was in charge of what aspect of the trade. This led to the subject of her own children, the oldest of whom was an executive in the firm. She gave name, age, marital status, education and occupation of each in turn, at the end of which he could remember only that there were two daughters and a son, and two grandchildren. Quickly, however, and with the same flashes of parental pride and pleasure, he ran through the corresponding recital of basic facts about his own two, Jane and Emily.

He was fascinated by the fact that this was Marica he was listening to, looking at, exactly the person he had known so many decades ago. Eyes, voice, gestures, turn of phrase, all unchanged, while at the same time everything, under the blow-torch of the aging process, was different. So much that had been latent was now realised; so much that had been lovely was gone; and yet it was Marica, indelibly. And as these thoughts formed themselves, crowding out the family details she was offering, and which he was pretending, and even seriously attempting, to take in, he wondered whether the same thought, the same perception, was passing through her mind as her disconcerting eyes watched him. Was there visible in him, too, such ample evidence of compensations for the exactions of time?

Now they were talking about New Zealand's new electoral system, Marica explaining how it worked and how it compared with the systems in Germany and Italy on which it was modelled. A commentary she'd read had said the Germans ran the system well and the Italians badly, and that so far New Zealand was tending to a Mediterranean performance. She said she found this surprising, and oddly reassuring.

'You know how it is for us,' she said, and he saw that she was speaking of her family. 'We've made a good fist of being New Zealanders. But we grew up believing that the Mediterranean's the centre of the world. Not Britain.'

'It's what the name means. Middle earth. But you've never been there.'

'Life's been too busy for travel overseas. And then, after

Gavin left me, I planned to go. Visit the aunts and uncles and cousins. It was all worked out and then this fighting started. I was advised not to go—to wait and see what happened. So far it's not looking good.'

So the husband had left her; and his name, which over the years Mike had found he couldn't remember, was Gavin. What he should keep in mind, he decided, as an aid to memory, was that each of them an M, Mike and Marica, had married a G, Gillian and Gavin.

Gavin. The name brought him a vivid image of the dark, handsome bridegroom smiling under the apple trees, and with that, the memory of a feeling like nausea that had mixed something close to grief and something even closer to hate.

'Not good, no,' he agreed. 'But it can't last, surely. You'll go one day.'

'But you've been,' she said.

'Landed in the middle of it.'

'It was brave.'

'It was ignorance.'

'What took you to Zagreb?'

'Stella called me in Oxford. She said you'd had no . . . That there'd been no news of Ljuba. I meant to go on down to the coast, but I couldn't get there.'

'You didn't go all that way for me—for us—did you?'

'No, no,' he lied. 'I was concerned for Ljuba. I wanted to know she was safe.'

Now they had something to talk about that took them out of themselves, away from the brooding ghosts of their past. He described Zagreb as he'd found it, and the view of the fighting as it appeared there—that this was not just symbolic sparring and skirmishing but the start of a real war, a win-or-lose conflict which would either subdue Croatia and rob it of its coastal region, or from which it would emerge bloodied but intact.

He described the feeling as battles were being reported nearer to Zagreb, the tension he'd felt in the city, the reports of refugees streaming towards it from the east and the south, the cry of 'Oba dva!' he'd heard on television when the militia shot down two Serb war-planes. He told her about Ira, who must be her relative, a cousin of a cousin, whose lover had been killed in Dubrovnik.

'The Auckland communities have been meeting,' Marica told him. 'Some of the young men are going back to join the army. They're born-and-bred New Zealanders, but now they feel they're Croatian and they should be there.'

So he got through his visit, filled what seemed a decent interval, put on display (he supposed) whatever modest peacock feathers Oxford and the world could be said to have added to his social plumage, took in the corresponding impression of Marica, the mature, intelligent woman and successful doctor, and took his leave. At the door he told her that Ljuba had asked him to visit Frano's grave. They'd hardly spoken of Frano. Mike had thought she might be willing to come with him to the cemetery; but now he failed to ask directly, and she didn't offer.

As he walked down the street he felt empty. It was as if he'd come to have something repaired, some piece of significant surgery, and was leaving with the knowledge that it couldn't be done, that the tear, or break, or hole was unmendable.

He didn't at once look for a bus or taxi but walked, found himself climbing the road that wound around Mt Eden, taking it slowly, taking in views of Auckland to the north, south, east and west as the turns led him on. Out of practice for such a gradient, he puffed on up, all the way to the summit. There he looked out on the city of his childhood and youth laid out in every direction, so much more densely built over now, and threaded through with motorways, but also more densely gardened, and still Auckland, with its green volcanic cones, its two harbours, its islands in the gulf beyond the North Shore, its blue hills to the west and to the south, its rain-clouds, grey over blue, blowing in and across and away again, leaving 'the wild sweet air' (as someone had described it) wilder and sweeter.

That evening Stella, home from bowls, still in her whites and her hat, but wearing a plastic apron that said GIVE ME ONE in red letters, did an ox-tail stew and made a chocolate cake, while Bruce, five years younger than Mike and seeming already like an old Kiwi codger who might give anyone anything except *that* (if, indeed, *that* was what was meant by the words on Stella's apron), showed him his pool-table and bar in the downstairs rumpus room, his BMW in the interior garage with the automatic doors, his ride-on Masport mower, his electric hedge-trimmer, his compost bins, the solar panel mechanism for heating their pool in winter, and its leaf-guard and filtration system.

After dinner they sat looking over old photograph albums, watching and not-watching television programmes so awful the innumerable advertisements that interrupted them came almost as a relief. Mike retired early, saying he had brought work and must do some of it. In the bedroom allotted to him, its walls still decked with posters of rock groups at rakish angles belonging to the last of his nephews to leave home, he tried to read. His book was a novel by a celebrated New Zealand writer whose twinkling eyes on the dust cover were as cheerful and homely and harmless as Bruce's—in fact his likeness to Bruce was uncanny—and whose narrative was full of despondency and raw violence.

Failing to concentrate, Mike sat propped up in the narrow bed, awake but with the light off. For a moment he allowed himself to wonder whether he was seeing his sister and brother-in-law as they really were, or whether he had them locked inside an old box or picture album marked 'New Zealand as I knew it in the 1950s', and wasn't letting them out. But even if that should be true, and he wasn't sure how it could be, the question remained—did he want to know Stella and Bruce 'as they really were'? They were as irrelevant to the life he had made for himself as he was to theirs.

He thought of Gillian and the house on Woodstock Road, and had to fight strong feelings of regret which the Zen of his new way of living, or of being, didn't permit. This visit to New Zealand was a mistake, he told himself, but a minor and harmless one. He must get through it, behave well, drink cautiously, talk sparingly, give no offence, do no harm, and get back as soon as possible to Oxford and what was now his home, his world.

After a time rain began to fall, softly, then more decidedly, more audibly. He slid down in the bed and lay listening to the white noise of its beating on corrugated iron roofs. This was one of the best of his childhood memories, the sense of losing self in sound, losing anxiety, identity, everything except the comfort of one's own body. It brought a feeling of drifting, then of plunging, almost of a lurch, down into another deep, abbreviated, jet-lag sleep.

THIRTEEN

Joe's Final Days

STILL WATCHING FROM THE RIDGE WHERE THEY'D CUT THEIR V-SHAPED slittie, Joe and his mates could hear the rattle and blast of engagements, some at no great distance, most further away, going on out of sight among the bamboos, through barley fields, olive groves and orchards, along stream beds, irrigation canals and ravines, and among the scattered houses. Many paratroopers, it seemed from where they watched, must have been dead before they reached the ground; many more before they were out of their harness. But the numbers, while the drop went on, had been huge. There had been a half-hour or more when the whole sky had been spattered across with drifting colours, like some dark parody of Walt Disney.

Now that there were German soldiers on the ground, the bombing and strafing eased off for a time. Some of the troop carriers had come in away to the west, beyond the airfield, where there were no defenders waiting to meet them. And what was happening to the east, towards Heraklion, where British and Australian troops were waiting, was out of sight of the New Zealanders.

Joe watched a late glider swoop over. Fire came up at it and there were perhaps one or two hits, but it swept on down to the beach area, went out of sight, and then could be seen in the

distance through a gap, skidding to a halt, men running from it
almost before it had stopped moving.

'Here's your chance,' O'Dwyer said to Boy Keratu.

Down at the camp he gathered a platoon together and they
were off at once, fixing bayonets as they went, crouching as they
ran under the olives. Up on the ridge Joe had had his moment
of fear—tightening stomach, dry mouth, urgent bladder. Now
what he felt was excitement. It was like a clear hard edge, a
sharpness. It was something he'd felt hunting pigs in the bush,
but this was keener, more dangerous.

The olive groves stopped at the road. On the other side the
soil was sandy, supporting grasses, tamarisk and weedy shrubs,
little that offered cover except in small tight patches. They
widened out into a well-spaced line and advanced on an abandoned house and garden. A burst of fire came from a window
and they went to ground, one of their number clutching his
upper arm and letting out yelping curses.

They kept low, closing in over a dune, making short forward
dashes and diving to fire from the ground. Fire came back at
them and they were held there, making no progress. Joe felt
unsafe, exposed to the skies. Two Messerschmitts swept over but
their guns were silent.

O'Dwyer sent his sergeant forward. 'Cover him,' he called.

They poured fire at the windows of the house and the
sergeant went in under it, bent almost double, but fast. He
disappeared among the jasmine, oleander and rhododendron of
the garden and for a time didn't move. Then Joe saw his back
and his helmet as he burst from cover, running straight and fast
to an open window. A grenade went in, another at a second
window before the first had exploded.

They could see him pushing himself flat, back against the
house wall so he couldn't be seen from the windows. There were
sounds of shouting from within. Something white was waved and
a deep voice called, 'Ve are hants oop, English.'

'Come out,' O'Dwyer called.

Five paratroopers came out, one wounded, helped, half-
dragged, by two others. The sergeant moved far enough from
the wall to throw in another grenade. Nothing moved in there.
He signalled the captured Germans up the slope and followed

behind while the platoon lay with eyes and rifles trained on them and on the house. They had their captives back across the road and were moving up through the olives when Joe thought he heard a sound away to their right and down close to the stream. He stopped, peered, thought he might have seen something move.

'Something down there?' O'Dwyer asked.

'Not sure, sir. Can I take a look?'

O'Dwyer nodded. 'Be careful.'

Joe moved away slowly, step by step, crouching to look down the long lines of sight under the olives towards the river, listening but hearing only the sounds of his platoon and their prisoners crunching away through the trees. He crouched, moved on, crouched again. Alone like this he felt soothed—by the place, the feel of it, the mildness of the spring air, the sound of the stream which he could hear now. There were bird sounds too, but as he listened they seemed to fall silent.

When the rattle of shots came at him he fell so quickly and so hard he thought for a moment he must have been hit.

Across a small clearing of red earth the German came towards him, not fast, carrying a machine pistol at the ready. He was wearing the baggy overall battledress and pudding-basin helmet of the paratroopers. There were big pockets in the trouser legs, and around his neck a pair of binoculars. He stopped and looked at Joe, peered across a space of ten or fifteen yards. Joe saw him see that the eyes of the man he thought he'd killed were open and looking at him.

At that moment, as the German lifted the barrel of his weapon, Joe rolled and was up running at him, running straight at and into the noise of the machine pistol. Where did the bullets go? In a few seconds the German was dead and Joe, unsure what had happened in that interval of risk, was looking down at him, wiping his bloody bayonet on the dead man's trouser leg. The eyes were squeezed shut, the lips pulled wide and thin and tight, the teeth and the whole face clenched in a grimace of horror and pain.

Joe took the machine pistol out of the dead hands and the binoculars from around the neck. He had to pull the head forward to free the strap that held them. The helmet came off, and his hand ran over blond hair, cut short and spiky, but soft on the warm head. From the pockets he took a map and a knife. Blood was seeping through the front of the overalls.

He heard steps among the trees and a whistle. It was Boy Keratu and Tu Shilling, sent to see what had happened and to give him support.

'Jesus, Hohepa,' Boy said. 'You speared one.'

Tu poked the dead soldier with his toe. He bent down and took a packet of cigarettes from a pocket and wiped the blood from it.

Halfway up the ridge they sat down and Joe rolled a cigarette. His hands shook. Everything in this grove was quiet and still. The birds were singing again. The sound of fighters and bombers could still be heard, but at a distance. They seemed busiest away to the west, and the troop carriers were already on their run back to the mainland. Joe handed Boy the tobacco and papers. Tu had lit one of the German's cigarettes and was pulling a face, spitting loose fragments of tobacco.

Boy grinned at Joe and let out a laugh that was like the whinny of a horse.

The remainder of the day passed in watching, waiting, hearing rumours. The battle was continuing east and west of the Maori positions. There was a feeling it must be going well, but no one was sure. In the evening a message came that B company was to head west towards Hill 107 overlooking Maleme, where 22 Battalion had come under strong attack and (the message went on) might not hold out without support.

Joe watched the company as it marched off into the gathering dark, taking the direct route west, straight down the road. He wished he was going with them and at the same time was glad he wasn't.

Just before breakfast and the return of the Luftwaffe, they were back, and Joe listened as their officer gave O'Dwyer an account of what had happened. They'd spent the night, the officer said, sometimes fighting full-blooded skirmishes, some-times watching the flitting shadows of lost stragglers (whether friend or enemy he'd had no way of knowing) trying to find their way back to their units, and all the time themselves hunting for the men they'd been sent out to help. Reaching Hill 107 at last, they'd found the trenches empty, abandoned. Later again, when it was almost morning, they'd found 22 Battalion all in one piece, withdrawn to safer ground. It was then they were told they were no longer needed and should go back to their own battalion.

'No "Thanks for offering us a hand,"' the officer said. 'Just "Fuck off we don't need you."'

Joe and his mates tried to guess what this might mean. It didn't sound good. How could the airfield be defended if the hill that overlooked it was given up? But none of them had more than a rough idea of what the larger picture might be; and if their officers knew more they weren't talking.

On this, the second day of the battle, more paratroopers were dropped. Some fell directly into the Maori area and were picked off before they reached the ground, or hunted down as they landed. A few were seen carried by wind gusts into the sea. But some landed out of reach and were out there somewhere, alone or in groups.

That morning another sortie was made to clear the beach. Some Germans were killed, others captured; but now the battalion was taking its share of casualties, and the enemy had footholds just to the west of them.

Twice the 'front row' were sent out with their platoon. On the first of these sorties they came on one of the olive groves where, the day before, the paratroopers had been hardest hit. Dead before they reached the ground, some bodies had simply folded or curled into tidy heaps, the chutes, spread wide, settling over them like candle snuffers. One, crumpled and broken, must have fallen like a stone and died on impact, his chute burning above him, only blackened shreds of it remaining by the time he reached the ground. Others hung in the trees. Entangled in their harness, arms spread, heads hanging back or leaning forward, they looked like a drama class persuaded into extravagant postures; or a collection of puppets hung away for the night. Some few had got clear of their chutes and had died fighting. Already the faces were beginning to blacken and the flies, buzzing, swooping, settling, taking off again, were putting on their own version of invasion from the air.

Up from a ravine shrouded by trees and shrubs came the call of a German soldier wounded and in pain, begging for help, for water, perhaps even for death. It was a pitiful, agonised cry. They looked at one another and kept going.

Not much came of this first patrol, but on the second Joe's platoon was suddenly in the thick of it, a desperate fight for survival in which they were scattered among the trees, through the lines of bamboo, around the outhouses of what appeared to be an olive oil factory, and in and out of an irrigation canal. As they fought their way back into some sort of formation a group of paratroopers, surrounded and outnumbered, attempted to surrender, but at the same moment grenades were thrown and in the heat of the fight no prisoners were taken.

They were almost back to their camp when Joe noticed that Boy Keratu was missing. They had lost some men in the skirmish, but no one had seen Boy go down. O'Dwyer was moving slightly ahead of them and Joe turned back at once, jogging, not asking permission because he wasn't sure he would get it. There was a moment when he thought he heard the officer's voice, kept low, calling him back, but he wasn't sure and in any case would not have stopped.

He found Boy sitting on the ground in a clearing, head hanging forward, rifle across his knees, helmet on the ground under them. There were three bodies lying nearby. 'You do this?' Joe asked.

Boy grinned at him and shook his head. He looked groggy. 'Something hit me.'

'You wounded, e hoa?'

'Not sure, Joe.' He touched his head and winced. 'Just a bang on the bonce, I think. Knocked me right out.'

Joe had a look. 'You got a big lump, that's all.'

They heard boots crunching among the trees not far away and German soldiers talking to one another, keeping their voices low. Joe pulled Boy to his feet. 'Come on. The bastards are looking for you.'

Bent forward, trying to make as little noise as possible, they pushed through undergrowth into a clearing, scaled a steep bank, passed through a citrus orchard, and found their way back to their base.

'You deaf, private?' O'Dwyer said to Joe; but he turned away, not waiting for an answer.

It was now they were told that Maleme had been lost, and 28 Battalion was to take part in a night counter-attack. It would be their job, along with 20 Battalion, to retake the airfield and the hill above it. The start was scheduled for one in the morning, so they should eat their evening meal and take some rest while they had the chance.

In battledress and boots, Joe lay under his blanket staring through olive branches at a thin moon and star-filled sky. Tu Shilling strummed a flat piece of wood, pretending it was a guitar, and he and Boy crooned popular songs in English and in Maori. Frogs croaked nearby, and in the distance, at intervals, a donkey brayed and a dog barked. There was the strong scent of some shrub or flower, mixed with the smell of smoke from cooking fires. When sleep came it was fitful, troubled by dreams and anticipations of the action to come.

Soon after midnight 28 Battalion was assembled and ready, spread over the area on the landward side of the road, waiting for 20 Battalion which was to move in unison with them along the strip between road and sea. While they waited they listened to gunfire offshore, increasing in intensity, with explosions and fires. They knew it must be the anticipated German invasion from the sea, intercepted, as they'd been told it would be, by the Royal Navy.

An hour passed, a second. The battle was ending out there, and nothing was coming ashore. That was good; it was very good—but what of their own battle? Where were the 20th? Even to men who had spent so much of the year learning that nothing in the army works as it should or happens when it's supposed to, this was worse than frustrating. Soon it would be light and the Luftwaffe would be back.

It was 3.30 before the men of 20 Battalion, held up by a failure of the trucks that had been meant to transport them, were in place. Now the two battalions, spread wide and thin across the landscape from the shore to the foothills, moved off together, with three battered old tanks trundling down the road that ran between. The moon was gone, but the stars were bright and their eyes were used to the dark.

The terrain Joe's group moved across was uneven. Sometimes it was easy going, through olive groves and orchards. Then a sharp ravine, running seaward, would cut across it, and they would have to scramble down into it and up the opposite side over stones and through trees and scrub. Lines of bamboo had to be got through, canals forded. Now and then hastily mounted machine-gun fire came at them from farmhouses and out-buildings. They responded with grenades, and chased unclad barefoot Germans, woken by the attack, scattering them into hiding or shooting and bayoneting them among the barns and in the fields. There were prisoners taken and sent back to the rear under guard, but not many. Once they found they were shooting at their own men, a detachment of Engineers camped in their path, who returned the fire, each side believing the other was German.

They were making progress, but it was obvious—had been from the start—that they would be beaten by the light. Already it was creeping into the sky behind them.

'Fucking stupid!' Years afterwards Boy Keratu would remember how angry his mate Joe Panapa had been as the sun came up. 'Why did we wait? We should have gone without them.'

A pink and grey dawn at their backs, its pale fingers reaching forward over their heads, they moved on, accompanied, they now saw, by some locals armed with old rifles and shotguns, men and boys, and even a few women, who had joined them silently during the night. There were also men from other battalions, whose ground they'd passed over, or near to, and who had joined the assault. The airfield was still ahead and to their right, Hill 107 ahead and slightly left. As the light increased, so did the fire directed at them, and their advance, no longer even-paced, was in short dashes from one sheltering tree or building or stone wall to the next.

Soon the fire coming down at them from Hill 107, and from Messerschmitts which with daylight were coming back into the action, seemed immense, the noise stunning. From a clearing on high ground Joe used the binoculars he'd taken from the dead German to get the larger picture; then handed them to O'Dwyer. They could pick out only one of the three tanks. Nose down in a ditch at the road's edge, a body lying nearby, it was holed and burning from what must have been a direct hit. The seaward side of the road was barren, which meant 20 Battalion had been able to move faster, but now had much less cover. Some of them, having skirted a village where fighting was still going on, had got very close to the outer perimeter of the airfield and could be seen scattered among sand dunes, still shooting, not in full retreat, but faltering under mortar and machine-gun fire. Some appeared to be edging south, crossing the road into the protection of the olives. Planes were beginning to come into the airfield from the mainland, unloading fresh troops who were deployed immediately in its defence.

'We're stumped,' O'Dwyer said. 'Can't take the airfield now. It's theirs.' He handed back the binoculars. 'This time round anyway.'

Joe said nothing. There was nothing to say. Would there be another time round? He must have doubted it, and must have known that O'Dwyer did too.

The idea of any further drive forward had to be given up, and the day settled into a grim test of nerves and courage in which the battalion, keeping under cover as far as possible against machine-gun fire from the hill and from the air, drove back each of the enemy's forward probes and held the ground it had gained.

As the afternoon went by the Germans appeared to be gaining in confidence. They came closer, pressed harder. Late in the day they could be seen among the trees on an opposite ridge setting up a wide banner, a swastika, on two poles.

O'Dwyer thought it might be to mark out their forward line so the Luftwaffe could see where friend and foe divided. But now they came pouring around either side of it into an attack supported by heavy fire from machine-guns and mortars, and then, as they got closer, using grenades which exploded with flashes of flame.

It was a fierce attack, meant to drive O'Dwyer's forward section from the ridge they'd been holding most of the day. For a few seconds there was a hint of dismay among the Maori, as if, shaken by this challenge and close to exhaustion, they might be ready to fall back; but then, unmistakably, the irresolute moment passed. Without any order, but as if some secret wiring bound them into a single force, and as if insulted by the idea that they might be driven off by fear, they got to their feet from their defensive firing positions and advanced on their attackers, steadily at first, then gathering pace, breaking into a run, yelling, firing from the hip. Men were going down but the charge went on, a sort of madness, or euphoria. The German line faltered. A strong defence would have been comprehensible, but this—meeting attack with attack—seemed like a departure from the script. They saw the bayonets, stopped, turned, scattered, ran, dropping weapons as they went.

O'Dwyer watched from behind. As his men came back, breathing hard, grinning, he reached out to touch those who passed close to him. 'Well done chaps,' was all he could find to say. 'Bloody well done.'

Evening came and there was relief from the incessant air attacks; an easing of the firing from the hill; and finally something approaching silence, a quiet in which they began to hear the usual night noises. Now Joe and his mates had time to think about food. All day they'd eaten nothing but chunks of bread and cheese brought with them in their pockets, and oranges picked from orchard trees as they'd moved through.

It was Tu who suggested the dead Germans might have food. Together the three went to search bodies lying among the olives. Others followed. Soon they were eating German field rations and smoking German cigarettes.

They were exhausted, and slept. The order was that they were to take turns, one man awake for every two sleeping. But the sentries slept, the waking detail slept, the officers slept. Men slept on their feet, leaning against banks or propped in the forks of olive trees to look as if they were awake and keeping watch. It was for most of them a deep, almost violent sleep, from which, however, some part of the brain opted out, so at the hint of an alarm they were ready again for action.

Before first light they were woken to the news passing down the line that there was to be a general withdrawal from the Maleme area. 28 Battalion was to be the rearguard, and O'Dwyer was to be in command of a composite group, ten men from each of the battalion's four companies, that would be the rearguard's rearguard.

No one in Joe's platoon was pleased. The counter-attack had

failed. They had recaptured neither Hill 107 nor the airfield. But they had made advances, got a lot closer, won good ground. Why shouldn't it be held, and forces sent to back them up and take the fight forward? Why give up now? They hadn't felt they were losing.

'The brass'll have their reasons,' O'Dwyer said.

When nobody spoke, he said, 'They'll be weighing up whether we can hold the island. If we can't, they'll want to get as many of us off as they can.'

'We could bloody hold it,' Boy Keratu said. His helmet was on the ground beside him; the lump on his forehead was huge and one eye was black and bloodshot.

O'Dwyer was silent a moment, looking down where this group of his men, sitting in a circle, had been sharing out field rations. 'It's a bad show,' he agreed. And then, feeling they should know: 'Our CO's not pleased. He'd like to stand and fight.'

The news had been hard for him to take. They were to withdraw—and that meant the whole New Zealand force—back to the line of the Platanias River, three miles from the airfield at Maleme. How could the land they were about to give up ever be regained? And if it couldn't, how could the island be held? Now the defeat of their sea invasion would hardly matter to the Germans. They could bring in all they needed, men and materials, by air.

So O'Dwyer's job as it appeared to him was no longer to let himself think of winning, but to keep his men together as a fighting unit and, as far as possible, to keep them alive. Their immediate job was to form a defence line through which the rest could escape. It meant standing firm, hitting your attacker hard, and then, as he reeled back from the blow, retreating fast to form another strong defence line which you held, striking the next blow before retreating again at speed.

This was how the textbooks explained it. A fighting withdrawal. It was sound in theory.

FOURTEEN

In the City of
the Dead

BUT MIKE'S DAYS WITH STELLA DIDN'T CONTINUE SO DESOLATE AS THE
first. Each morning he went with her while she walked her dog,
a fox terrier not unlike Marica's, through pleasant suburban
streets, and what they found themselves doing was putting
together memories of their childhood. It was their only common
ground, but a fruitful one which, alone, they could enjoy without
fear of boring others. They talked especially about their parents
who, like Ljuba Panapa, had left Henderson when the orchards
and vineyards began to be sold and replaced by suburban
housing. They had moved to an acre of land among small farms
north of the harbour, near Albany, only to be overtaken again
by the spread of the city. Both had died in their late sixties, the
father first, of a weak heart, then the mother, it seemed of a
broken one; and Mike remembers his flying visit to see her in
her last days—an experience blurred by haste, jet-lag, a sense of
being torn at short notice from work and family, and grief at the
knowledge that, however they might conceal it, he was seeing
her for the last time.

'You seemed more foreign to us then,' Stella said.

'More?'

'Than you do now. We all felt you'd changed.'

'I was becoming an Oxford man,' he said. 'It's hard work at first.'

'And what about now?' They had stopped under a tree, waiting for the terrier (called Spot-the-dog) which had found something so interesting at the base of a lamppost his nose seemed glued to it.

'Now? I suppose now I am one, and I can forget it.'

That evening Marica rang. Was he free on Sunday—for the whole day? Could he be down at the old central railway station at 9.45?

He was free, and he would be there. So where was she taking him?

'Out west,' she said. He was to ask no further questions.

What surprised him first that day was the station itself. The main building, which in his childhood had represented almost his only idea of architectural grandeur, was closed, and the surrounding land—rail approaches, sidings, tracks for out-of-use rolling-stock—all had been made over (or Marica thought it was so) to the local Maori tribe, the Ngati Whatua, who had claimed the land was rightfully theirs, and who were now selling or leasing it to developers. The platforms, and their connecting underpasses, were derelict, their once handsome tiles cracked and broken, covered in mould and graffiti.

'Rail's not used much any more,' Marica said as they made their way to Platform 4. 'There are still services on these tracks, but roads have pretty much taken over. Anyway, Mike, this is a nostalgia trip.'

A steam train built in the 1930s had been stoked up and was to take them out on the line west through Henderson and on, north, to Helensville. There would be wine served, and a stop for lunch at Swanson. At intervals they would get out to hear readings by local writers and talks by local historians.

So he got alternating glimpses of the familiar and the unfamiliar, with whiffs of real train smoke in nose and eyes that sent him hurtling back across the decades. There was the climb through lower Parnell to the tunnel that went under the Domain and brought them out close to Newmarket station. Here the engine did a backing-and-filling manoeuvre he remembered from the past, seeming to run a train's length on to the line south, then shunting and turning west through the points—after which it was slow- but plain-sailing, past the Mt Eden jail, through Mt Eden station (everything derelict, closed) to Morningside, Mt Albert, Avondale, New Lynn, Glen Eden, and on around the back of the Waikumete Cemetery to Henderson. Most of the old wooden stations and their signalboxes were still there, some falling into disrepair, others restored, some shifted from one location to another and given a new life as relics of the past.

At times Mike found himself looking out on white weather-board houses that looked back at him with astonished recognition; at others he seemed to be travelling through a wilderness of small factories and dingy apartment blocks especially designed to punish with in-your-face ugliness any rail-user who dared to make eye contact. He was jolted equally and indiscriminately by painful familiarity and distressing alienation. His feelings—nostalgia, confusion, delight, revulsion—were stretched and pulled, and this not unwelcome buffeting was, he supposed, what Marica had intended.

Beyond Henderson the last of the suburbs petered out into small farms, pine plantations and orchards. At Swanson they were served lunch in a restaurant, plied with local wine, and read to by local poets. After that, for an hour or more, he and Marica sank, side by side, into somnolence. The food, the wine, the readings had relaxed them. There was no need to talk.

But on the return journey, as the line took them once again past the back of the Waikumete Cemetery, Mike found himself remembering Frano's funeral. 'I didn't know then,' he said, 'and I've never known since, what to believe about his death—whether it was an accident, or he meant to kill himself.'

'Or whether,' Marica said, 'he didn't know what he meant to do. The way he rode the Norton sometimes—it was Russian roulette.'

Mike went a little closer to what they hadn't so far spoken about. 'But he had a reason.'

'To kill himself?'

'He'd seen us together.'

Looking away she said, 'Yes,' but with an inflexion that made it more a question than an affirmative.

'He'd told me to stay away from you.'

'I didn't know that.'

'But you knew he was in love with you.'

She didn't answer.

Now he told her what at the time he'd kept to himself—about the wild ride up from the Henderson Valley to the Scenic Drive on the night of Frano's death, the stop in the dark along the Piha road, the painful hand-grip, the anger, the insulting farewell, and Mike's long trek back on foot in pouring rain.

She was silent for a time, staring out at gum trees and clay banks; or perhaps at her own reflection now the daylight was fading and lights had come on in the carriage. 'He was disturbed,' she said. 'But it might have been an accident.'

'You didn't think so at the time.'

'Didn't I?'

'Or if you did, why did you let it come between us?'

She shook her head and turned away again towards the window. Was that a denial? Or was she saying this was something she didn't want to talk about?

He changed tack—reminded her about Frano's head injury at school; told her of his strange behaviour when they used to ride their bicycles around the suburbs. 'He'd ride at a wall. Then he'd say he'd had a blackout.'

'I'd forgotten about the concussion,' she said. 'And I'm sure I never heard he was having blackouts.'

'I used to think he was acting—otherwise why did he always turn away at the last second? Why didn't he ever crash?'

She stared at the ceiling, looking, he thought, like the medical person she was, considering an unusual or difficult case. 'People with head injuries do sometimes behave unpredictably.' After a while she said, 'Why didn't you tell me?'

'There wasn't any reason to. We never talked much about Frano. And after his death, when I suppose I had reason to tell you, you wouldn't talk to me.'

'Wouldn't I?' She patted his hand. 'I was upset, Mike. So were you, of course. But I wasn't the right age to behave wisely or consistently. Most of the time I told myself I'd killed him. Or we'd killed him—you and I. It was girlish melodrama, I suppose. But it still distresses me when I remember. And we'll never know the truth of it because Frano's not here to tell us.'

'What we do know is that it blew our ship out of the water.'

'Yours and mine? Oh no.' She shook her head emphatically. 'We don't know that.'

Mike thought they did. That if they knew anything they knew that. But it was obvious she didn't want to accept it, or even talk about it. And perhaps, he reflected, there was a sense in which she was right. With or without Frano's death, she would have gone south to what was then the only medical school in the country; he would have got his scholarship to take him overseas. They had both been very young. Who could say what would have become of them if Frano had remained alive?

So the subject was left there—except that this talk, bringing them closer, allowed him to ask the question he'd failed to ask before: whether she would come with him to visit the grave and tidy it for Ljuba.

She said that of course she would, gladly, and they agreed on a time.

Two days later she called for him and they drove to Henderson, taking the new (or new to him) north-western motorway that ran out from Point Chevalier to North Te Atatu across some of the inner harbour's shallow tidal bays. There were horizontal striations of colour—olive-green mangroves, white sand, yellow mud, blue water—and such skimming, water-level views, long and clear down the miles of the harbour, it was as if the eye was drawn over it, fast, with the graph of the city skyline showing up on one side, and on the other the summit of Rangitoto, an inquisitive neighbour, looking over the fence the low-lying land made between Mt Victoria and North Head.

Seen from sea level, or equally from above, Auckland had a way of simplifying itself into patterns of land and water; and Mike was reminded of those paintings in Marica's house that had surprised him with their fresh abstractions of form and colour. That it was a beautiful location seemed to him true beyond question, and it was only a pity it had been inhabited, not by a race of gods, but by fallible mortals, first the Maori, who had called it the Place of a Thousand Lovers but made of it an inter-tribal killing field, then the Pakeha, who seemed hell-bent on turning it into a thoroughfare.

Everywhere now they were invaded, Mike especially, because

he'd been away so long, but Marica too, by the recollections that are hidden, like traps waiting to be sprung, in the places of childhood and youth. They turned off the motorway at Te Atatu Road and stopped at Bridge Avenue where he'd so often 'doubled' her on his bike for a swim. The water flowed there still, under the motorway—in with the tide, out with the flow of the Whau River—and there was a marina, and many yachts moored to poles.

They went on up Te Atatu Road, identifying old houses, trying to remember what had been there before the new ones had been built. Everywhere orchards, vineyards and farmland had been subdivided and sold, to be replaced by suburban houses and gardens. They parked where once there had been the gate with the sign LICENSED TO SELL TWO GALS, and walked down the hill to stand silent, side by side, looking into the grounds of the school he and Frano had gone to. The buildings Mike had known, one in concrete, the other in white weatherboard, both with high-pitched ceilings and sash windows, were gone, replaced by undistinguished prefabs. But the setting, blue hills in the background, stream running past the lower grounds and under the road, was unchanged, and he was overwhelmed by its familiarity, as if he had come around a corner and run headlong into his long-dead mother.

Back in the car they drove to Waikumete, through the main gates, Marica following the path she knew would take them to the place where her family had their graves. The cemetery stretched away over rolling land, a city of the dead whose urban sprawl, Mike reflected, should make its inhabitants feel at home. They passed the crematorium building where a caretaker, enacting a haiku, was sweeping up rose petals from the front courtyard with a brush and pan. Everywhere the graves were adorned with fresh flowers and coloured plastic windmills, making him think of *le jour des morts*, the day of the year in France when everyone remembers and visits the graves of their dead. But in fact, Marica explained, Waikumete was like this every day, since the flowers left at the crematorium after each service were gathered up before the next and distributed around the graves.

They went over a hill, down into a hollow, and then climbed

the other side where tombs, strange to Mike, were built on either side of the narrow roadway—square or oblong box structures in marble or stone or plastered concrete, each like an infant-school drawing of a house, with a heavy iron door right in the middle, and two 'windows' of black marble, one on either side of the door. In large letters over the door was the name of the family to whom the tomb belonged—Marsich, Boracich, Frankovic, Dragicovic, Nobilo, Radich, Stipe, Marinkovic—some of them decorated with patterns of vines or of interlocking oak leaves. The names of the internees were inscribed on the black windows over the words '*Pocivali* (or *Pocivala*, or *Pocivao*) *u miru*'—the Croatian form, Marica explained, of Rest in Peace. Among them was a tomb with the name Selenich over its door.

'I don't remember these,' Mike said as they got out of the car and walked along what seemed like a street of pretend houses, reinforcing his earlier thought about a city of the dead.

'They weren't here then,' she said. 'That's prosperity for you, Mike. It brings on the pharaoh syndrome.'

'Will you be put in there?'

'Oh no. I'll be cremated. I don't think the dead should take up space. Of course if you could see through black marble, it's what a real estate agent would call a prime position. We're like the Maori. We like a view of the sea for our dead.'

He turned and looked where she was looking, and there, sure enough, was a long view to the harbour and all the way down it to the city skyline ten kilometres away, the business towers and the hump of the harbour bridge standing out clear in morning light. And then, as his eye ranged about, near and far, he looked down the slope they were on, beyond the house-like tombs, over an area of lawn cemetery, all plaques inset flat into mown grass, to a neglected hollow where weeds and rank grass had grown up around older tombstones. He turned to her. 'Frano's down there.'

She smiled. 'So you remember.'

'And over there was where . . .' He didn't go on, but pointed away to the left. Most of the pines were gone, but there was a grove still standing.

She half nodded and turned away. It was just an acknowledgement, no more than that, but it was enough.

Back at the car she opened the boot and took out a trowel, a rake, a small shovel, a scrubbing brush, some plants in plastic pots. 'Help me, Mikie,' she said, and together they carried all this down into the shadowy hollow and walked about there, swishing through weeds and grasses, scraping at headstones, calling out dates to one another, until they found a line of graves dated 1952, and among them, Frano's.

'Frano Heta Panapa,' Mike read. '1933–1952. Dearly Loved and Always Remembered Son of Ljuba Maria Panapa (née Selenich) and the late Joseph Parata Panapa. *Pocivao u miru.*' There was a photograph of Frano, faded now, water-stained, inset under perspex in the concrete headstone. A passage from the Psalms, 'O God, thou art my God, early will I seek thee', was repeated in Maori, 'E te Atua, noku koa Atua; ka moata taku rapu i a koe', and in Croatian, '*O Boze, ti si Bog moj; gorljivo tebe trazim.*'

To Marica, who was standing at his shoulder, Mike intoned, 'O Dog thou art my Dog, early will I seek thee.'

She smiled and put a hand on his arm. 'You two were such silly boys.'

The small plot in front of the headstone had been neglected, and for half an hour or more they worked on it, weeding, loosening the soil inside the concrete perimeter, putting in the shrubs and ferns and flowers Marica had brought, scrubbing dirt and moss from the stone, clearing the long grass from round about that might close in and engulf it again. They were pleased with their work, it looked very good, and they took photographs, he of her, she of him, standing beside the grave.

'Ljuba will be pleased,' Mike said.

'Imagine if Frano could see us. What would he say?'

'He'd say fuck off, wouldn't he?'

'Yes, I suppose he would. But he wouldn't mean it. He'd be pleased.'

'You used to be scared of him.'

'Frano? No, never.'

'That's how it seemed.'

'I was scared of hurting him. Hurting his feelings. You didn't understand that, Mike, and I never felt as if I could explain it to you.'

As she said that she looked puzzled, and young. Her youthful face showed through for a moment, like a face at a window, and then the curtain of the present came down. Mike stared at her.

'What is it?' she asked.

'What's what?'

'You were looking at me as if . . .'

'I was remembering.'

'Oh.' She waved him away. 'Don't do that.'

'Knocked down by a speeding memory in the city of the dead.'

He turned and looked towards what remained of the pines. He would have liked to go there, hunting for the place where they'd first made love, but he didn't suggest it.

That evening they went together to a restaurant in Parnell and then drove along the waterfront to sit in the car looking out across the water where Rangitoto appeared and faded as the moon moved fast and purposeful as a sheep dog through flocks of cloud. They held hands.

'Life's a bitch,' he said, after a silence that had lasted so long he wasn't sure what he meant.

'Only if you think it is,' she said; and he silently rebuked himself for a lapse in his Zen discipline.

'Are you still a Catholic?' he asked.

'Are you still a New Zealander?'

'It's like that, is it?'

'It's not a question of believing.'

'Of loyalty?'

'Not even that.'

'Identity?'

She laughed at his persistence. 'I suppose . . . Yes. Identity will do.'

He said now, and surprised himself—it seemed out of character—that he'd been wondering whether they should spend the night together. She didn't appear surprised. It was as if for practical Marica the possibility, although unspoken, had been there all the time.

'No,' she said. 'We shouldn't.'

'I don't mean to . . . Not to . . .'

'I understand.'

'Although it would be nice if it happened. Of course. But I was thinking more of the comfort.' When she didn't speak he added, 'Of physical contact. The companionship.'

'Comfort, contact, companionship,' she repeated. 'All the Cs.'

He could think of a few more, but didn't say so.

'You miss them, living alone,' she said. 'That's why I have a dog and two cats.'

'I didn't see the cats.'

'They were there, out on the deck under the bougainvillea. Debbie and Lion.'

'Good names.' They were good, too, he recognised it at once, but for the moment couldn't think why. And in any case he didn't want to lose the thread. 'But they don't go to bed with you, do they?'

'Oh yes, they do. Especially in the cold weather.'

'Well, I think it would be nice to be Debbie or Lion for a night.'

'Yes, Mike. But not us. Not now.'

He felt she was right, but didn't know why. 'Because?' he asked. 'Is there a because?'

'I might say fear of attachments that don't last—but being an egotistical male, you might think that meant I'd want it to last.'

'That's complicated.'

'Not complicated at all. Very simple. But in any case it's not the sole reason.'

'Give me the other.'

'Oh . . . I suppose really it's because I don't want the present to replace the past. And in any case . . .' She hesitated. 'It couldn't.'

When he didn't respond she said, 'We're not what we were, Mike. I know I'm not. And you look much too eminent for bed.'

'Something more for the piano top, you think?'

'Or a heavy frame.'

'Well, I'll try not to be insulted.'

'Don't be.'

'And it's a faded eminence—if that's what it ever was.

158

I haven't had a fresh thought in years.'

'That I don't believe.'

'No. And it's not entirely true. It's just that the thoughts don't any longer quite fit the profession.'

'That sounds like freedom.'

He smiled at that, leaned back in his seat, and put an arm around her. 'Come closer.'

She rested her head on his shoulder and they remained like that a long time. He thought, even, that he might have caught the bird of sleep on the wing, so quickly and briefly she hadn't noticed and he wasn't sure.

'Maybe you should have got yourself a younger woman,' she said.

'Like Gary.'

'Gavin,' she corrected. 'But since you haven't . . .'

'Since I haven't—what follows?'

'It's not for me to say, of course. But shouldn't you go back home to your wife—to Gillian? Make your peace.'

He ignored that, stared out at the hulking shape of the island, silent.

Suddenly he said, half-shouted it, with an American accent. 'Duterra! Du-terr-a! You remember that? Long and slow. *Du-terr-a!*'

'I don't think so. Should I? What is it? A war cry?'

'It's in a cowboy movie. *The Law and Jake Wade.* Richard Widmark. Didn't we see that together?'

She shook her head. 'If we did, I don't remember it. The one I remember is *Les Enfants du Paradis.*'

'Oh well yes, of course.' And he called soulfully, 'Garance! *Garance!*'

'It was so romantic. I thought life should be like that.'

'I thought life was like that,' he said. 'That's what I didn't like about it.'

'About the movie?'

'No, stupid. About life.'

FIFTEEN

Dolphins and the Sacred Head

'I'M SORRY TO KEEP YOU STANDING HERE, YOUNG NEWALL.'

'Not at all, Bertie. Just take your time.'

They have come through North Parade from Gee's and are now in the churchyard beside Church Walk where Winterstoke, who has neglected to take a 'precautionary slash' (as he calls it) before leaving the restaurant, is now taken short on the walk home. But taken short in his case doesn't mean wetting himself. It means, apparently, a terrible urgency combined with an inability to relieve it.

'Most of the serious business of the Lords is conducted like this,' he says. 'Peer pressure, I call it. Affairs of prostate.' There are some grunts and snorts which might signal effort or pain, or perhaps both. 'We're like horses,' he goes on. 'Spend half our days standing about in the stalls waiting for the starter to open the gates.'

It's true, Mike thinks, there is something horse-like about Bertie, standing patiently, his penis hanging limp, seen and not seen in the changing tree-filtered light that comes from Woodstock Road.

'But you have women peers now,' Mike reminds him.

'Yes, yes, but I suspect they have prostates too.'

And now a thin hay-coloured stream begins. 'Aaah, here we go,' he whinnies. The stream grows stronger, steam rising from it, and a faint aroma that has indeed something of the stables about it. Bertie's head goes back and he stares up, sighing his gratitude at the heavens. A breeze rustles the leaves. It is a moment of satisfaction, of deep peace.

'The relief of Mafeking,' he murmurs, shaking off and stowing the instrument away. 'As a child I used to wonder what it meant. I now believe Mafeking was an elderly peer.' His knuckles are swollen and clumsy as they tug at the zip. 'I've been meaning to ask. What was so good about Debbie and Lion as names for cats.'

Mike explains that the two principal brewers in New Zealand are DB and Lion. 'And the little dog's name was Sel—short for Selenich.'

'I see, I see. Brewery cats and a vintner's dog.' He takes the walking stick Mike has been holding for him and leans back against the churchyard wall, turning his face once again towards the night sky and, eyes closed, breathing deep through his nostrils. 'And now, Michael, I think you can tell me at last, can you, about Joe Panapa's death?'

Mike takes up a comfortable position alongside him. 'All those years ago,' he says, 'O'Dwyer said he'd killed Joe Panapa, and one day he'd tell me the whole story. But time passed and it didn't happen. A few times we got close to it. Once he seemed right on the brink—it was at the Gardener's Arms, and he'd been talking about the Battle of Crete—but then Camille came in and joined us and he clammed up. A couple of other times I thought he was going to talk about it and at the last moment he seemed to funk it—made a joke and changed the subject. Or suddenly discovered it was late and he had to go. And he'd send out warning signals . . . At least that's how I read them. That I shouldn't come too close, shouldn't push him, shouldn't ask direct questions. Maybe he regretted ever having said anything to me about Joe's death. Or maybe I was too tentative. Not brutal enough. Didn't press home the enquiry. Whatever the reason, decades passed and still I had no more information than he'd given me when I first knew him.'

Winterstoke opens his eyes but doesn't take them away from

the faintly sprinkled haze that is a clear night sky in Oxford. 'But in the end, you got the truth.'

'I got one account of what happened—and then I got another.'

'Different?'

'Yes, different. And the first didn't come from Don. It came from Helen.'

'Oh yes. You mentioned she wrote something. A story.'

'It was when she was in London, at UCL. It was published in a student magazine. One of my girls brought it home and I came on it by accident. It was fiction. I was only flicking through in the way one does with student publications, but it took my eye because it was by O'Dwyer's daughter; and then because it was about an officer in the war fighting the Germans in a place that wasn't named but I could see might have been Crete. There was a terrible battle, bullets, grenades, shells flying in all directions, aircraft overhead bombing and strafing, men being wounded, men being killed, and in the midst of all this one of the Allied soldiers steps on a land mine. He's hideously wounded. Can't possibly survive. They're retreating from the Germans. The wounded soldier's in agony. They can't take him with them and he doesn't want to be left. He begs the officer to shoot him.'

'Ah,' says Winterstoke. And then, solemnly, 'I see.'

'The officer asks whether this is really what he wants, and the soldier says yes it is. And then he says, Kia tere, e pa.'

'Maori.'

'Yes. That's what seemed to make it clear . . .'

'Where the story came from. And the words in Maori—they mean?'

'I'm not sure she got it right, but roughly they mean, Please hurry, sir.'

'I see. I see.' The noble equine nods. His face is creased, as if he's wincing from an anticipated blow. 'And the officer, he . . . Does he? Shoots him?'

'The enemy's closing in through the trees. There's no time to argue or even to think about it. He puts his revolver to the soldier's head, turns his face to the heavens, says "Thy will be done", and pulls the trigger.'

Bertie nods, a long, silently repeated inclination of the

head—imagining it, taking it in, the horrible reality of it. 'What a burden to have carried,' he murmurs.

'When I read that story I thought now at last I could get O'Dwyer to talk. I don't think it was just idle curiosity on my part. This was someone I'd known, the father of my dead friend . . .'

'Quite so. The young soldier who'd given you the clasp knife.'

'So next time I found myself alone with Don I told him I'd read Helen's story. "What story?" he says. Very gruff. Now that put me in a cleft stick. Either he knew what I meant and he was signalling very clearly that he didn't want to talk about it. Or— and this was equally possible—she'd written it without telling him.'

'Difficult,' Bertie concedes. 'Damned awkward.'

'So I backed off. Went vague. Said I'd seen something of hers in a student mag. Couldn't remember it's name. He didn't press me.'

'And you were no for'arder.'

'No. Except that it seemed what was in the story must have been pretty close to what had happened. Don had said, "I killed your friend's father." I'd never thought there was any way this could be simply and literally the truth. But here was a way. I supposed he must have told Helen. Or he'd told Camille who'd told Helen. And the girl had put it into a short story, probably without telling him.'

'And it would explain the mac thing. The curse.'

'I thought so, yes. But I couldn't be absolutely sure and I didn't feel I could ask. So that was one further thing I had in mind for myself when I made my visit to New Zealand. If I couldn't confirm the truth direct from O'Dwyer in Oxford, there might be a way of doing it in New Zealand.'

'How would you do that?'

'Visit Joe's Maori family. Talk to them, ask them what they knew—why their Auntie Pixie had put the hex on O'Dwyer.'

The two are moving again now, back in the direction of Southmoor Road, Mike intending to see his friend safely to his door. They've crossed Woodstock Road and are turning into Plantation Road. Seven minutes late, the church clock, that has just overseen the easing of the Winterstoke bladder, is sounding the hour, and Mike is returning to the story of his visit to New Zealand.

❧

It had always been his intention that one day he would go back and see the place in Northland where he'd spent those childhood holidays with Frano. Now he had this further reason for going. And since he and Marica were friends again, and the terms of their relationship, including its limits, seemed agreed upon, or at least accepted, his idea was that she should come with him.

It was when she delivered him back to Stella's house, after they'd sat looking over the harbour, that he suggested it. Marica remembered the story of the Maori curse—the two boys on the verandah seeing Frano's Auntie Pixie naked, chanting in the rain. She remembered envying Frano his holidays in the north, and the fact that he and her Aunt Ljuba took Mike, the boy next door, with them, and not Frano's girl cousin.

'It's a kind thought, Mike,' she said. 'It would be nice, but no . . . I think it has to be thanks, but no thanks. Not this time.'

Her reasons didn't seem to him very good. She still worked, but no longer full time. Debbie and Lion had to be fed, and Sel fed and walked. She'd told him a son lived nearby. Couldn't he do it? But Mike didn't suggest this; didn't persist.

Next morning, however, remembering a conversation about their past when she'd described him as 'indecisive', he phoned.

'Marica,' he said, 'I've made a decision. You're coming with me.'

There was a silence.

'You're not in prison, are you?'

She laughed. 'This is unusual, Mike.' When he didn't reply she said, 'All right. Yes. Why not?'

Stella and Bruce were happy for him to take their second car, and he and Marica set off early—over the harbour bridge and north towards Whangarei, where they stopped for lunch on the verandah of a restaurant that looked out on yacht moorings and an inlet of the sea. Then it was on up the main north road, leaving it beyond Hikurangi and entering a region that was still remote and undeveloped.

As they drove along he asked, 'Doesn't this remind you of something?'

'This landscape?'

'No. Driving together. You don't remember the truck in the orchard?'

'Ah, that. What's strange, Mike, is that I have no recollection of the truck. None at all. But I remember you asking me the same question.'

'Not . . .' He had a fear of forgetfulness, of repeating himself. 'You don't mean on this visit.'

'No, no. Long ago. In fact it was when we were . . .'

She stopped, and he prompted her. 'When we were?'

'Lying in the pines.'

'At Waikumete.'

'Yes.'

'When it rained on us.'

'Yes.'

It was mid-afternoon before they reached their goal. The marae that Mike remembered from childhood was still there, and the beach, the headlands, the pohutukawas. The meeting house had new tukutuku panels, new windowpanes, new fences, new carvings on poles at the front; but the old carving, so terrifying to the child, was gone. A Maori man in a track suit and wearing industrial ear-muffs was driving a motor mower, much like Bruce's, up and down the lawn at the front. There was no one else. The place seemed deserted—no old kuia and kaumatua sitting on the verandah talking and laughing.

Up and down the long straight road where previously there had been shelter-belts and pasture and unused land infested with dock, thistles, gorse, blackberry, manuka, there were now holiday houses and ten-acre plantations. An estate agent's sign advertised 'lifestyle blocks'. The Panapa grandparents' house was gone, and Mike could no longer be quite sure where it had been. Along the beachfront, which had been almost empty in his childhood, there were now baches and what were probably the homes of people retired from farms and from the city. The old wooden store had been replaced by one built in concrete blocks.

They drove to the end of the beach and, where the road had previously come to an end, it now rose steeply over the headland

and down the other side. But there, at the next beach, it stopped. Wheel tracks ran along the sand where once there had been the prints of horses' hooves. It was clear that the locals still used the beach as their road; but Mike, worrying about Stella's car, and uncertain about the tides, decided they should park and walk.

When they came to the next headland, the rocks below it, close to the cliffs, had been covered with a very rough coating of cement, so at low tide you could drive over the reef and around to the next beach. Once again there were wheel tracks along the sand; but at the end of that beach these ceased. There was no way forward except on foot.

Mike and Marica walked on over rocks covered with healthy oysters and littered with long fragile shells and shell fragments of iridescent green. At the next beach there was only one building and Mike recognised it at once. It was the cottage that had been Joe and Ljuba's first and only home together. The paint had peeled away, the iron of roof and water tank was rusted into holes, the outhouse had been blown sideways into the shape of a parallelogram, the shelter over the long-drop had collapsed— but there the cottage sat, unused and neglected beside the stream that still ran fast and clear and fresh, emerging from rushes to meander and fan out across the sand.

They stood side by side looking at it. 'Why did Joe want to go to the war?' Marica asked. 'You know he was a volunteer.'

'I think all of that first lot were.'

'I suppose there's no why. It's what men did in those days.'

Mike turned and looked down the long wide harbour to the part of it that opened to the ocean. 'It was the world out there. There weren't many ways of getting to see it.' After a moment he added, 'And it was a good cause.'

Marica shook her head. 'I don't think Aunt Ljuba thought of it like that. She accepted his going, but I doubt it made much sense to her. The Seleniches had come here to get away from all that stuff in Europe.'

Back at the store they asked the woman behind the counter where they would find the Panapa family. Not here, she told them. Not any longer. The Panapas had sold up and moved across the harbour. They were all on that side now—those that hadn't moved down to Whangarei and Auckland. And she named the place, Ngawari Bay, where they could be found.

It would be a long drive to reach the opposite shore, and it was unlikely there would be anywhere to spend the night. They decided they would drive on north, spend the night at Russell, and return in the morning to the other side of the harbour.

So that evening, after a meal and a bottle of wine at a restaurant on the Russell seafront, they found themselves a motel unit that offered twin beds. Pleased and also faintly apprehensive, Mike wondered whether this was bringing them closer to an intimacy he supposed he must want. Was this to be another situation calling for the decisiveness she'd told him he once lacked?

Lying in the dark, wondering what the next move of a 'decisive' Mike Newall might be, attempting to think how he might engage Marica in what he entertained himself by thinking of as the intercourse that leads to intercourse, he recognised from her breathing that she was already asleep. And in a short time so was he. He woke once in the early hours of morning from a dream in which the Bardolph's butler was explaining to him that the candle chandelier in the panelled room where dessert was taken was to be 'electrified'. He had replied that he found this 'unacceptable', and appealed to the Master, but Seb Straw had turned away, fiddling with his umbrella. It took Mike a few moments to remember where he was, and that it was the friend of his youth, Marica Selenich, breathing audibly in the next bed.

Ngawari Bay, when they reached it late that morning, was a remote and beautiful curve of beach overlooked by a single hill whose deeply cut terracing showed that it had once been a fortified pa. Along the shore ran a narrow road of loose metal and a single line of houses. Maori children wearing crash-helmets rode mountain bikes up and down. Three once-were-warriors wearing gang patches sat or sprawled on the tray of a broken-down truck staring at a gleaming new motorcycle as if, having acquired it, they were stunned by its beauty and didn't know what to do with it. There was a camping ground with no tents or caravans, a changing shed with no swimmers, and a store with no customers. In the store a Maori in a baseball cap, who told them he was also the local policeman, sold them ice creams and answered Mike's questions.

Yes, he assured them, the Panapas lived here in the bay; and yes he'd heard that one of the family had been killed in the Battle of Crete. 'Here,' he said, coming around the counter and going with them to the door. 'You see the white house with the Norfolk pine? The kuia in the wheelchair? That's Wikitoria. She's a relation. She'll know all about it.'

Wikitoria Paul, as she explained when they talked to her on her verandah, had been married 'to a half-brother of the man who married Joe Panapa's youngest sister'. They were, in other words, part of the same whanau. She could show them photographs—and she got them to wheel her indoors.

Mike stared at the one of Joe (ebony hair cut short and gleaming with Brylcreem, tie neatly knotted, cap tucked into the shoulder flap of his battledress) hoping that recognition would flood over him, but feeling only uncertainty. Marica, on the other hand, recognised it at once. It was the same photograph her Aunt Ljuba had kept in a frame on her dressing table.

Wikitoria Paul was old, perhaps in her eighties, but well preserved, with a flat round 'Japanese' face, like a brown dinner plate, friendly eyes painted on to it, wide nostrils and warm welcoming lips. She was shy but not unwelcoming, and her answers came readily enough until Mike asked, in a voice that might have sounded too much like a chief inspector's, what she knew about the circumstances of Joe Panapa's death. At that moment the dinner plate lost its smile and went still, neutral, silent. When he repeated the question it said, in a flat dinner plate voice, 'You better ask Ricky.'

Mike pressed on. What about Auntie Pixie?

There was just a flicker of a glance at him after which the eyes wouldn't meet his. Auntie Pixie was dead, she said, in a tone that might have suggested he was to blame.

'I met her once,' Mike said, trying to get the conversational engine back on its rails. 'That was a long time ago, of course.'

'Ricky,' Wikitoria repeated. 'You try him, eh? He might know.'

Ricky—or perhaps it was Riki—was, she explained, a kaumatua and a tohunga. He lived over the hill. You followed the road up there, turned left towards the sea, missed the next five or six farm gates, and looked for the stockyard. Ten minutes past the stockyard (ten minutes on foot, on horseback, by car, Mike wondered, but didn't ask) Ricky lived in the yellow house in the gorse. They would recognise it because there was a whetu marama painted on the door.

Having given out these directions the brown dinner plate fell silent, closed its eyes, and appeared to sleep.

They weren't good or helpful directions, and might have been intended to confuse. Mike and Marica had a long hunt for the house, which was indeed in the gorse, and yellow in that it reflected the gorse flowers in the sun, but unpainted, or had long since lost its paint. Its steel pipe and wire mesh gate stuck to the ground and had to be lifted and wrestled open. The orange clay track to the door was steep, slippery with recent rain, and encroached upon by gorse; and when they knocked no one answered. But a crescent moon and star—the whetu marama of the Ratana movement—signalled that this was the house the old woman had directed them to.

All windows, and the two doors, front and back, opposite each other across a single room, were locked. Through dusty panes they saw a sofa, two armchairs, an ancient radio with a fretwork Peter Pan over torn fabric, a varnished sideboard with mirrors, a steel and Formica table—furniture that had long since died in its sleep. It was hard to believe anyone had lived there for a very long time.

Back at the bay they saw the policeman in the baseball cap coming away from the store. 'How did you get on?' he asked.

'Not well,' Mike said.

The policeman laughed. He wasn't surprised, but he didn't offer any suggestions. 'Have a nice day,' he said, and walked down the road past the men in gang patches who in the meantime had discovered the trick of making a gleaming new motorcycle disappear from sight.

'It's the makutu,' Mike said. 'They're afraid to talk about it because they believe in it. It scares the hell out of them.' He was ready to give up. 'Let's swim,' he said.

They changed in the shed and lay on sand in the sun until the heat drove them towards the water. As they approached it Mike saw curved grey-black fins moving in circles, a dark gleaming body rising and rolling, another leaping clear and splashing down, a sharp double tail smacking the water.

'Dolphins,' he said, breaking into a run.

Marica hung back in the shallows. 'Are you sure?'

He was. He swam towards them and for ten minutes the dolphins circled him, swam under him, rolled alongside him, swam straight at him like torpedoes, veering away only at the last moment. He dived and joined them under water, where he thought he heard them whistling and calling to one another. They came very close, but were past him and out of reach so quickly he never managed more than a touch.

Then, as if one of those whistles was a signal from their wing commander, they curved away from Mike in a single graceful aerobatic movement and were gone.

Later, when Mike and Marica were coming from the dressing sheds a young Maori couple came towards them. They introduced themselves. The woman's name before she married had been Panapa. Their kuia, Wikitoria, had sent them. From her verandah she'd watched Mike swimming with the dolphins, and she'd told them it meant he was tika. It had been a signal, letting her know.

'She couldn't be sure,' the man said, as if he too thought the attentions of dolphins proved a point.

Perhaps seeing something in Mike's eyes that suggested scepticism, even amusement, the woman said, 'That's how the old people decide things. It's their way.'

'Of course,' Mike said. 'And the dolphins were right.'

The message these two brought was that if Mike and Marica liked to come back to the old lady's house, they could have a cup of tea with her and she would answer their questions.

What they learned from Wikitoria Paul that day was, or seemed to be, a confirmation of Helen O'Dwyer's story. Of the three local boys who had gone away with the first Maori Battalion, Joe Panapa and Tu Shilling had been killed; only Boy Keratu had come back. Asked about the deaths, Boy had said that during the retreat from the failed counter-attack on Maleme, Tu had been killed by a shell from a Bofors gun the Germans had captured at the airfield, and that Joe had stepped on a mine laid by engineers of the 7th Field Regiment—so both had been killed by weapons of their own side.

That, so to speak, was the official line, and it confirmed what the families already knew. But later, drinking in a pub, Boy told some of his friends that Joe had been shot by their officer, Captain Don O'Dwyer. This story soon got back to the marae.

Questioned when sober, Boy first refused to say any more. He said O'Dwyer was a great officer, and that he owed him his life. He regretted having talked too much. But later, under pressure from Joe's family, he admitted that something bad had happened. Joe had been seriously wounded, his feet were destroyed, he was in pain, probably dying, and had asked the officer to shoot him. And so it had been done.

'So why the makutu?' This was Mike's question. 'Surely under the circumstances, in the heat of battle . . .'

Yes, the old woman agreed. All that was acknowledged. And that was what the family had divided over, and even come to blows about, on the terrible night when Auntie Pixie, taking the law into her own hands, had put her curse on the Captain. Those who agreed with Pixie could accept that the officer had had to make a snap decision, and that he'd thought he was acting humanely. It was not for the shooting itself, though that was serious, that the makutu had been put on him, but because Captain O'Dwyer had shot Joe in the head.

Mike stared into Wikitoria Paul's grave eyes. 'Because he shot Joe in the head?'

'That was the mistake,' she said. 'It was wrong. The head is tapu. It is sacred. The Captain should not have shot him in the head.'

SIXTEEN

Men Die and Women Weep

'NO GOING BACK.' THAT'S WHAT WINTERSTOKE SAID ON THE DAY OF O'Dwyer's funeral when they were having their lunch at the Trout; and he says it again now as Mike takes his elbow and helps him up the wet concrete steps to his door in Southmoor Road.

But Mike knows that; knew it, and relearned it on his visit to New Zealand two years ago. 'Of course, Bertie, you're right,' he says, as his friend drags out his huge ring of keys and, in the light cast from the street, stares at them, unable for an Alzheimer (or perhaps merely alcoholic) moment to remember what they're for. 'It's one of those things one knows but has to prove to oneself all over again.'

There was no going back. But sometimes there was such a thing as going forward; and although Mike doesn't try now to explain it to Winterstoke (who is showing signs of remembering the relation of key to keyhole) that's what he was left feeling he'd achieved with Marica. They went forward. By the time he was ready to return to Oxford he knew that he liked her, admired her, was glad to have her as a friend—and believed all this was reciprocated. They got on well. But they also stood apart, independent and self-sufficient. And although each would be sorry to say goodbye, neither was going to be greatly upset by it. Was this, then, the Third Age (there were now organisations calling themselves Universities of the Third Age), when the iron lock which the necessities of sex and procreation put on couples was at last left behind? If it was, there was something to be said for it.

He came back to Oxford knowing also that for better and worse this was where he would live out his life. He felt refreshed by the change, clearer in his mind about himself, and ready to get on with things. But there was something that remained to be done. At some convenient time, when the fighting in Croatia was over and he could get away from Bardolph's, he would go back there—to see Ira again, to visit Ljuba and see the Dalmatian coast, taking Marica's greetings and the photographs of Frano's grave.

With that in mind, his eye went always, after his return, to news from the Balkans. At first the fighting in Croatia that had continued during his time away grew worse. Then the United Nations intervened, and though the killing went on in Bosnia, and sometimes along the borders, in most of Croatia things seemed to settle down. Mike was able to get through by phone to Ira in Zagreb, and even to Ljuba, who was no longer on her island, but in the village close to the town of Sibenek where her two half-sisters also lived.

Twice during the eighteen months after his return from New Zealand, Mike was free of college duties and ready to make his visit. Both times it was Ira who put him off. Serbs, she said, had created a state within the new state, and still held large parts of what Croatia considered to be its own. Roads from Zagreb to the Dalmatian coast were blocked. There were problems with oil. For these reasons alone—and there were others—Ira was sure the fighting wasn't over.

'What about the UN?' he asked.

'What about it?' she replied.

'Isn't it keeping the peace?'

'Wait and see,' she said.

Ira was a journalist and must have known more than she was prepared to say. When the fighting began again it came without warning, and was swift and brutal. In lightning pushes, Croatia's new army reclaimed its territory, first to the east, and then between Zagreb and the Dalmatian coast. In less than six months its borders had been re-established and a peace accord was signed. The following summer vacation Mike flew once again to Zagreb.

He spent two days talking in hand-signals to Ira's aunt, Grozdana, and walking about the city while Ira worked to finish assignments. On the third day she was free and they set off in her noisy, dependable Skoda on the road to the coast.

They hadn't gone fifty kilometres when they came to their first evidence of the fighting, and after that the sights came thick and fast—isolated farmhouses, whole villages, parts of towns, bullet-riddled, burned out, shelled, destroyed. In some villages of twenty or thirty houses along either side of a country road, surrounded by the crops and pasture and woodlands that had sustained it, the tanks had gone through firing into a house, setting it on fire, then moving to the next and the next until all were burning. There were only blackened shells left, pock-marked walls, collapsed roofs, and neither people nor animals. Now and then a family could be seen trying to survive among the wreckage of their former life. In one ruined village, as they hurried through, Mike caught a glimpse of a small child alone in a blackened doorway. Somewhere there must have been (or so he hoped) a parent, but he could see no other human being anywhere.

These were sights that had become, after a time, so familiar on television he had hardly stopped what he was doing in Oxford to look at them; had watched them while eating a meal alone, or taking drinks with colleagues, anxious for his Croatian friends, feeling a somewhat abstract, or abstracted, concern, but in truth (he now realised) untouched. So the new sense of shock was itself a shock. Reality and television, it seemed, were not the same. How many had died here? How many there? Had they been driven out as refugees, or left dead in their cellars, or taken into the woods and bludgeoned, stabbed, shot? Who were the perpetrators in this place? Was it Serbs or Croats had been living in this village or that?

These were questions he wanted to ask; but at first, and for quite a large part of the journey, he felt an inhibition, a kind of solemnity that prevented it. He thought, too, of taking photographs, but didn't like to suggest it in case it should give offence.

And meanwhile Ira drove on, not grim exactly, but purposeful, seldom looking to left or right, playing a tape, first one side, then the other, then back to the first again, of an Italian singer whose haunting, quavering, mysterious voice would, Mike knew, keep coming back into his head, and would bring with it always images of this rich green countryside, pastureland, woodland, its roadsides bright with wildflowers, its houses like sooty skulls with burned-out eyes.

After a time he took out his camera and loaded it. She glanced at it on his lap. 'You want to take pictures?'

'What do you think? Would it be insensitive?'

She shrugged. 'When the Serbs were doing this we wanted the world to see.'

'It was done by Serbs?'

'In this part, yes. South of here, in the Krajina—that's another matter.' On a straight stretch of road she slowed and stopped. 'It's OK to take pictures. But please, be careful.'

He got out of the car, walked a few paces, hesitated, turned back. What was it he should be careful of?

Probably nothing, she told him. She had a fear of open spaces, that was all. But she thought he shouldn't wander far from the road. There could be mines. And just occasionally in places like this there was a madman—someone with a gun and a grudge who felt like taking shots at anyone who came to look.

He smiled. 'Oh, is that all!'

So he made his way down the road slowly, watchfully. Soon he was photographing the scene, the burned-out houses, feeling that it was faintly indecent, that he was a trespasser, but doing it anyway.

It was very quiet. There was no traffic on the road, no one among the ruins. The crops were running to seed. There were no animals grazing the pastures. He saw a black dog, all ribcage and backbone and hangdog head, scavenging in a grassy ditch. He whistled to it and held out his hand, but it loped off on three legs among rows of corn that were drying out unharvested. He could hear birds, a breath of wind among the trees, a river rustling under a bridge. The peace which followed war, it seemed, was more peaceful than the peace of human occupation. Nature raised no objection to ethnic cleansing.

Back at the car he found Ira smoking a cigarette. She smiled wryly at him.

'You think I'm a tourist,' he said, thinking it was true, and not feeling she would condemn him for what he couldn't help.

She shrugged. 'I'm a journalist. There's not a whole lot of difference.'

She was also, he remembered with another twinge of guilt, a woman who had lost the man she loved in this war.

'And you're not a tourist,' she was saying, switching on the engine. 'You're a philosopher. An expert on the *Tractatus Logico-Philosophicus.*'

'You remember.'

'Of course. Why wouldn't I?' She engaged the gears and drove on.

'On that visit,' he said, 'I wasn't sure how much you noticed. I felt I wasn't quite real to you.'

'You were real to me,' she said. 'I thought you were not quite real to yourself.'

'Ah.' He absorbed that. 'My marriage was flying apart.'

'And now?'

'I'm getting used to it. To being alone. I've absorbed the shock, I think—most of it. What about you, Ira? Your friend was killed. Josko.'

She cast him a sideways glance. 'So you remember too?'

'I do.'

She shrugged. 'I'm OK.'

'You look as if you are. In fact, you look great.'

'Compared to how I was? But you can't see my soul.'

'If I could, what would I see?'

'I'm not sure. I think it's still wearing black.'

Later she said, 'When you were here two years ago we didn't say a lot to one another, but I felt as if we'd had conversations. And then—at the airport, remember?—you told me the final sentence of Wittgenstein's book.'

'What we cannot speak about we must pass over in silence.'

'I have that sentence pinned above my desk at the office. But in German.' And she quoted, '*Wovon man nicht sprechen kann, darüber muß man schweigen.*'

'You know German as well? I'm impressed.'

'When it comes to languages,' she said, 'English-speakers are easily impressed.'

In the afternoon they left the fertile lands behind and followed a road that zig-zagged up into mountains—steep bare slopes, with few trees, littered with white stones. Coming down on the far side of this divide Mike began to recognise the signs of a Mediterranean landscape—vines and olives, pines and cypresses, orange-red roofs and yellow-orange walls, and at last the sea, pale aquamarine inshore, dark yet intensely blue further out.

Dalmatian. The word had figured so often and so casually—so carelessly—in his childhood. Dallies. Dally plonk. In a rush of excitement he put his hand on Ira's knee and said it. 'Dalmatia.'

She smiled. 'It's beautiful isn't it?'

There were some signs of bombardment; but for the most part everything seemed to be intact. They were going east now along the coast road. Just short of Sibenik they turned inland, following an arm of the sea. Ahead, where the estuary came to an end, they could see a church spire and the houses and cafés of a compact village, with painted fishing boats moored on the glassy water.

Ljuba and one of her half-sisters, Ana, with whom she now lived, were waiting for them. In old age Ljuba was the same tall strong healthy woman he remembered from his childhood. Her hair was still thick, held in place by a headband; and even its colour had not gone entirely into greyness. She hugged him, held him at arm's length, hugged him again. 'So this is my Micky Savage. You're a big boy now, Micky.'

'A big old boy,' he said.

'Yes. I can't imagine it—when I think of Frano . . .'

'No. Frano stays young, doesn't he?'

'Frano and Joe. The two young men in my life.' She smiled, her eyes were bright, there were no tears. Mike could see, could imagine, that she had burned through all that—all the pain of it. It was her history, and it was accepted.

Indoors he was introduced to Ana, who spoke no English, but who wished him '*Dobro dosli*,' and whose broad smiles and welcoming eyes were multilingual. Glasses of plum brandy and a dish of almonds were on the table—the traditional welcome of the region. While Ira talked to Ana in Croatian, Mike told Ljuba of his visit to New Zealand, of Marica, of what they had done to Frano's grave. When Ljuba looked at the photographs her eyes filled with tears. 'It's not the death,' she said. 'It's just the passage of time. When you reach my age you weep, and most often it's yourself you're weeping for. Your past self, your lost self.'

But already she was smiling again. 'Come, Micky,' she said, taking him by the hand. 'You must see what we do here, Ana and I.'

She led him out the back door, through a courtyard paved with cobbles, past a pen occupied by hens, goats and a donkey, and up a hill, terraced and planted in vines. He had trouble keeping pace with her up the steep slope. At the top the land levelled out and there were fruit trees and a vegetable garden. All this had been Ana's and her husband's; but now, a widow, beginning to stiffen in the joints, Ana couldn't do the work on her own, so Ljuba was living with her and together the two old women farmed the little holding.

'This is where I'll see out my days,' Ljuba said. 'And when they bury me, it will be over there.' She pointed across to the opposite hill where he could see, above terraced olive groves, the headstones and cypresses of a graveyard looking out over the roofs of the village and down the estuary.

That evening they were all to go to the house of Ljuba's other half-sister, Jaka, who would be preparing supper. The day had been hot and humid, and as evening came on the air seemed to press down until rain began to fall, warm, heavy, drumming on the vine leaves outside the window—Auckland rain, Ljuba called it, Waitakere rain, but with forked lightning and cracks of thunder close overhead, as if branches of the World Ash, or some other giant tree of local legend, were snapping. Under umbrellas they splashed down the narrow flooded street into the village.

Jaka had prepared a meal of soup followed by three kinds of fish, bought from the boats that morning, each cooked in a different way, with a bowl of courgettes and kale rich in garlic, and her own wine which was taken (according to the local custom) with water. Soon the sisters were exchanging reminiscences about their early years before Ljuba had gone to New Zealand, and while this continued, Ira translated for Mike. They were from a peasant family, born to poverty, subsistence and hard work. Ana and Jaka had been partisans during the Second World War and had married partisans. In the postwar years they had been good communists and had prospered. Now they were, they said, loyal Croatians, but not happy that independence had been achieved at the cost of so many lives.

When they said goodnight to Jaka and came out into the street the rain was gone, the sky was clear and full of stars. The village, with its church, its cafés and fishing boats, repeated itself in the perfect mirror of the estuary.

'I can see why you've had no regrets about coming home,' Mike said to Ljuba as they walked back.

'Oh, but I have regrets,' she said. 'What sort of a life is it if you have nothing to regret?'

That night Mike slept well, but woke at intervals to a strange conjunction of summer night noises coming in at him through the open windows—a snoring giant in a nearby house, a chiming clock loud enough to suggest it belonged to the giant, roosters crowing at the moon, the clatter of goat hooves on cobblestones, and loudest of all, Ana's donkey with its ancient lamentation about the length of its ears and the weight of the loads tomorrow would expect it to carry.

Next day Mike followed Ljuba as she climbed the hill to her vegetable patch. Hearing him coming she stopped and waited. 'Micky,' she said, standing hands on hips as he toiled towards her.

There was a wooden seat on one of the terraces. 'Can we rest a moment?' he suggested, and they sat recovering their breath, looking down on the tiled roofs, fig trees, vineyards, vegetable plots, and at the olives and cypresses on the opposite hill. He was holding a large brown envelope. It rested on his lap. Ljuba looked at it.

'You have something for me.'

'Yes.'

'Something from the past? To do with Frano?'

'To do with Joe.'

'Ah.' She stared away into the distance. 'Such things—they make me . . .'

She looked at him squarely. 'But go ahead. Tell me.'

'While Joe was away overseas he kept a notebook.'

She knew. She'd given it to him when he was leaving. Joe had mentioned it in his letters. 'But it was lost,' she said. 'It never came back.' She looked again at the envelope. 'So it was not lost.'

'Don O'Dwyer had it.'

'The Captain.' She absorbed that. 'Why did he not . . .'

'After the war, on his visit to the marae—he brought it. He meant to give it to you. Then the makutu was put on him . . .'

'Did he expect a medal?'

'You knew about Joe's death.'

'Only then I was told. On that visit—not before. It was terrible. Such a shock. All I could think of was how to make sure Frano didn't hear. And you, Micky. You were there.' She fell silent, remembering. 'I can see how it happened—the death. That it had to be. That the Captain had no choice. I've had a long time to think about it. But at the time . . . It was too much for me. Too brutal. Too sad. And even now I can't understand why he would have come to the marae.'

'He thought no one would know. He felt guilt. He came because in his own way he wanted to face up to it. He wanted to see Joe's parents, his widow, his child. He meant to rub his own nose in what he'd done.'

'He didn't know Boy Keratu had talked?'

'He had no idea. They had some kind of agreement— O'Dwyer and Boy. That nothing would be said. Boy hadn't meant to talk . . .'

'But the beer talked. I know. It would have been better if we hadn't been told.'

'So O'Dwyer just had to tough it out. And then there was too much booze—he couldn't handle it. There was the argument in the family about the head being tapu. There was Auntie Pixie's makutu. It was a disaster. In the morning he just had to get out of there. When he reached Auckland he found he still had the notebook.'

'How do you know all this, Micky?'

'You know that O'Dwyer lives in Oxford. Two weeks ago he decided it was time to tell me the whole story. He's dying. Cancer. He heard I was coming to visit you and he wanted you to have the notebook. He wants me to say to you that he's sorry.

That he's never got over it, never forgiven himself.'

She nodded, unable to speak, and took the envelope, rested it on her lap, patted it, staring into the distance, her eyes filling with tears. 'I don't weep about it these days,' she said. 'I used to, a lot. Then I stopped. Enough, I decided. Enough tears. In my heart I said goodbye to Joe, goodbye to Frano, goodbye to Henderson. I came back here to my roots. To my half-sisters. To a peaceful old age.' She laughed, her eyes still flooded, her cheeks wet. 'And look what happened. War. My own house destroyed. And such killing, Micky. Such brutality.' She shook her head. 'Human beings.'

'It's called Original Sin, isn't it?'

She said, 'I call it bad behaviour.'

They sat in silence until she said, 'You will be seeing the Captain when you return. I'm sorry he's dying. You can tell him I bear him no grudge. That's all. I can't forgive him. Only God can do that. Only God will know whether there's anything to forgive.'

Later that morning, back at the house, she brought him a sheaf of Joe's letters, and in the days that followed he read them all.

That afternoon Mike and Ira walked up the hill on the other side, to the cemetery, where he thought he might see tombs like the ones he'd seen with Marica at Waikumete. It was as they followed the curves of the cemetery paths around the hill slope that they heard the wailing which seemed to Mike instantly familiar, as if it came out of his past. On the path directly below them a young woman, at once comforted and restrained by her parents, shouted her distress, throwing herself about, tearing at her hair and clothes.

The scene held them, concerned, fascinated, staring down unseen through the screen of trees.

Mike asked what she was saying. Quietly, Ira translated for him. The young woman's husband had been killed in the recent fighting, and she was speaking to him in his grave, asking him why he had left her, saying she loved him and couldn't live without him.

It was, Mike told Ira, or it seemed, as if he was hearing the same lament he'd listened to in the orchard all those decades ago, the sound of Ljuba giving vent to her feelings at the news of Joe's death.

'The world's supposed to be different,' Ira said, 'but nothing changes. Men die and women weep.'

SEVENTEEN

Donovan O'Dwyer's
Worst Day

'DEAR BOY, POINT OF CLARIFICATION, D'YOU MIND?' THIS IS
Winterstoke.

'Certainly, Bertie. Am I scrambling the egg instead of boiling
it?'

'You're making a very nice omelette, Michael. But there's a
small matter I think you haven't come clean about.'

'I know. I'm sorry. I've been saving it up.'

After their dinner at Gee's, Mike has delivered Winterstoke
to his door in Southmoor Road, but has then permitted himself
to be enticed inside, partly for a taste of malt, but as much for
the promise of any number of large cups of tea from the pot he
thinks of as Bertie's Brown Jug, a magic brewery which delivers
the English infusion more exactly to his taste than any except
his own. The house smells faintly of moist carpet and rising
damp, but has been beautifully cleaned and tidied by its owner's
help, a Mrs Cratchett, whom Bertie refers to variously as Mrs
Scratch It, Mrs Cat Shit, and Mrs Back Chat, but whom he
claims he secretly adores, and to whom he has bequeathed (or
so he says, though Mike allows himself a secret doubt), his
Greenwich sword and two hundred pounds.

'She'll be so surprised,' (this was late in their dinner at

Gee's). 'I want an afterlife just so I can watch her eating all those black words spoken behind my back.'

'But you told me you don't intend to die.'

'Quite right, I don't. There's the trick of it you see, Michael. I have it both ways. I leave her something in my will, but she'll never get it. Or, if something goes wrong with my plan to live for ever, I have the pleasure of giving her one helluva shock.'

But what Winterstoke wants now is for Mike to explain whether Helen O'Dwyer's version of Joe's death, which he now runs through to make sure he has it right, was indeed what happened. 'Joe steps on a mine. He's wounded, dying, in pain, afraid to be left. He begs his officer to shoot him. O'Dwyer puts the gun to his head, says "Thy will be done," and . . . bang.'

Mike asks, 'Does it strike you as unlikely?'

Winterstoke puts on his beak-face, weighing things up. 'The "Thy will be done"—that's out of character, perhaps. Of course in my line of business you hear a lot of stories. Nothing's surprising. And in the heat of battle, anything's possible. Anything at all.'

'I detect a doubt though, don't I?' Mike asks.

'I have a nose for what's . . .' He hesitates. 'Plausible, I suppose.'

'And Helen's story?'

'If you tell me it's true, I'll believe it.'

'Until just a few weeks back,' Mike says, 'I thought it was. My visit to New Zealand seemed to confirm it. It was what Wikitoria Paul believed. It was the reason for Auntie Pixie's makutu—because he'd shot Joe in the head. And I suppose Helen had heard it from Camille. But just before I went back to Croatia, O'Dwyer summoned me. He wanted me to know the truth.'

'And the truth was different.'

'Yes.'

'And you were chosen to hear it . . . Because of the New Zealand connexion?'

'I suppose so. The connexion with Joe.'

'This was before you talked to Ljuba?'

'Yes it was.'

'And she believed the story as Helen tells it.'

'There was no point in telling her the truth. It would only have upset her.'

'So the truth was worse.'

Mike thinks about that. 'It was more dramatic.' After a moment: 'But yes, worse. Undoubtedly worse.'

He sniffs his glass of Glenfiddich, takes a very small sip which he leaves lying on his tongue while he pours himself another cup from the brown teapot. Swallowing, he goes on, 'In the counter-attack on the Maleme airfield so much had gone wrong. They'd had their long wait to get started. They had to fight skirmishes in the dark along the way; and by the time they got within sight of the airfield and the hill overlooking it . . .'

'Hill 107,' Bertie murmurs.

' . . . it was daylight. They were exposed to fire from the air, and from the hill. They dug in as best they could among the olives, held their ground right through that day, fought off a German attack with a bayonet charge that was so courageous he couldn't tell me about it without weeping . . .' Mike pauses. 'Can you imagine Don in tears?'

'I can imagine it,' Winterstoke says gravely, 'but not with pleasure.'

'That night,' Mike continues, 'they were still hanging on, still hoping for reinforcements. They knew there were plenty of their own men in reserve. And any number of Aussies and Brits east of Hania—thousands of men not too far away to be rushed into the fray. They'd fought their way this far and the last thing they wanted was to give up. But when the order came in the early hours of the morning it was to retreat.

'Don's first reaction was to tell himself that Freyberg was gutless. But of course he knew that wasn't true. Freyberg had won a VC at Gallipoli. He had so many scars from so many battles he could have played Coriolanus without help from the makeup department. But he had the whole New Zealand contingent there on Crete. He had to decide whether he wanted to risk losing them all. If he'd elected the gamble, O'Dwyer's sure he would have won. The airfield was still there for the taking.'

'But it would have seemed like playing with someone else's chips.'

'Exactly. He could risk his own life. He'd done it often. But could he risk theirs? Freyberg wasn't a gambling man, and he decided he couldn't.'

So in the dawn light the rearguard was formed among the olives, ten men from each of the four Maori companies, an officer in charge of each, and O'Dwyer in charge of them all. They were to cover the retreat of 20 and 28 Battalions, and of two other New Zealand battalions, 22 and 23, that had been in the area since the first day. They would hold their ground, fight hard, retreat fast, defend again, and so on in backward steps, while in the shelter of this action the rest of the force would be high-tailing it for a line running inland from Platanias where there was still safety in numbers.

O'Dwyer gave himself three or four hours for this task. He planned to have his men, or those who survived, back in the safety zone by midday.

So many years later O'Dwyer still remembered two things from that morning. The disappointment of the order to retreat, and the joy of breakfast. They'd had so little to eat the day before, mainly field rations taken from German dead. But now, he didn't know how, tins of food were got up to the line. He shared a tin of bully with his sergeant and another soldier, and had a whole tin of beetroot to himself. And Joe and Tu had gone foraging before first light and come back with their shirts full of oranges, like schoolboys back from a raid on an orchard. Bully, beetroot and oranges, with water from the stream—O'Dwyer remembered it as one of the great culinary experiences of his life.

As the order to retreat spread, there was disbelief, grumbling, and finally a scramble, mostly undisciplined, and in places close to panic. Fighting men told to retreat cease to be fighting men. No manual can teach them how to run away like heroes. O'Dwyer was glad the day required him to stand and fight; and none of his men complained of it.

Soon the Germans were coming close, testing, but tentative. The bayonet charge of the night before was what saved the rearguard—O'Dwyer was sure of that. It had given the enemy such respect for, such fear of, the Maori infantry, they couldn't, right through that morning, quite bring themselves to take the opportunities that a retreat offered them.

O'Dwyer had them, his 'forty thieves' as he called them, with a few extras, Pakehas who chose to stay 'just for the scrap', stretched out in a long line, ten paces apart. He'd told them to save their ammunition, to hold their fire until there was something to shoot at, to snipe with care, and use the Brens in short bursts. As the paratroopers closed on them he ordered the two outer groups back to a ridge, while the centre held their ground. Then, as the centre retreated, the flanks covered them.

Moving back through the groves and orchards they saw and smelled the dead of the past few days, lying where they had fallen, or hanging in trees, their faces black and swarming with flies. That there were many more German dead than New Zealanders confirmed the feeling that they'd been ahead on points. And the recognition of some of their best men lying there, killed during the counter-attack, added to the bitterness of the retreat.

All O'Dwyer could do now was to see that order was maintained and the textbook adhered to. But the trees and the uneven ground, which were their protection, also made it hard to be sure of the larger picture; and as the morning went on, and the Germans came closer, his anxiety was that the rearguard, together with the tail-ends of the retreating battalions, might be caught in a pincer movement. He was catching glimpses of Germans down on the road keeping pace with his line, dragging a Bofors anti-aircraft gun captured from the airfield, which they would soon be using as an artillery piece. And green flares from the higher slopes meant a German unit was making its way through the olives up there, signalling progress to the men down on the road.

Mid-morning, as the centre held its ground and the two outer sections retreated again, the fighting was suddenly intense. Paratroopers, darting from tree to tree under the canopy of the olives, were so close O'Dwyer could see their faces, hear them calling warnings and encouragement to one another. He was with the centre group, spaced out along the length of a low stone wall, when the Germans charged. The rearguard's firing was accurate and the charge faltered. But half a dozen paratroopers led by an officer burst suddenly into open ground, shouting and firing machine pistols. At just this moment, when it seemed the rearguard was going to be breached, one Maori soldier jumped the wall, a grenade in each hand. He was a little to the Germans' right, distracting them, causing them to hesitate, and in that instant two fell to rifle shots. One grenade, perhaps hit by a bullet, blew up in the Maori soldier's hand. He glanced at it, threw the other, bringing down a German who was wrenching at his gun as if it had jammed, and was back again in the cover of the wall.

The soldier didn't speak, simply thrust what had once been a hand at his officer, as a small child might hold out a cut finger to its mother. Beyond the wall the frontal assault had been given up. O'Dywer pulled a leather lace from the soldier's boot, tied it around the wrist and twisted it tight with a small branch of olive wood. He took a knife from his pocket, cut away the shredded flesh and sinew and splintered bone, all that was left of the hand. Around the stump he packed a field dressing and tied it in place, hoping it would staunch the blood.

The soldier said nothing, seemed to feel nothing. It was as if he had fainted but was still semi-conscious. He was very young, eighteen or nineteen. O'Dwyer laid him down in the shelter of the wall. 'You did well,' he said. The soldier didn't speak. 'Lie there. Don't move. We're going to leave you here. D'you understand?'

The soldier nodded and closed his eyes. Tears squeezed out at the edges.

'Listen,' O'Dwyer said. 'You've lost a hand but you're going to survive. They'll take you prisoner. They'll look after you.'

He hoped it was true. So there couldn't be any mistake that the soldier was out of action he took away the rifle that was lying beside him.

He looked over the wall. The Germans had pulled back, looking to their wounded. He patted the soldier's cheek. 'Courage, brother. When we're back in New Zealand you can buy me a beer.'

He signalled up and down the line and once again they were running, at first bent almost double under the olives, then clear of them, sprinting over tawny grass and bright flowers, then smack into a stand of bamboo which broke their line, some pushing through, others finding a way around, up towards the hills or down towards the road.

O'Dwyer forced his way through. It took time and when he came out on the far side he found himself alone, his path checked by a canal. The water was opaque but he thought it must be shallow, that he could wade it. Climbing down to test its depth he felt his feet slide from under him. It was a feet-first unstoppable slither, leisurely, like a disaster in slow motion, and gave him the sense of his own considerable weight. The water closed over his head, his gear was heavy, and for a few moments, his hands clawing and sliding uselessly on green slime, he thought he was going to die, not heroically in battle, but absurdly by accident.

A voice came down to him. 'Grab it, sir.' It was Tu, crouching at the canal's edge, holding his .303 down so that its muzzle pointed straight at him.

Was the safety-catch on? O'Dwyer didn't ask. He took hold of the muzzle, shut his eyes tight, propped and scrambled with his feet, and felt himself hauled from the water. When he opened his eyes he saw that Boy and Joe were there too. They were grinning, three sets of uneven teeth.

'Saved by the front row,' he said. A volley from a machine-gun shivered and chattered through the tops of the bamboo, the boom of the Bofors gun came up from the road, and a Messerschmitt went over, heading for the heights of Galatos.

They led him along to where the canal ran underground, crossed it there, and climbed to the ridge that was to be their next line of defence. O'Dwyer was wet to the skin, and foul-smelling. He had felt some moments of fear, some moments of excitement. Now he was exhausted and depressed.

Again the German troops pressed hard, and again the line held, even drove them back, despite mortar fire, and now and then a shell exploding too close for comfort.

O'Dwyer estimated they had covered at least three-quarters of the planned retreat, and would soon have been moving under cover of protective fire from the Platanias line, when Joe Panapa stepped on one of the mines that had been laid by their own men of the Field Engineers. They had been making one of their dashes back to a new defence line. Tu, running beside Joe, stopped, calling to Boy, who came back. O'Dwyer, bringing up the rear, stopped too. Joe's feet were gone. They were just shreds of flesh and leather and torn trouser. Between ankle and knee one leg was bent at a right-angle and pumping blood. Joe groaned, muttered something in Maori, half raised himself, crawled a few steps on hands and knees. His eyes rolled, and he fainted.

'Leave him there,' O'Dwyer told them.

They ignored him and heaved Joe up, pulling one of his arms around each of their shoulders. As they moved, what remained of his lower legs at first hung clear of the ground. Then, as they slowed and bent under the weight, the legs dragged, smearing bright blood over green grass, along bauxite red earth and through twigs and leaf mould.

They stopped to rest. O'Dwyer looked back. Their pursuers weren't yet in sight among the trees, but it wouldn't be long. The Germans down on the road had got ahead of the rearguard, and the ones up on the higher ground were keeping pace with them. The pincer was ready to close.

Joe's eyes were shut tight. O'Dwyer put a hand to his throat. There was still a pulse. 'Come on,' he said. 'Just leave him there.'

Tu and Boy looked at him and looked away. He said, 'Please chaps, leave him, or we'll all be dead.' When they ignored him again and began to heave Joe up O'Dwyer found himself blustering. 'Fuck it, didn't you hear me? I said put him down. That's an order.'

It might have been an order but it didn't have the ring of a command, not even to O'Dwyer, and they ignored it. There was a burst of machine-gun fire that sounded close, and the crump of a mortar. The rest of the rearguard were now a long way ahead, up on the next ridge. Tu and Boy were slowing again, pulled down by the dead weight of their unconscious comrade. Following behind, O'Dwyer pulled out his revolver. 'Put him down.'

Recognising the note of urgency, perhaps of something like hysteria, they looked around, still holding Joe with an arm pulled over each of their shoulders and clamped by the wrist. They looked down the muzzle of the revolver, turned, and went on without a word, exhausted, stumbling, pig-headed, loyal.

O'Dwyer raised the revolver, aimed it at the back of Joe's head, and fired a single shot. A shudder went through the body, and it hung there, limp, dead.

What happened next O'Dwyer remembered only as confusion. Boy and Tu must have thought that Joe had been hit by a stray bullet. But as they lowered him to the ground they saw O'Dwyer still there, the revolver in his hand. Boy's face showed astonishment, Tu's instant anger. But as Tu took a step towards his officer, paratroopers appeared down the long slope among the olives, darting as before from tree to tree.

'Move,' O'Dwyer barked. 'We've got a job to finish.'

One Bofors shell exploded, and a second, the noise huge, shrapnel knifing through the trees. The paratroopers were checked, not wanting to come in close where shells were landing. When O'Dwyer turned again he saw that Tu was on the ground, half his throat torn away, one eye gone, blood coming through a wide tear in the front of his battledress tunic. He didn't have to check that he was dead.

'Move,' he shouted again. Boy ran and O'Dwyer followed.

When they reached the rearguard again they found they were in a wooded area at the bottom of a steep slope. At the top of the slope was the ridge marking the Platanias line. From up there Bren and rifle fire was pouring down over their heads, keeping the Germans back; but if they were to reach it they would have to go out into the open, up a bare slope. The two dozen men surviving of the rearguard went down in a long line to a stream, waded along its shingle bed, then climbed again. But it was the same—a wooded area protecting them, and beyond, a bare slope up to the safety of the ridge.

It was a question of whether they should sit it out, waiting for nightfall and hoping the German mortars and field guns wouldn't get a fix on their position, or make a dash for it, risking the open ground. They decided it was every man for himself. Each would make his own decision how and when to go. Few intended to wait for nightfall.

Resting among the trees, getting his breath back, hearing the covering fire going over, O'Dwyer found himself sitting, back against the trunk of an olive tree, beside his sergeant. In his head, the moment of his shooting Joe Panapa was being repeated, vivid and ghastly, with feelings that were strange—something like exhilaration mixed with horror. He told the sergeant what had happened.

There was a silence while the sergeant, leaning forward, tugged at his bootlaces. And then, 'I wish you hadn't told me that, sir.'

O'Dwyer felt himself blinking on what might have been tears. What he said, however, was staunch. 'If I'm wounded, sergeant, and holding up the rearguard, that's what you must do to me.'

In ones and twos, sometimes three together, sometimes four or five, they made their dashes—out from the trees, up the grassy slope, past a white shrine on level ground, then up a final steep incline and over the top to safety—with the covering fire from above redoubled as they ran. A few were hit; most got through. The sergeant was almost at the top when a Bofors shell exploded so close it blew his head off. His body collapsed, slid down the hill a few feet and lay still while the head went on rolling and came to rest beside the white shrine.

When Boy ran, O'Dwyer went with him. Boy was faster, fitter, but not far short of the top he was hit and fell. O'Dwyer reached the summit, tumbled into a shallow trench and lay there recovering his breath. He could hear Boy groaning and cursing. The cursing sounded healthy. He called to him. 'How bad is it, private?'

There was no answer. He called again. 'Keratu, can you hear me? How bad's your wound?'

A voice came back, muffled but unmistakable. 'Go and fuck yourself, sir.'

O'Dwyer took off his helmet, unbuckled his webbing, shed his holster, put aside his rifle, tied a dirty white handkerchief around his upper left arm. He stood up and, step by step so he wouldn't slip, made his way down the slope. He was in full view. All around him the firing stopped. Everyone was expecting him to go down. He was expecting it himself. But the Germans weren't firing either.

'Afterwards,' Mike says, looking into his empty glass, 'the men who'd seen it were never able to agree. Had the Germans believed he was wearing a Red Cross armband, and that meant they had to let him rescue a wounded soldier? Or was it just that they respected his guts and no one wanted to be the one to kill him?'

Winterstoke nods. 'No way of reading such things, is there? War's like cancer. Nasty. But it can go into remission at any time.'

'I think at that moment,' Mike says, 'O'Dwyer was ready to die. He wanted to offer himself—that's the phrase he used when he told me about it. Let death take him or leave him. He was available. His men watched. The Germans watched. He went down the slope, took a look at Boy's wound, and somehow encouraged him, helped him, dragged him, back to safety. Boy was taken off that night with the wounded from Suda Bay.'

'So he saved the life of the one surviving witness to his crime.'

Mike lifts the brown teapot, tests its weight and decides it's empty. 'I suppose that's what it was—a crime.'

'In law?' Winterstoke says. 'Oh yes, surely.' He stares at the ceiling. 'An odd one though, isn't it? If he'd killed one of the others . . .'

'Tu or Boy.'

'Failure to obey a lawful command—he'd probably have been in the clear.'

There's a silence, which Bertie is the first to break. 'Can't imagine the military wanting him court-martialled. They'd want it covered up.'

'He wrote an official report,' Mike says. 'Got nothing back. No reply, no acknowledgement, nothing. It went into someone's files.'

'Or waste-paper basket.'

Mike stands up. 'Bertie, this was meant to be an early night.'

'Yes of course.' He scrambles to his feet out of the depths of his ancient fireside chair. 'You must go.'

As they walk towards the door he says, 'So the other version of the story—Boy Keratu's—that became Don's story too. Why didn't he leave it like that—let sleeping dogs and so on?'

'He was dying.'

'Getting it off his conscience.'

'And into the record perhaps.'

'Ah, you think so?' Winterstoke considers. 'But Joe might have survived.'

'Of course. There are famous New Zealand examples. Colonel Bennett—he was OC Maori Battalion. Walked with a stick for the rest of his life. And General Kippenberger. Lost both feet in the Italian campaign.'

'So why, then?'

'I don't think there's a why. He didn't try to explain it. He just told me what happened.'

Winterstoke nods. 'Brave chap. I always knew he had guts.'

In the hallway, buttoning up his coat, Mike says, 'You remember at the service when we spoke to Camille, she said she wanted to see me? She called yesterday to remind me. I went around in the afternoon and we had a chat. Looked at photos and talked about Don. What she had to tell me was that just before he died Don said he wanted me to take his ashes to Crete. To be scattered on Joe's grave.'

'Oh I say!' Winterstoke looks disconcerted. 'Seems a bit . . . You know. Don't you think?'

A bit what? Mike wonders. Dramatic? Melodramatic? Un-English, perhaps? But then, how English is an Irish-New Zealander?

'I wondered what the Maori protocol might make of it,' Mike says. 'And then I thought, fuck it, that's what he wants, that's what I'll do.'

'Good man,' Winterstoke rumbles. 'Wishes of the dead and so on.'

'But I've persuaded Camille to come. She wasn't going to. Said Don hadn't asked *her* to do it. That he probably wouldn't have wanted her there. But I insisted. Made it a condition. And I'm working on Gillian to come too.'

'Gillian? That's a rattling good idea.'

'She and Camille are old friends. And I think you should be there, Bertie.'

'Good God, why me?' But as he says it, fiddling with his earpiece which has begun to whistle a tune, it's apparent he likes the idea.

'A return to one of your fields of endeavour,' Mike says. 'And you and Don were mates.'

The two men smile at one another.

'More the merrier sort of thing,' Winterstoke says.

As he opens the front door to his departing guest they see that it's raining again.

EIGHTEEN

The Soul Without a Stitch

IN THE DAYS THAT FOLLOWED THEIR WALK IN THE CEMETERY WHERE they heard the young woman wailing for her lost lover, Mike and Ira went about together—into Sibenik, along the coast to the ancient peninsula town of Primosten, and further south to Split. They went by ferry to spend a day on Prvic, the small island from where it was said many had gone in the early years of the century to live in New Zealand, and where Ljuba had retreated after her house had been destroyed in the fighting.

They swam every day, sometimes twice in a day. They ate in restaurants, walked, talked. The talk was of books, politics, ideas, philosophy, Zen. It was also of two lives, his and hers, two histories so different it was surprising they had so much ground on which to meet and feel at ease together.

'When do we find the thing we have to pass over in silence?' Mike asked one day. They'd been talking again of the Wittgenstein dictum.

'Don't you think we've found it?'

He was surprised by that. He was lying on his stomach on a red-brown bed of needles in the shade of pines that filled the air with their scent, and only metres from the bluest of blue seas in which they'd been swimming. As a breeze came and went, little blades of light cut through the branches. Ira was on her knees, crouched over him, massaging his back. It was something they'd discovered they both liked so much there was an agreement to take turns after swimming, one to give, one to receive the massage. Ira's hands and fingers were strong. She pressed hard into his shoulders, up around his neck and beyond into his scalp. The sensation was so deeply pleasant he found it hard to talk, even to think, but she'd aroused his curiosity. 'You mean there's something we can't speak about? What is it?'

'Because we can't speak about it, I must pass over it in silence.'

He heard the smile in her voice. What could this mean? The possibilities made him nervous, which seemed to prove her point, so he let it pass. But he went on thinking about it, then and in the days that followed.

Once, as they walked down to the village for coffee on the seafront, they talked of driving down the coast all the way to Dubrovnik. It was Ira who mentioned it first, and it was an idea that appealed to him. But as they talked he could see that although she wanted to see it again, and wanted him to see it, she couldn't bring herself to make the decision. 'I'm afraid of what I'll find there,' she told him.

'The destruction?'

'Yes. And the things that would remind me of Josko.' She had stopped and was staring at the figure of a white stone virgin inset in a wall as a wayside shrine. 'Not that all the memories would be happy ones.'

'No?'

'He used to lie to me.'

'What about?'

She laughed, moving on again towards the seafront. 'What do you think, Mike? About his wife. About other women.'

Mike gestured in a way that was meant to signal, did signal, he was a novice in such matters. They walked on in silence until he said, 'But you were his wife.'

'I'm the wife of any man I'm in love with. That's why I've never been married.'

Later, over the coffee, she said, 'Josko was nice. He was clever, he was witty, he had a million friends, and he was a bastard. When he lied to me I hated it. When he told me the truth, that was worse.'

'But you loved him.'

'Of course. Otherwise it wouldn't have been so painful.'

One day when they'd been wandering about the churches, squares and narrow streets of Sibenik's old quarter she stopped, looked around, recognising where she was. 'Come with me,' she said, turning up a narrow alley that became a flight of stone steps. 'I'm going to show you something I shouldn't.'

She led him up into a courtyard where she knocked at a blue-painted door with a huge earthenware jar on one side and a green chair on the other. It was answered by an old woman wearing the peasant widow's traditional black. There was an exchange of pleasantries in Croatian before the woman disappeared a moment and returned with an envelope.

'This,' Ira told him, holding it up, 'is the key to an apartment. It belongs to my friend, Mare. She works with me in Zagreb.'

He followed her up another flight of stone steps. At the top she unlocked a door and stood back to let him go in ahead of her. The apartment was not large, but it was so well designed and beautifully furnished, it gave a sense of space. The floors were tiled, the walls whitewashed stone. In addition to the living room there was a bedroom with tiled bathroom attached, a small modern kitchen, and a wide terrace that looked over roofs towards the port and the sea.

Ira went into the kitchen and made them coffee, and they sat together at a table on the terrace, in the shade of a canvas awning. 'Is your friend rich?' Mike asked.

'No. Only this.' Ira waved a hand towards the apartment. 'This is her wealth.'

'And why did you say you shouldn't show me?'

'There's a story goes with it. It's not that I shouldn't show the apartment. It's that I shouldn't tell the story.'

'But you will.'

She smiled. 'Why are you so sure?'

'Well . . . You brought me here.'

'It's true,' she said. 'I must trust you.'

Two years before, Mare had had a lover whom Ira called K.

'Some kind of banking lawyer,' she said, 'with connexions to the HDZ. He had a wife and two children but they were living in Italy. This was after the end of the communist period when there was a lot of buying and selling of state assets, and K was making a lot of money. Then the fighting started, and he was making a lot more. Mare thought it was from buying and selling arms, but she didn't ask. Didn't want to know. K began to go about with a bodyguard. He travelled a lot. He'd go out into the country-side with this big protector—or maybe over the border somewhere, away for days or weeks, and when he came back there would be his usual travelling bag, and a suitcase.'

'Ah,' Mike said. 'The suitcase.'

'Yes. Like in the movies—full of deutschmarks, dollars, sterling. Mostly marks. Mare tried not to see, but she couldn't—you know?—avert her eyes. He was careless. There would be something to pay for and he would open the case and take out a bunch of notes. Even I saw that happen. I met him a few times. He was very nice. I don't think Mare was in love with him, but she's young and she was having a good time. He was fun, he was a good cook, he liked jazz, he was a good lover. But she was frightened of the bodyguard. Not so much that he would harm her—but that he was there.'

'That he was necessary.'

'Yes. And she worried about the suitcase. One day he went off with the bodyguard. I don't know where exactly. Somewhere in Bosnia, I think. Anyway they were killed. Blown to bits. A shell hit their car and they were worse than dead. They didn't exist any more. Someone who'd been involved in what they were doing got word to Mare. She panicked—decided she should get out of his apartment before the Zagreb police came snooping around to see what he'd been up to. She went back to live with her mother in Samobor. That's a village outside Zagreb. She came in to the office each day, but she was in a bad state, expecting the authorities to come asking questions. But nothing happened. After about six months she started to feel safe and her curiosity got the better of her. She went back to the apart-ment . . .'

'And K was there,' Mike suggested.

'No. Not that. He really was dead. That was true. What she

found was that the apartment was exactly as she'd left it. No one had been there. Nothing was changed. Her last cup of coffee was still where she'd put it down, half empty on the kitchen table. She gathered up a few things she'd left and she was looking around for a bag to put them in, and there, under the bed, was . . .'

Ira stopped, and like a conductor bringing in the brass or the woodwind, signalled to him to finish the sentence.

'Oh I see,' Mike said. 'You mean a suitcase.'

'A suitcase. Exactly. *The* suitcase.'

'Full of money.'

'It was locked. She took it and ran. She had it at her mother's house, but she couldn't bring herself to open it. A few months went by and finally I said, "Come on, Mare, let's just have a look."' Ira waved a hand around the apartment. 'This is what she bought with it.'

'How much?'

'She never told me exactly how much. It was in marks. Obviously a lot.'

He nodded, looking around. 'She spent it well.'

Ira said, 'I suppose it's what's called blood money. But you know . . .'

'When there's a lot of blood . . .'

She laughed. 'Yes. There's a lot of money.'

The coffee was drunk, the heat of the sun had been burning through the canvas of the awning, and they'd moved to a couch which faced out through the sliding glass doors to the terrace.

'Now it's my turn,' he said.

'Your turn?'

'To tell a war story. One that I shouldn't tell and one you mustn't ever mention to Ljuba.'

What he told her was the story of Joe Panapa's death—first as Ljuba knew it, then as O'Dwyer had told it to him just before his departure to Zagreb.

When he finished Ira was solemn, shocked. 'He didn't want you to tell the real story to my aunt?'

'No, no. I'm sure he didn't. All he wanted, I think, was that someone should know.'

'But why?'

'I'm not sure. But I feel as if I understand. I think he felt what happened was too momentous just to be expunged from the human record. Something like that.'

They were side by side looking out over the rooftops towards the sea. Ira threw an arm over his shoulder. 'And do you understand why he shot Ljuba's husband?'

Mike held out his hands in a gesture of helplessness. 'It's one of those things that's just a fact. It happened.'

'It happened, and it's sad.'

'Oh yes. Infinitely sad.'

She looked at him, at his profile, and pushed a strand of hair away from his brow, hooking it behind his ear. 'Another thing that has to be passed over in silence.'

That evening they found a restaurant in Sibenik. It was in a courtyard enclosed by an ancient stone wall but open to the skies. A small fig tree that had taken root in the wall had pushed its way through the masonry and hung out almost horizontal over their table. As the sky darkened they could look up through its leaves and see the stars. Ira still ate sparingly, but it was not as it had been during his first visit, when she seemed not to eat at all. They shared a seafood risotto with salad, and followed it with ice cream. There was a bottle of wine. Soon her cigarette was alight.

'Why don't we stay here,' she said.

'Here?'

She laughed. 'That frown! The philosopher asks himself, What does this woman mean? She means *here*. In Sibenik. At Mare's apartment.'

There was only one bed in the apartment. That morning they had stood a moment too long, side by side, staring at it. He asked, 'Is this the thing you said we've had to pass over in silence?'

'You guessed?'

'I hoped. I feared.'

'I'm glad you hoped. Why did you fear?'

'You haven't noticed my age?'

'I've noticed you refer to it rather often.' When he didn't reply to this she asked, 'Why is that?'

'Vy is that?' he mimicked, but she waited for an answer. 'I suppose,' he said, 'because I think it's embarrassing when a man reaches a certain age and allows himself to forget how he appears to women who are two decades younger.'

'How you appear to me, for example.'

'For example. Yes.'

'You want to know how you appear to me?'

He sat up straight, mimicking again. 'Please, yes. I vant.'

'Like a man with more defences than he needs.'

He smiled. 'Oh, I'm sure that's true. More than anyone needs.'

'You don't want to spend a night with me at Mare's apartment?'

'You must know I do.'

'I think I do know that, yes. Otherwise I wouldn't have suggested it.'

There was another silence. He was aware he might seem ungracious; but he was embarrassed, and found it difficult to speak.

'Come,' she said, putting her cigarettes and lighter into her handbag and waving for the bill. 'Enough of this. Herr Professor Wittgenstein is right. We must pass over it in silence.'

'No, wait.' He leaned across the table and took both her hands, 'I've thought lately,' he said, looking down at his hands holding hers, 'that my sex life is over. It's more than two years now I've been living alone. I don't think I . . .'

She interrupted. 'Men, of course, are insane.'

He absorbed this. 'Yes,' he said.

When she didn't go on he said, 'What you've just said constitutes in logic the first premise of a syllogism. Men are insane. Mike is a man. Therefore Mike is insane.'

'Quite right,' she said. 'That is what I meant.'

'And now I think you want to tell me—don't you?—in what way Mike, and all men, are insane.'

'About sex, of course.'

'Of course? Yes. Of course.'

'Listen, Mike.' She sat up straight, half amused, half exasperated. 'I didn't say to you let's have sex.'

'No,' he agreed. 'You didn't say that.'

'I didn't say will you please fuck me. Did I?'

'No. That would have been interesting. Exciting. But no, it's not what you said.'

'I said why don't we spend a night together. To me that means let's see what happens. Maybe you will learn something. Maybe I will. Maybe we will have a good night's sleep. Maybe you will discover whether your sex life is over, or not over, or just starting. Maybe you will discover I'm a man.'

'And that I'm gay.'

She laughed. They both laughed. After a moment he said, 'Thank you for asking me, and yes. The answer is yes. All the answers are yes.'

She squeezed his hand. 'Would you like me to give you a massage?'

'You know I would, but it's your turn.'

'I'll make you a present of my turn. Just this once.'

'Then you have to let me pay the bill.'

What Mike discovered principally that night was that his sex life was not over. After that he found himself counting the days remaining, and that they clicked by too fast. Ljuba didn't ask where they had been on the night they didn't come home. If she noticed that they went each night to their separate rooms in her house, but that one or the other didn't stay there, she made no comment. The giant in the nearby house snored and the giant clock struck the hours and the quarters while they tumbled and groaned together, and talked and slept. The donkey brayed. The goats clattered on the cobbles. The roosters crowed at the moon. The black cypresses in the cemetery on the hill, and the white stone virgin in her shrine on the road below the house, kept their chaste, or chastened, silences. The world revolved and held exactly to its planetary course. Nothing changed and (though slightly, subtly) everything changed.

'What becomes of us now?' he asked once, as a grey light came in at the window and birds started up among the vine leaves.

'Nothing,' she said, with an emphasis that might almost have been angry. 'You go back to your life in Oxford. I go back to mine in Zagreb. We write one another nice e-mails. We send one another cards on birthdays and at Christmas. We keep fond memories. We hope our paths cross again.'

'Is that all?' he asked. And then, feeling tears on his cheek that were not his own: 'But of course you're right.'

Each morning he climbed the hill with Ljuba and sat with her on the seat up there, talking about the past, about Henderson, about Auckland and Northland where now (he told her) a big sign on the main road read WELCOME TO THE NORTH, and then HAERE MAI, and finally DOBRO DOSLI.

One day she got out old photo albums and he looked again into the dark handsome face of his childhood friend who when angry had called him Pakeha, and with whom he'd wrestled at night in the orchard, enjoying it, even the pain of it, almost as an act of love. Had he been in any way responsible for Frano's death? It was something he'd asked himself over the years; but it was an academic question, not one he'd been able to feel as a weight on his intellect or his conscience. He and Frano, it was true, like Donovan and Joe, had been part of a bigger story which, when it went by the name of History, would attribute cause and perhaps apportion blame, but which to the participants was simply memory, or What Happened, and to the philosopher who had learned and unlearned his trade at the feet of the Master Wittgenstein, was a set of facts which, without enlightenment, was without meaning.

On their last night in Dalmatia Mike and Ira walked down into the village to an outdoor café that looked over the breathless mirror of the inlet on which the fishing boats sat up straight like good children, posing for a photograph. A klapa group, six young men in white shirts, black trousers, and dark embroidered waistcoats, sang traditional songs in three-part harmony, sometimes unaccompanied, sometimes accompanying themselves on guitars, zithers, mandolins. Love songs, songs about war, songs about the seasons and about leaving home for ever—Ira translated for him, and later wrote out the words of one he especially liked because it made him think of the people who had gone from this region and whose children had been friends and neighbours of his childhood:

> In vain my mother told me
> The sea never returns what it takes
> Not the people and not the ships.
> In vain she told me

In vain she wept.
The sea was stronger
And my ship sails tonight.

As they were walking back that evening Ira said, 'You have to let me say thank you, Mike.'

He began to say that she was the one to whom thanks were due, but she stopped him. 'Listen to me. When we were driving down here I said if you could look into my soul you'd see it was still wearing black—do you remember?'

Yes, he remembered that. Of course he did.

'And can you see it now?'

'I think I can.'

'What's it wearing?'

'Not black any more.'

'Bright colours?'

'Bright, yes. Bold colours.'

'Bold. What about yours, Mike. The armour's gone, isn't it?'

'Oh yes. That's gone.' He smiled, thinking about it as they walked along. 'Actually, I don't think I have a soul.'

'You have a shadow.'

'It's true. I've noticed. Does that mean I have a soul?'

'I think it does, yes.'

He nodded. 'OK. I suppose I can live with that.'

'So what's it wearing?'

'Before I came here it rather fancied the idea of saffron.'

'Like a Buddhist monk?'

'Zen,' he explained. 'Zennish. Zen-tending.'

'And now?'

He turned her towards him and pulled her close. They had stopped again and were standing on the road below Ljuba's house. The little white stone virgin, head bowed in her shrine, was praying for a lover. The cemetery's heaven-pointing cypresses had become darkly phallic.

'Now,' he said, 'right at this moment, it's not wearing anything at all.'

She laughed. 'Naked?'

'Not a stitch,' he confirmed.

NINETEEN

'Is it I, God, or Who, that Lifts this Arm?'

MIKE WAKES TO LIGHT IN FINE LINES ON THE PATCHED AND PEELING yellow-painted wall of his room in the Hotel Lucia on the seafront at Hania. It strikes up from the harbour through slats of the french windows' green shutters. Although the harbour is like glass, it is a glass that imperceptibly moves, causing the lines to shiver and glitter.

He lies watching them move on the wall, enjoying the green of the slats through which they come. The room, with its balcony looking over the harbour, and its own tiny bathroom, is basic, even dingy—cheap, and entirely to his liking. From the promenade come the sounds of morning—trade vans making deliveries, early workers exchanging '*Kali méra*' and '*Ti kanis*', brooms on tiled floors, cane chairs being re-arranged, a few early strollers and breakfasters from the hoard of tourists most of whom are still sleeping.

From eight each evening until well past midnight the promenade, every inch of it taken up with tavernas, estiatorios, cafés, bars, has been loud with talk, singing, quarrels, laughter, amplified music, none of which, since his arrival three days ago, has kept him from sleeping. Much later, at three and four in the morning, sudden noises in the silence—a rubbish truck, a singing drunk, a lover's quarrel—have woken him briefly; but the continuous noise of the promenade at full pitch has been for him, after a meal and wine with his friends, a cradle in which sleep has been easy.

He gets out of bed, opens the shutters and looks out beyond his balcony. The promenade runs around three sides of the harbour. A breakwater completes the enclosure, leaving only the sea entrance, narrow, but sufficient for the Venetian galleys the harbour was built to receive and protect. At the end of the breakwater overlooking the entrance stands the pharos. Beyond, the Aegean leads the eye away into a blue that doesn't alter as it becomes sky, so the horizon line, though it must be there, is an item of knowledge, a guess rather than an observation.

Over to the right is the Mosque of the Janissaries, a relic of the Turkish occupation which replaced the Venetian one, and lasted until the end of the 19th century. Beyond it are the five or six remaining *arsenale*, elegant dockyard buildings in which the galleys were built, stored and repaired. Until 1941 there were perhaps twenty, most destroyed in the bombardment the Luftwaffe unleashed on the town—whether in revenge against a civilian population that had declined to welcome the German invader, or simply as practice for the assaults on Russian towns that were about to begin, no one has been able or willing to say. As pointless and random as it was vicious, that bombardment reduced Europe's most ancient city to ruins—windowless shells, walls of ancient stone—many of which remain, softened by time and swallows, trees and wildflowers, in the narrow streets behind the rebuilt harbourfront.

Mike's room is on the third floor. Two floors down Gillian and Camille have rooms also looking seaward. At ground level a few doors from the back of the hotel, away from the clamour of the seafront, Bertie Winterstoke has his quarters, a wide room looking out on a cobbled lane and a pale wall from which the windows were long since blown out and the roof brought down. Tall trees have grown up through the ruin, and the chairs and tables of the garden restaurant Bertie has made his HQ are set out there, open to the skies.

'You're a naval man,' Mike tells him. 'You should be on the seafront with a spyglass and a wooden leg.'

But Winterstoke is happy there, shaded in the daytime, quiet in the evenings. 'I'll have a word with the sea at an appropriate time,' he says.

Mike has spent many weeks organising this mission, something O'Dwyer made clear to Camille he wanted his fellow-New Zealander to do alone, but which Mike has, by persistence, many phone calls, and a refusal to be managed from beyond the grave, turned into a small pilgrimage. Already Marica, persuaded that the time has come to make her long-delayed visit to Croatia, is down on the Dalmatian coast with her Aunt Ljuba, and tomorrow will arrive with her at Hania's new airport. And before leaving New Zealand, she has told Mike by phone, she has visited Northland again and spoken to the old kuia, Wikitoria Paul, who has given her the words of a karakia she is to say over Joe's grave.

On their second day in Crete, while Winterstoke took himself along the seafront to Hania's naval museum, Mike and Gillian and Camille took the bus towards Maleme. On the seaward side of the road almost everything—villas, hotels, resorts, cafés, swimming pools, tennis courts—seemed new, or recent, certainly postwar, and designed for tourists. On the other side the land, rising into foothills of the mountain chain that bisects the island, was as it must have been fifty years before. There, among the olive groves and citrus orchards, the stands of bamboo, the irrigation canals, the grassy slopes bright with wildflowers, the sudden ravines through which streams ran seaward fast and clear over stones and shingle, had occurred the most violent, the most brutal, the most heroic actions of the ten days that were the Battle of Crete. Yet the slopes looked as if nothing had ever happened to disturb their calm and fruitfulness. To Mike, staring through the dusty windows of the rocking, fumy bus with its loud taped music, its shouting, semi-peasant passengers and chain-smoking driver, it was a reality he struggled with and failed to grasp. Time covered its tracks. Life, normality, the seasons, the natural world, were irrepressible—and he remembered Bertie beside the Thames at Binsey marvelling at the planet's capacity for renewal.

He helped Gillian and Camille down from the bus and together they climbed a narrow country road towards, and up into, the hill which military maps had designated 107, and which the Germans themselves, after their victory, had made their *soldatenfriedhof*, their war cemetery. The day was hot and they took it slowly with many stops. A fighter jet, one of the Nato force now stationed at Maleme, roared overhead and fired a rocket, and the sound of a distant explosion floated up to them. Five minutes later it happened again. They were high enough now to see down to the airfield. On a raised target area between the far edge of the airfield and the sea, a white puff of smoke rose, slow, thin and tall, leaning seaward with the breeze.

The road became a path, over which loomed a black cross. There was an elaborate entrance in dark marble, and beyond it, steps up to the graves. A plaque recorded that 4465 German soldiers were buried here, 3352 of them killed between 20 May and 1 June 1941. The graves too were in dark marble, the headstones flat to the slope of the ground, surrounded by waxy flowering plants, one stone to each two names. It was a solemn place, built in part to make a point at the time of the occupation, and to last.

As for the hill and the strategy of the battle, Mike could see it now quite clearly. Who controlled the hill controlled the airfield; who controlled the airfield controlled the island. Out there to the north was the sea where Bertie's ship had joined in the defeat of the seaborne invasion. Directly below and to the east was the territory 20 and 28 Battalions had fought over in their attempt to retake lost ground. But the crucial error had been made within the first twenty-four hours of the invasion, when a New Zealand officer had withdrawn his troops from these slopes and left them to invading paratroopers.

Beside the entrance to the cemetery there was a café under trees, and after looking at the graves Mike and the two women sank into canvas chairs and ordered cooling drinks. An elderly man spoke to them in German, but turned the conversation over to his wife when he discovered they were English speakers. The wife was brisk, bright. She deplored the loss of life, and seemed embarrassed by the large number of German dead, explaining that serious tactical errors had been made by the high command.

'The mistake was being here, wasn't it?' Mike said, but she seemed not to take his point.

Gillian explained carefully. 'We are here in Crete because a friend of my . . .' Mike could see that she was about to say husband, but corrected herself. 'Because a New Zealand soldier known to this gentleman was killed in the battle. And . . .' She gestured towards Camille, 'my friend's late husband fought here, also with the New Zealanders.'

There was a quick exchange between the German couple. 'My husband vishes me to say,' the woman said, 'zat he is pleased he vas not in Crete. He vas in Russia.'

Gillian flared. 'Does that make it better?'

Turning back to Mike and Camille, still speaking audibly, she said, 'I can accept what happened during the battle. But not the occupation. Every time there was resistance they rounded up men and boys in the nearest village and shot them.'

The German couple were gathering up their things, standing up, moving away from the table. 'It's peace now, isn't it?' the woman said. 'Ve are all Europeans.'

Showered, shaved and dressed, Mike goes out on to the balcony and looks down. Gillian and Camille are already at a table at the café below. They wave up and ask whether they should wait for him but he tells them to carry on, have their breakfast. He's going for a walk and will see them later.

He sets off into the old town's maze of cobbled streets behind the seafront, cool, forbidden to cars, and at this time of day uncrowded. He buys a hand-painted blue milk jug at one shop and at another a miniature of a Grecian urn, or amphora, into which he thinks he will transfer the ashes of Donovan O'Dwyer. At present they are in something that looks like a cigar box—in Mike's luggage, not Camille's, because, she insists, her husband was emphatic that it was to be Mike who would take them to Crete, Mike who would scatter them on Joe Panapa's grave.

The urn, terracotta coloured with black edging, has elaborate designs, part abstract, part representing horsemen galloping and birds flying in endless self-pursuit around the circumference. But the central picture is of two warriors wearing breastplates and helmets. One has fallen, and the other is about to kill him with a sword. Yes, Mike thinks. This will do. This is right.

Not sure where he's going, he walks on and comes to the seafront again, beyond the harbour and the walls of the ancient bastion. Across the street is a modern memorial—a gigantic metal hand and forearm rising heavenward in mute appeal out of what appears to be a circular pool. Looming over the hand are shapes which at first seem abstract, but which, against the background of the Aegean, take on the appearance of the prow and super-structure of a sinking ship. So this, Mike supposes, must commemorate those lost at sea in the war.

He crosses the street to look more closely. The pool is empty and there are cans, bottles, plastic bags, newspapers, littering its tiles. Graffiti which he can't read are scrawled around its rim. Palm fronds, laid there on some commemorative occasion, have dried, turned brown, and withered.

To the young whose weapon is the spray-can, Mike reflects, the German invasion must seem as remote as the Turkish and the Venetian occupations. Yet, on the other hand, Bertie has said that in the naval museum there is a display of recent paintings by schoolchildren in which the skies are full of German para-troopers, and the fields full of Cretan peasants, men and women, rushing out to kill them with pitchforks, axes, hammers and knives.

Mike stands in the shade of dusty ragged pines and looks back across the street. Along the front of a psarotaverna, octopi are strung out on a cord, attached by plastic clothespegs. The buildings on that side are three- and four-storey modern apart-ments, but with some ruins from the war, and some fragments of the ancient city wall. The colours are mostly yellow, orange, brown—earth colours—but there are also some whites, pinks and vivid blues. Everywhere, on balconies, among ruins, through the stones of crumbling walls, flowers spring up.

Turning away from the sea again, he buys an English newspaper and finds a verandah café loud with the repetitive quavery strains of Greek music and bright with flowers in baskets. He decides for a change he will try the English breakfast, which will cost him the equivalent of £2. It is brought and put before him with many flourishes, as if only a powerful magic could bring such stuff into existence, and only a magician would want to eat it. There are pale, half-cooked bacon rashers curled into symbolic waves, and fried tomatoes, out of which the fried or poached eye of an egg stares at him. The toast is thick white bread, finely singed but only on the surface. There is frozen butter and tepid jam to go with it. The choice of coffee is Greek, strong as an ox in a small cup, with space left for many spoons of sugar—or Nescafé. He elects the real thing, drinks it down, and feels almost at once the effect of its caffeine-and-sugar hit.

He gets back to the harbour-front in time to see a taxi pulling up outside the hotel. Marica gets out and then leans in to give a hand to Ljuba, who climbs out smiling and full of energy.

Mike hurries to greet them. There is a third person. Ira.

'I'm an old woman,' Ljuba says, noticing his surprise. 'I need help, and I couldn't load it all on to our visitor from New Zealand.'

'Ljuba's my excuse for being here,' Ira says.

'Why would you need an excuse?' Mike takes her by the hands and kisses her cheeks, first one: 'Welcome!' Then the other: '*Dobro dosli.*'

Since his return to Oxford from Croatia he and Ira have exchanged at first a cascade of letters, cards, books, e-mails, back and forth; and then, as if embarrassed by their own excess, and thwarted by the recognition that living and working as and where they do their chances of seeing much of one another are not good, they have lapsed back into brevities and silences. There has been, even, a faint note of petulance, or complaint, as if each would like unreasonably to blame the other for the discomfort of a broken attachment.

But Ira's smile as she meets his is warm. He knows his pleasure must be evident and that she's glad of it, and glad to have taken him by surprise.

He hugs Ljuba, hugs Marica, and then manages to clamp them, all three, into a wide embrace. 'Now come and meet the others of our party.'

So Mike finds himself with the Englishwomen on one side, the Croatians on the other, a Siegfried introducing two Rhinemaidens to three of the Valkyrie, while Winterstoke, Wotan with the broken spear, looks on, bewildered but benign. Gillian and

Marica laugh and exchange greetings with an immediacy that comes of having known one another, figured in one another's lives, without ever having met. Ljuba's silent, broad, wide-smiling face blesses them both. Ira watches. The feeling all round is good and bodes well.

Mike has rooms booked for Ljuba and Marica in the Amphora, a hotel just along from the Lucia. But now one must be found for Ira. In a short time he has found a rather superior room, quiet, though without a sea view, in an alley just up from the naval museum.

In the afternoon, after lunch together on the seafront and a brief siesta, all seven of them set off in two taxis for the Allied war cemetery at Suda Bay. The lunch has been jolly, not least because Winterstoke, at first wary of the preponderance of female companions, has begun to enjoy himself and to show off a little. But now they are quiet, driving through a rural landscape, bougainvillea over walls and balconies, vegetable gardens and farmlets of goats and poultry. They pass through a village, turn left along a narrow road, and after two or three kilometres, come to a stop among olive trees.

Ahead is the entrance to the cemetery. Tall trees, mostly Australian eucalypts, enclose it on three sides. The fourth is open to the blue of Suda Bay which all the graves, row on row of them in long lines, look towards.

Mike has been here already, on the day the group from Oxford arrived, and has located Joe's grave. Now he takes Ljuba to it, leaving the others in the shade of the olives. She holds his arm in a strong grip. 'Help me, Micky,' she says.

Having climbed with her to the garden and vineyard behind her house in Dalmatia he knows the strength she's needing is not physical. 'I'm here,' is all he can think of by way of reply.

There is no one about, no sound but the wind in the trees. The graves are beautifully tended, the grass cut close, with roses, carnations, daisies, fuchsias—flowers of every kind and colour—planted around them.

'Flax,' Ljuba murmurs, as they approach the New Zealand section. 'That makes me remember.'

He leads her to Joe's grave and she stands in front of it, very still, clinging firmly to his arm. He can hear her breathing.

39492 Private
J. P. PANAPA
N.Z. Infantry
24 May 1941 Aged 29 Years

Under the inscription there is a silver fern curved around the words 'New Zealand' and contained within a wide, indented cross.

The moment goes on and on. There is only the swish and fall of the wind, the slow sad sway of branches overhead. At last Ljuba nods and speaks, still looking down at the headstone. 'He was such a lovely fellow.'

Mike says, 'I'm sorry, Ljuba.'

She takes a deep breath and rallies herself. 'We have this strange thing we must do.'

'You don't mind, do you?'

'I don't mind, no. If Camille doesn't.'

So Mike signals and the others make their way down to the grave. They range themselves around in a half-circle facing the headstone, backs to the sea, and Marica chants the karakia she has memorised. It's not a Maori voice—loud, harsh, like something torn from her in pain. It's not even (Mike thinks, remembering Ljuba's long-ago wailing, and the recent cries of the young woman in the Dalmatian cemetery) a Croatian voice. It's an incantation, but the note is quiet, clear. He's moved by its reticence. Through his own mind are running the lines of the Catullus graveside poem—*Multas per gentes et multa per aequora uectus / aduenio has miseras, frater, ad inferias*—Across lands and seas I've come, brother, to take of you this last leave.

He glances around at his friends. Camille's expression is anxious, as if she's afraid of what feelings may come to engulf her.

The face of Winterstoke, inheritor of traditions of empire, is conscientiously unruffled. 'Karakia. Of course of course,' it might be saying (if only it knew the word). 'Quite right too.'

Ljuba is visibly moved. Ira is weeping beside her. Gillian's eyes are closed.

Marica has finished. No one speaks. Mike goes down on one knee and takes from the bag he has been carrying the little amphora on the side of which is the picture of the standing warrior putting the fallen warrior to the sword. He removes the cover he has taped over its mouth.

The Catullus poem completes itself in his head—*Atque in perpetuum, frater, ave atque vale.* And now he is shaking all that's left of Donovan O'Dwyer into the flowers growing on the grave of Joe Panapa, the man he killed.

When he stands and looks at his friends he sees that Winterstoke has turned his back on them and is staring away into the distant sky beyond the treetops. Camille is weeping now. Ljuba has taken her hand.

Later, as they are wandering about looking at the graves, Mike goes over to Marica. 'You did the karakia beautifully.'

'Did I? I hope it was alright.'

'I was moved.'

'I was thinking of Frano.'

'Of course. So was I. Do you know what the words mean?'

'It addresses the atua whiowhio—they're the gods, or the dark spirits, that whistle in the reeds. It asks them to speak once, clearly, and then to leave this place for ever.'

'So it's a lifting of the makutu.'

'Yes, well . . .' There was something like a shrug. 'I think Wikitoria Paul thought that had worn itself out long ago.'

'So this is just a precaution.'

'It's an observance.'

He nods and squeezes her arm. 'I'm so glad it was done—so far from home.'

Winterstoke, his walking stick laid against the low wire fence that divides the cemetery from the bay, is standing squarely at ease—shoulders back, hands clasped behind, feet planted at the regulation twenty-inch separation—staring at the sea in which he once very nearly drowned. 'Bloody hell,' he says as Mike ranges up alongside him. 'When does life stop taking one by surprise?'

Gillian comes up and puts an arm around Mike's waist. 'Such a beautiful place,' she says. His arm goes around her, and for a moment they stand there side by side, as if nothing has changed between them (and indeed, he thinks, nothing has!), admiring the great sweep of the bay it looks out on, and the dramatic forms of the hills that look down on it.

He turns and looks back. Ira is still standing with Ljuba and Camille at the graveside.

That evening the G7, as Winterstoke has decided they should call themselves, eat together, outdoors again on the seafront, this time at the innermost end of the harbour beyond the Mosque of the Janissaries. As they sit down the swallows are still swooping and twittering across walls and the façades of buildings and down over the water. Soon, before the swallows have quite given up and gone to their roosts, the bats, their dark doubles, arrive for the night-watch. Briefly the doppelgängers, feather-sheened and leather-black, swoop and twitter across one another's flight-paths. Then darkness comes more decidedly down, and the bats, which seem to favour the ruin that looms over this end of the harbour, have it all to themselves.

It's a large meal of many good Greek dishes shared around—dolmades, taramasalata, hoummus, yoghurt and cucumber, all with pita bread; then a Greek salad with olives and fetta; then a klephtiko and a stifhado (some of each for everyone) with aubergines and stuffed capsicums; and finally a choice of baklava or rice pudding—all of this with bottles of the local wine which nobody quite likes but everyone partakes of liberally.

There is talk (when is there not?) about O'Dwyer. When the klephtiko is brought Camille tells how, after the evacuation was complete and O'Dwyer, wounded in the thigh, had been left on the island, one of the abandoned ones, and had escaped capture by hiding in caves in the hills, locals found him there, exhausted and feeling as if he was close to starvation, and brought him this dish in an earthenware pot.

'His two favourite memories of eating,' she says, 'were the breakfast before the retreat from Malame . . .'

'Bully and beetroot,' Winterstoke says, remembering the story Mike has told him so recently.

'Yes. And klephtiko in the cave.'

'And he got away in the end,' Winterstoke says. 'Courtesy of the Royal Navy, I have to say.'

'It's a traditional Cretan dish,' Camille says. 'Don used to say Cretans were best at cooking lamb. He thought their lamb was always slightly tough. But the animals graze on herbs, and those flavours get into the meat. He'd even heard it said you don't need much salt with mutton from Crete. Sea salt comes with it, in the meat.'

A man with a red flower behind his ear entertains them at their table, cranking out tunes on a barrel organ while his wife takes around the hat. As he wheels his machine away through the crowd, the sad and self-pitying—or are they sad and self-mocking?—repetitions of Greek love songs come out at them again from the interior of the taverna.

Winterstoke says, 'I'd like someone to tell me what it is about Cretan women and bulls.'

'We don't know, Bertie,' Mike says, looking around the table. 'You're going to have to tell us what you mean.'

'Europa and the bull,' Bertie says. 'It happened right here.'

Gillian says, 'But the bull was Zeus, wasn't he?'

'He was Zeus in the form of a bull.'

'And he raped her.'

'He did,' Winterstoke confirms. 'Case number one. And then there's Pasiphaë. She grumbled to Aphrodite about her husband's infidelities. Aphrodite made her fall in love with a bull.'

He stops, but Gillian encourages: 'And then?'

'Well, Pasiphaë got someone—might have been Daedalus—to make a fake cow. She got inside and positioned herself so when the bull . . .' Bertie waves a hand. 'You see where this is heading.'

'An early example of artificial insemination,' Mike says.

'It's the bull's testicles,' Ira says. 'They're so . . . visible.'

'You mean women fall in love with them?'

'I mean men make up stories about women falling in love with them.'

When the meal is over and they have lurched together back to their end of the harbour, Mike climbs to his room and stands looking at himself in the smudged mirror that hangs in a chipped green frame on the wall. 'Are you sober?' he asks. And although he knows the right answer might be, 'Not entirely,' he is also sure that he's not drunk. He is in the grip of something, but it's something distinct from alcohol.

He sits on his bed, takes his shoes off, stares at them on the floor between his feet, and puts them on again. Along the promenade below his balcony the tourist season's endless party is raging on. He goes down the three flights of stairs he has just climbed (there is no lift in the Hotel Lucia), turns left along the promenade and walks, steady and determined, through the crowd. As he approaches the alley beside the naval museum he can see a light in what he knows, or believes he knows, is Ira's room.

For a moment he asks himself, as if the answer is really not known to him, whether that is where he's going. But though his legs have slowed, and his head turns to keep eyes on the light up there, hoping to see her shadow against the curtain, the walking doesn't stop.

Soon he's on the road that runs beside beaches west of the harbour. The rhythm and pace of his walking pick up. He is becoming better coordinated, getting his second wind. He leaves the town behind and is on the dark road to Maleme. Sure now of a direction, if not of a reason for it, he hails a taxi and asks to be driven west.

'This will do,' he tells the driver when he sees a sign for Platanias. He pays, gets out, and keeps walking in the same direction.

It's well past midnight when he turns left off the main road. The side road, running south into the foothills, takes him through olive groves and vineyards, past stone farm buildings and cottages. He walks perhaps half a mile, still obeying some inner— or is it outer?—pressure, and at last the moment comes when it seems right to stop. Very tired, he sits down under olive trees.

'Here,' he tells himself. 'Somewhere very near here. Within the empathy-field of this space. This is where it happened. This is where the shot was fired.'

Feeling the strength and strangeness of this conviction, he lies down on his back and looks up at faint stars in gaps between the branches. Time passes—he has almost no sense of how long or short a time, nor whether during it he may have slept; but at last he feels himself released, free to go.

He walks back to the main road thinking he will return now to Hania. But at the crossroads he turns left and continues west. Outside some shops he finds a coin machine that dispenses cans of cold drink. He chooses Seven-up. The machine takes his money and rolls down to him the soft-and-heavy-sounding can.

He walks on, drinking as he goes.

Now and then a car goes by, a voice comes from a house, a dog barks, a night bird calls. There are lights in the hotels and resorts on the seaward side, and distant sounds of music from the beach. His legs carry him forward and he rides along on them, step after step. They're aching now, but they keep walking.

When he reaches the outskirts of Maleme village he knows he must turn right soon if he wants to reach the shore. Beyond the village the airfield lies between road and sea and can't be crossed. So he takes the next right, a long straight narrow road between holiday villas and motels, cafés, tennis courts and swimming pools, that brings him to the beach.

He finishes his can of Seven-up and settles down under a pine, his head on a fallen branch. Listening to the quiet hiss and flap of waves, he hears, as if from underneath that sound, the noises of war, coming from far away, unmistakable but receding, becoming faint. Straining to hear, he drops off to sleep—sleeps well, rolling on to his side and curling up as the night grows cool, but comfortable on the dry, grainy sand.

When he wakes it's beginning to be light. The blue of the sea is streaked dark and light in perfect horizontal lines. The sky is another blue, edged with rose and quite distinct. The horizon has been drawn across with a ruler and dark pencil. The sand is grey, at an angle to the horizon. So the three—land, sea and sky—make an abstract composition, austere, but of immense simplicity and beauty. It occurs to him that everything in life could be like this if only one were . . .

Were what, though? Dead is probably the answer. Free of attachments. Dead, but with consciousness.

His mind goes to the next graduate seminar he will take when he gets back to Oxford. It's to be on the question of how Wittgenstein's mature thought helps, if it helps at all, with philosophy's traditional problem of mind and body—the problem of identity illustrated by the age-old question Captain Ahab asks in *Moby Dick*: 'Is it I, God, or who, that lifts this arm?'

He gets up, stretches, takes a pee under the pines, and heads back towards the main road. As he goes he's thinking about human organ transplants. No one seems to think that identity is compromised by the receipt of another's heart, another's kidney, another's cornea, or bone-marrow, or blood. Limbs will follow soon. But what about the head? Suppose the sergeant's head that rolled down the hill near Platanias had been transplanted on to the body of Joe Panapa. Or the brain. Who would wake from the operation? The sergeant, or Joe Panapa?

I think of *my* limbs, *my* body, *my* organs. They are *mine*. But who is the *I* who possesses them, and is willing to accept replacements?

I am my consciousness. And the head is tapu.

He reaches the main road again. Early workers are waiting for the bus into town, and he joins them, remembering Winterstoke, his feet planted, his blue English eyes playing who-will-blink-first with the blueness of the Aegean, asking when did life stop taking one by surprise.

A large dark-eyed woman says something to him in Greek and he replies in English. 'Yes, it's going to be a cracker.'

She seems not dissatisfied with this and says something more, again incomprehensible. The bus is pulling up at the stop. The door swings open and the people surge forward.

'The dead have had their share of me,' he tells her, moving with the crowd. 'Now it's time for the living.'

Villa Vittoria

C. K. STEAD

From a resort town on the Italian Riviera, to London, to a lonely farmhouse in the west of France, the pace of *Villa Vittoria* steadily quickens. Why are a professor of literature and a London photographer being pursued? What is the secret hidden in the forbidden photograph of the reclusive former mistress of the famous poet and sympathiser to the Fascist cause? What is the Mussolini connection? Why should this be related to the collapse of a major Italian bank? Whose lives are at risk, precisely — and from what unknown enemies?

Part thriller, part love story, this surprising novel from C. K. Stead is almost unbearably gripping as the story unfolds and as lines of romantic entanglement weave a web of half-truth and misunderstanding all of their own.